T0333752

Estimating illicit financial flows

Estimating illicit financial flows

A critical guide to the data, methodologies and findings

ALEX COBHAM AND PETR JANSKÝ
JANUARY 2020

OXFORD

UNIVERSITY PRESS

OXFORD
UNIVERSITY PRESS

Great Clarendon Street, Oxford, OX2 6DP,
United Kingdom

Oxford University Press is a department of the University of Oxford.
It furthers the University's objective of excellence in research, scholarship,
and education by publishing worldwide. Oxford is a registered trade mark of
Oxford University Press in the UK and in certain other countries

Published in the United States of America by Oxford University Press
198 Madison Avenue, New York, NY 10016, United States of America

British Library Cataloguing in Publication Data
Data available

Library of Congress Control Number: 2019945448

ISBN 978–0–19–885441–8

Printed and bound in Great Britain by
Clays Ltd, Elcograf S.p.A.

Links to third party websites are provided by Oxford in good faith and
for information only. Oxford disclaims any responsibility for the materials
contained in any third party website referenced in this work.

For our families

Preface

The last decade has seen growing concern over 'illicit financial flows' as a threat to human progress. This culminated in 2015 in the global agreement to set a target in the UN Sustainable Development Goals to reduce illicit flows. What was lacking then, and remains lacking as we write in 2019, is consensus on the indicators and measurement for this target.

In this book, we survey the landscape, and aim to offer a critical review of the many methodologies and estimates for various aspects of illicit flows. We have had the privilege of being actively involved in this research agenda as it has developed, and also of participating in many of the international policy processes. By sharing the draft chapters online as we wrote them, we were able to obtain inputs from across the generous community of expert scholars.

We have benefited from discussions, comments and collaboration from more people than we can name, including Charles Abugre, Dereje Alemayehu, Annette Alstadsæter, Owen Barder, Stephanie Blankenburg, David Bradbury, James Boyce, Peter Chowla, Michael Clemens, David Cobham, William Davis, Alex Erskine, Valpy FitzGerald, Maya Forstater, Daniel Haberly, Gamal Ibrahim, Charles Kenny, Mushtaq Khan, Alice Lépissier, Steve MacFeely, Jan Mareš, Mick Moore, Alvin Mosioma, Vera Mshana, Savior Mwambwa, Léonce Ndikumana, Miroslav Palanský, Sol Picciotto, Rakesh Rajani, Pooja Rangaprasad, Peter Reuter, Thomas Tørsløv, George Turner, Ludwig Wier, Harry Wood, Gabriel Zucman, as well as seminar and conference participants from Addis to Oslo and Lima to Jakarta by way of Beirut and New York, and the many expert colleagues at the Tax Justice Network, Global Alliance for Tax Justice, Financial Transparency Coalition, COFFERS project, Open Data for Tax Justice and the Independent Commission for the Reform of International Corporate Taxation (ICRICT).

In addition, we are grateful to a number of organisations that have provided financial support for elements of the underpinning research, as well as spaces and platforms for engagement and discussion. We would especially like to thank the United Nations Conference on Trade and Development (UNCTAD), the UN Economic Commission for Africa (ECA), the African Union/ECA High Level Panel on Illicit Financial Flows from Africa, the

Tana High-Level Forum on Security in Africa, the Joffe Trust, Norad, the European Commission and the Ford Foundation.

Research on illicit financial flows is now developing apace. This is a very welcome change after a long period of undue neglect; but it does have the disadvantage of making this book an attempt to hit a moving target. We have sought to ensure full coverage of current work, while recognising (and hoping!) that new data and new methodologies will continue to emerge.

The common features of illicit financial flows are that they are deliberately hidden, made opaque to obscure their true role; and that they drain resources from states and/or make states less responsive to their peoples' needs. As things stand, too much remains hidden for it to be possible even to judge whether any progress is being made on the SDG target to curtail illicit flows. In this book, we identify a set of the most promising channels to improve methodologies and data.

We believe the very act of measuring illicit flows more accurately will contribute to reduce their level—just as failure to measure has allowed them to balloon. The failure thus far to translate the UN target into a measurable framework with global and national accountabilities is deeply disappointing. It is our hope that with a continuing international policy focus on reducing illicit flows, this book may contribute to more rapid progress. This should include substantial shifts in the international policy architecture, to ensure that countries at all income levels are fully included in the benefits of new standards of transparency and cooperation. We hope that academic and policy researchers in the field may also benefit from this work, as we have benefited from theirs, and continue the process of strengthening understanding and analysis in this critical area.

Contents

PART 3 PROPOSALS FOR IFF MONITORING

List of Figures

List of Tables

Introduction

By 2030, significantly reduce illicit financial and arms flows, strengthen
the recovery and return of stolen assets and combat all forms of
organized crime

UN Sustainable Development Goals Target 16.4

Global agreement in 2015 on the Sustainable Development Goals framework,
to guide worldwide progress in the period to 2030, includes for the first time a
target to reduce illicit financial flows (IFF). But the challenge is this: without
agreement on methodologies to measure the scale of IFF, how can the target
be met? How, indeed, can it even be attempted, or monitored?

'Illicit financial flows' is an umbrella term, which came to policy prominence during the period of the Millennium Development Goals (2000–2015).
Its success, in part, was due to its breadth. The term allowed a shared agenda
among, for example, people who variously saw either kleptocratic leaders or
rapacious multinational companies as a critical obstacle to development
success. The common elements, of hidden behaviours that strip resources
and weaken governance, were sufficiently clear that an irresistible momentum
developed to ensure prioritisation within the Sustainable Development
Goals (SDGs).

There are, however, important differences in the political sentiments underpinning support to tackle the various elements under the illicit flow umbrella.
Consensus at the headline level does not necessarily imply consensus on each
element.

At the technical level, there is equally great variation in the channels used
for illicit flows and in the approaches to estimation and measurement that
have been applied. And so while many SDG targets left open the question
of definition and measurement, this is perhaps especially true in the case of
16.4. Which flows fall under the umbrella term? How will progress in reducing
them be measured? How will that progress be *achieved*? Who should ultimately be held accountable for progress, and can the choice of indicators ensure
they are?

Estimating illicit financial flows: A critical guide to the data, methodologies and findings. Alex Cobham and Petr Janský,
Oxford University Press (2020). © Alex Cobham and Petr Janský.
DOI: 10.1093/oso/9780198854418.001.0001

In this book we provide a critical survey of the evidence base to answer these questions, and present our own proposals. The book is laid out in three parts, as follows.

In Part 1, we discuss the rise of 'illicit financial flows'. We chart the political rise of the term, and lay out the ideological differences that have to some extent been obscured. We present a typology showing the breadth of the underlying phenomena, and also highlight the important common elements and impacts. We distinguish between tax-abusive and market-abusive IFF, which tend to involve illicit transactions with capital of legal origin; and IFF related to theft and criminal markets, where the capital itself is illegal.

Overall, we confirm the substantive importance for development of illicit financial flows, and the tendency to undermine both the level of resources available to states, and the likelihood of states using their resources efficiently and for inclusive benefit. But we also confirm the inherent difficulties of tracking progress against phenomena that are, by definition, deliberately hidden from view.

For this reason, Part 2 provides a survey of the extensive literature on estimation and measurement of illicit flows. As well as underpinning the subsequent proposals, this is intended to provide a standing resource for researchers, students, policymakers and activists on the relative merits and reliability of different approaches to key elements of IFF. Each chapter in Part 2 follows a consistent format to allow easy use. For each methodology, a separate treatment is given for the quality of the data and the robustness of the methodology. These include assessments of the scope for improvement and/or the likelihood of access to better data. Each section, and each chapter, also include overview and conclusion sub-sections with key findings which can be read as standalone summaries.

First, chapter 2 evaluates the literature on trade-based IFF. Separate sections address the literature using national-level data; that using commodity-level data; and that using transaction-level data. Chapter 3 focuses on estimates based on capital accounts anomalies, with separate sections addressing the approaches of Global Financial Integrity; of Ndikumana and Boyce (e.g. 2000; 2008); of James Henry (2012; 2016); and assessing the estimates that combine trade-based and capital account components. Chapter 3 also evaluates leading estimates of undeclared wealth held 'offshore' specifically, the approaches associated with James Henry and with Gabriel Zucman (2013, 2015), respectively. Chapter 4 addresses the much larger and more varied literature on the extent of multinational profit shifting—from international organisations including UNCTAD, the IMF, and OECD, and key individual authors such as Kim

Clausing (e.g. 2016) and Gabriel Zucman and co-authors (e.g. Tørsløv, Wier, & Zucman, 2018).

The intention in this volume is not to provide a comprehensive overview of estimates of every IFF component, nor of every IFF channel. We focus on the main areas of the literature—academic and beyond—in which rigorous, replicable methodologies have been developed. In general, we give priority to those approaches generating global estimates based on country-level findings. We also prioritise those estimates that have been most salient in policy discussions, and those which we find to be most robust—although these are, sadly, not always consistent categories.

As a result of this approach, since estimates of illicit flows associated with illegal markets are generally made at the national level, and tend not to be widely replicated across countries, this literature is largely excluded from consideration. Estimates of undeclared assets held offshore are included, however, and these include much of the ultimate proceeds of illegal market IFF. We also do not address the literature on national tax gaps. This is in part for the same reasons of global comparability and policy salience, and in part because tax gaps may be purely domestic rather than necessarily reflecting the cross-border transactions that characterise IFF.

We reach a number of conclusions from Part 2. The most extensive, rapidly developing literature, with relatively robust results, relates to multinationals' profit shifting. Of the many approaches here, those which provide most confidence are based not on regression analyses but on direct measures of the gap between where economic activity takes place, and where the resulting profits are declared. This insight also provides an indication, exploited later, of how scale measures could be constructed for other IFF.

In Part 3, we look beyond the current estimates and set out various alternatives, including our proposed new, direct measures of scale for use as SDG indicators. In chapter 5, we consider two main types of non-scale alternative IFF indicators. First, we present a set of policy-based indicators that were originally proposed before the SDG process settled on a scale measure. These offer the scope to track global progress on transparency measures that are key to curtailing illicit financial flows, and also offer the jurisdiction-level disaggregation to support accountability for policies that maintain opacity.

Chapter 5 also includes two related sets of IFF risk measure, which follow the same logic but combine the policy-created opacity of jurisdictions with bilateral data on economic and financial transactions between jurisdictions, in order to evaluate the exposure of each country to IFF-facilitating secrecy elsewhere. Both approaches build on the global ranking constructed by the

Tax Justice Network, the Financial Secrecy Index. The first, pioneered by the High Level Panel on Illicit Financial Flows out of Africa, emphasises granular analysis of each countries' vulnerabilities to IFF, to support policy prioritisation. The second, operating in a similar way, is a Bilateral Financial Secrecy Index, replicating the global approach at the national level.

In chapter 6, we present our proposals for SDG 16.4, which were developed as part of the UN process. These proposals build on the findings in relation to scale estimates, and on insights from the non-scale approaches. We propose two indicators. Both are direct measures, rather than estimates, in keeping with the conclusions from Part 2 on the robustness issues of many of the estimates.

The first proposed indicator relates to tax avoidance by multinationals. The proposal follows the stronger of the approaches surveyed in chapter 4 in preferring a measure of the broader phenomenon of profit misalignment, to a less certain estimate of the somewhat narrower phenomenon of profit shifting. It is proposed to construct the measure on the basis of newly available data following the introduction of a country-by-country reporting requirement for multinationals. Alternative 'workaround' approaches are also discussed, should data access prove problematic.

The second proposed indicator takes a similar approach, constructing a direct measure which also works on the basis of newly available data—in this case, data resulting from the introduction of multilateral, automatic exchange of tax information between jurisdictions. Following the insights of Henry (2012) and others surveyed in chapters 2 and 3, we propose an overarching measure for a common result of most illicit flows other than multinationals' profit shifting: the volume of undeclared offshore assets.

The two proposed indicators share a valuable feature of the policy- and risk-based measures set out in chapter 5. This is that they can be fully disaggregated to the jurisdiction level in a way that will support accountability both for jurisdictions that benefit from provoking illicit outflows elsewhere, and for effective policy responses from those that suffer.

Finally, chapter 7 presents the overall conclusions of the book and makes recommendations for the most promising directions for future research, and the most pressing and realistic priorities for data collation and data access. We highlight the most robust estimates currently available, and draw out the implications of our analysis for target 16.4 of the Sustainable Development Goals. Recognising the growing momentum for wider UN measures, we also identify related proposals to improve the data infrastructure and policy instruments.

PART 1

ILLICIT FINANCIAL FLOWS

1

History and overview of 'IFF'

1.1. Context and Motivation

The emergence of a global 'tax justice' movement, following the formal establishment of the Tax Justice Network in 2003, has had a powerful impact on international policymaking.[1] By 2013, a range of innovative policy proposals had risen onto the agendas of the G8, G20 and OECD groups of countries. And by 2015, the UN Sustainable Development Goals (SDGs) themselves had come to embody that shift also.

Most obviously, tax appears as the first 'means of implementation' in the SDGs (target 17.1). This stands in stark contrast to the predecessor framework, the Millennium Development Goals, which contained no single reference to tax as a source of finance for development. In addition, the closely related issue of illicit financial flows has also gained major policy traction.

The illicit flows agenda emerged in a fair degree as an opposition to a view which saw corruption as a problem largely, or even exclusively, of lower-income countries. Raymond Baker, the US businessman who worked for decades in sub-Saharan Africa before setting up the NGO Global Financial Integrity, popularised the term 'illicit financial flows' in his 2005 book, *Capitalism's Achilles Heel*. The key selling point of the book was Baker's ballpark estimates of the scale of flows, with 'commercial tax evasion' many times larger than flows linked to the bribery of, and theft by, public officials.

Baker's first chapter is starkly titled 'Global capitalism: Savior or predator?', and the emphasis is clear from the first paragraph (p.11):

'I'm not trying to make a profit!' This rocks me back on my heels. It's 1962, and I have recently taken over management of an enterprise in Nigeria. The director of the John Holt Trading Company, a British-owned firm active since the 1800s, is enlightening me about how his company does business in Africa. When I ask

---

[1] This chapter draws from our earlier papers (Cobham & Janský, 2017b, 2017c), and from Cobham (2014, 2018).

Estimating illicit financial flows: A critical guide to the data, methodologies and findings. Alex Cobham and Petr Janský, Oxford University Press (2020). © Alex Cobham and Petr Janský.
DOI: 10.1093/oso/9780198854418.001.0001

how he prices his imported cars, building materials and consumer goods, he
adds, 'Pricing's not a problem. I'm just trying to generate high turnover.'

Baker goes on to lay out powerfully how the abusive behaviour of multinationals of the period led to massive trade mispricing, and stripped lower-
income host countries of their taxing rights—despite the often desperate need
for revenues to support public spending on health, education and infrastructure.
For the same reason, a key plank of the Tax Justice Network's policy platform
is the proposal for public, country-by-country reporting by multinationals
(Murphy, 2003) to lay bare the discrepancies between where economic activity
takes place and where taxable profits are declared.

Illicit financial flows encompass much more than multinational tax
abuses, however. The opacity of corporate accounts that hides profit shifting
finds a parallel in the financial secrecy offered by 'tax haven' jurisdictions—
and this, too, is a critical driver of illicit flows.

In 2007, the Tax Justice Network began the process to create the Financial
Secrecy Index, which identifies major financial jurisdictions like Switzerland—
which typically does very well in international perceptions of corruption—as
central to the problem of producing and promoting corrupt flows elsewhere
(see Cobham, Janský, & Meinzer, 2015). A narrative that sees corruption in
lower-income countries only will miss this central driver of the problem—
and so an important element of the illicit flows agenda is that it recognises the
centrality of financial secrecy in particular, often high-income jurisdictions,
to the undermining of revenues, the undermining of good governance in
countries all around the world. Rather than saying 'Why is your country
corrupt?', it asks, 'What are the drivers of corruption—and where?'

Underpinning most major cases of corruption around the world, and many
major cases of tax abuse, can be found anonymously owned companies, from
the British Virgin Islands to Delaware; opaque corporate accounting, typically
in the biggest stock markets in the world, that cover the degree of profit-shifting
and tax avoidance; and deliberate failures to exchange financial information
that protect, even now, banking secrecy.

As such, international cooperation is needed—at least as much as domestically focused efforts. The global agreement on a target (16.4) in the SDGs
committed to the reduction of illicit financial flows (IFF) is therefore particularly
significant. Politically, the target can be traced back to the work of the High
Level Panel on IFF from Africa, chaired by former South African president
Thabo Mbeki, which worked with the UN Economic Commission for Africa
to build the case for urgent action both on the continent and globally, and

obtained unanimous African Union backing. It was natural that the subsequent report of the Secretary-General's High Level Panel of Eminent Persons on the Post-2015 Development Agenda, co-chaired by President Susilo Bambang Yudhoyono of Indonesia, President Ellen Johnson Sirleaf of Liberia, and Prime Minister David Cameron of the United Kingdom, also clearly identified IFF as an issue to be included in the new framework.

Despite this broad backing, however, the IFF target has proven to be one of the most difficult to pin down. Even now in 2019, there is no specific indicator or group of indicators finalised as the basis to track progress. Worse, there has been a concerted effort to subvert the target by removing multinational companies from the scope, despite the consistent emphasis on their tax avoidance practices in the academic and policy literature and in the reports of the two high level panels that set the basis for global agreement on the target in 2015.

With UNCTAD and the UNODC now leading a technical expert process to identify and agree proposals, there is the potential—but not yet the certainty—of ensuring the target has indicators which both reflect the original policy intention, and also create appropriate accountability mechanisms to support genuine progress.

The current indicator title is this:

16.4.1 Total value of inward and outward illicit financial flows (in current USD)

Setting aside whether such an indicator is most suitable to support progress and accountability, or sufficient on its own, the process to identify a methodology for *this* indicator is severely complicated by the absence of agreement on how to measure the scale of illicit financial flows. A specific aim of this book is to provide a basis for rigorous comparison of current approaches to estimating IFF, that can support national and international policymaking and global accountability for progress towards SDG 16.4.

Our more general motivation is to provide a reference tool for scholars, students, activists and journalists. 'Illicit financial flows' is an umbrella term for a broad group of cross-border economic and financial transactions, each of which have different motivations and a range of varying impacts. For activists and journalists, for example, this makes it important to distinguish when estimates refer to one IFF component or another, for example, as well as to have a robust basis for preferring one estimate over another. For researchers and experts in one area of IFF, who will not necessarily be as familiar with issues related to another component, an up-to-date guide to methodological and data questions should have clear, practical value.

1.2. Definitions

There is no single, agreed definition of illicit financial flows (IFF). This is, in large part, due to the breadth of the term 'illicit'. The (Oxford) dictionary definition is: 'forbidden by law, rules or custom.' The first three words alone would define 'illegal', and this highlights an important feature of any definition: illicit financial flows are not necessarily illegal. Flows forbidden by 'rules or custom' may encompass those which are socially and/or morally unacceptable, and not necessarily legally so.

This is in line with developments in criminology, which has seen a growing zemiological critique (e.g. Hillyard (2004) and Dorling et al. (2008); zemiology being the study of social harms). The critique emphasises a range of short-comings in the crime-led approach, among them that crime is a social construct based on value judgements and so varies across time and geography—thereby undermining it as a consistent basis of comparison; and that crime as a category excludes many serious harms (e.g. poverty or pollution). A related point, first raised by Blankenburg & Khan (2012) and further developed by Khan, Roy, & Andreoni (2019), is that a legally-based definition requires a legitimate state actor. Cross-border flows could be declared illegal by an illegitimate state (a military dictatorship, say). But would they therefore be illicit? As such, working on the basis of harm done (or risk thereof) can provide a more consistent basis for the definition.

To take a specific example, commercial tax evasion affecting a low-income country where the tax and authorities have limited administrative capacity is much less likely to be either uncovered or successfully challenged in a court of law, than would be the same exact behaviour in a high-income country with relatively empowered authorities. A strictly legal definition of IFF is therefore likely to result in systematically—and wrongly—understating the scale of the problem in lower-income, lower-capacity states. In contrast, a zemiological approach would clearly support the inclusion of multinational profit shifting since the revenue impacts and related harms in the grey area of 'possibly legal but untested' avoidance are indistinguishable from those which are firmly in the 'unlawful' category.

For these reasons, a narrow, legalistic definition of IFF is rejected. *The phenomenon with which we are concerned is one of hidden, cross-border flows, where either the illicit origin of capital or the illicit nature of transactions undertaken is deliberately obscured.*

The most well-known classification stems from Baker (2005). In Baker's assessment, there were three components: grand corruption accounted for just a few per cent of illicit flows; laundering of the proceeds of crime between a quarter and a third; and the largest component by far was 'commercial tax evasion', through the manipulation of trade prices, accounting for around two thirds of the problem.

A somewhat extended classification, from Cobham (2014), identifies four components of IFF, distinguished by motivation: 1—market/regulatory abuse, 2—tax abuse, 3—abuse of power, including the theft of state funds and assets, and 4—proceeds of crime. The third and fourth components map onto two of Baker's. The tax abuse category makes explicit an issue that is sometimes obscured in presentation of Baker's categorisation, namely that tax-motivated IFF include not only the actions of multinational companies but also those of individuals. The first category, of market/regulatory abuse, is largely additional to Baker's categorisation. These IFF reflect cross-border flows in which ownership is hidden, for example to circumvent sanctions or anti-trust laws. Circumvention of (legal or social) limitations on political conflicts of interest may fall here or under abuse of power.

This categorisation allows in turn the identification of the major actors in IFF:

- private actors (individuals, domestic businesses and multinational company groups committing tax and regulatory abuse, and the related professional advisers—tax, legal and accounting)—these are the leading actors in IFF types 1, 2 and 3;
- public officeholders (both elected and employed)—these are important actors in IFF types 3 and 4, and may be involved in type 1; and
- criminal groups (a term used here to indicate both those motivated primarily by the proceeds of crime, and those using crime to fund political and social agenda)—the leading actors in IFF type 4.

Table 1.1 provides an overview of the underlying transaction types. It is unlikely to be comprehensive because there is potential to engineer an illicit flow in any transaction, and the range of potential illicit motivations is wide indeed; but nonetheless demonstrates the breadth of IFF phenomena. As the final two columns indicate, all four IFF types are likely to result in reductions in both state funds and institutional strength—that is, both in the funds available for public spending and in the likely quality of that spending.

There is substantial overlap in the mechanisms used for IFF, regardless of motivation. The opportunity to hide, where it exists, is likely to be exploited for multiple purposes. For example then, the legal use by a multinational of highly secretive jurisdictions may both provide cover for illegal use of the

Table 1.1. A typology of illicit financial flows and immediate impacts

Flow	Manipulation	Illicit motivation	IFF type	Impact on state funds	Impact on state effectiveness
Exports	Over-pricing	Exploit subsidy regime	2	↓	↓
		(Re)patriate undeclared capital	1	↓	↓
	Under-pricing	Shift undeclared (licit) income/profit	2	↓	↓
		Shift criminal proceeds out	4	↓	↓
		Evade capital controls (including on profit repatriation)	1		↓
Imports	Under-pricing	Evade tariffs	2	↓	↓
		(Re)patriate undeclared capital	1	?	↓
	Over-pricing	Shift undeclared (licit) income/profit	2	↓	↓
		Shift criminal proceeds out	4	?	↓
		Evade capital controls (including on profit repatriation)	1	↓	↓
		Shift undeclared (licit) income/profit	2	↓	↓
Inward investment	Under-pricing	Shift undeclared (licit) income/profit	2	↓	↓
		Shift criminal proceeds out	4	?	↓
		Evade capital controls (including on profit repatriation)	1	↓	↓
	Over-pricing	(Re)patriate undeclared capital	1	?	↓
	Anonymity	Hide market dominance	1		↓
	Anonymity	Hide political involvement	3		↓
Outward investment	Under-pricing	Evade capital controls (including on profit repatriation)	1		↓
	Over-pricing	Shift undeclared (licit) income/profit	2	?	↓

Flow	Manipulation	Illicit motivation	IFF type	Impact on state funds	Impact on state effectiveness
		Shift criminal proceeds out	4	↓	↓
	Anonymity	Hide political involvement	3		↓
Public lending	(If no expectation of repayment, or if under-priced)	Public asset theft (illegitimate allocation of state funds)	3	↓	
Public borrowing	(If state illegitimate, or if over-priced)	Public asset theft (illegitimate creation of state liabilities)	3	↓	
Related party lending	Under-priced	Shift undeclared (licit) income/ profit	2	↓	
Related party borrowing	Over-priced	Shift undeclared (licit) income/ profit	2	↓	
Public asset sales	Under-pricing	Public asset theft	3	↓	
	Anonymity	Hide market dominance	1		↓
	Anonymity	Hide political involvement	3		↓
Public contracts	Over-pricing	Public asset theft	3	↓	
	Anonymity	Hide market dominance	1		↓
	Anonymity	Hide political involvement	3		↓
Offshore ownership transfer	Anonymity	Corrupt payments	3	↓	↓

Source: Cobham (2014). 'IFF type' is defined as follows: 1—market/regulatory abuse, 2—tax abuse, 3—abuse of power, including theft of state funds, 4—proceeds of crime.

same secrecy, and also inadvertently legitimize such behaviour. Identifying illicit flows in a particular mechanism will tend to be insufficient to specify the type of IFF in action.

Table 1.1 shows a roughly equal number of potential IFF in each of the first three categories, and rather fewer for the proceeds of crime; but this rests on an assumption made for descriptive clarity which is unlikely to hold in practice: namely, that businesses operating internationally are not used to launder the proceeds of crime. This distinction in turns highlights a more important one: namely, that IFF can take place with capital which is anywhere on a spectrum of legality. At one end are criminal proceeds and stolen public funds, with legitimate income and company profits at the other.

A second spectrum exists in relation not to the capital but rather the transaction itself. At one end there are clearly illegal transactions, such as bribery of public officials by commercial interests; at the other end, transactions which are likely to be legal (at least in the sense of not having been challenged successfully in a court of law) but may well be illicit; in this category would be, for example, some of the more aggressive transfer pricing behaviour of multinational companies.

Figure 1.1 provides a rough plotting of the four IFF types identified, on a quadrant diagram showing the spectra of transaction il/licitness and capital il/legality. The historical emphasis of both research and policy has been on those IFF types that are furthest, in general, to the northeast quadrant (i.e. where both the capital origin and the transaction are in question); and least attention to those in southeast (i.e. those where the capital origin is less likely to be in question than the manipulations involved in the transaction.

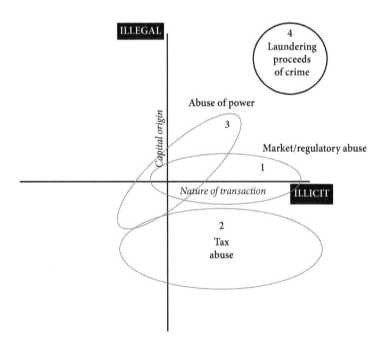

Figure 1.1. Main IFF types by nature of capital and transaction.
Source: Cobham (2014).

Most attention, in other words, has been paid to the clusters relating to abuse of power, and more recently to the proceeds of crime—at least in relation to efforts against 'terrorism financing' subsequent to the World Trade Center attacks of September 2001. The areas of market abuse and tax abuse have been relatively neglected in terms of policy focus, with the result that the dominant discourse has largely excluded the role of private sector actors in driving illicit flows—at least until the financial crisis affecting many countries that began in 2008.

It is worth reiterating that in all cases in the typology, the behaviours in question are in some sense reprehensible. They rely on being hidden because there would be substantial negative ramifications to their becoming publicly visible. These ramifications might be legal or social—that is, they may reflect violations of law or of 'rules and custom'—and in each case are sufficiently powerful to justify any costs of hiding. As such, it is inevitable that estimates of these deliberately hidden phenomena exhibit a degree of uncertainty. Moreover, since different IFF types use the same channels, estimates of particular channels will inevitably combine some IFF types to some degree; and since different IFF types use multiple channels, 'clean' estimates of individual IFF types may be difficult to obtain.

It is worth deviating somewhat to highlight here what IFF are *not*: they are not equivalent to capital flight. The literature on capital flight, which dates back several decades further, focused on the element of unrecorded funds as calculated from capital account statistics (the IFF aspects of which we survey in chapter 3). This literature over time came to present the issue as one of (legitimate) portfolio investment responses to capital controls and problems with (typically lower-income, often African) countries' investment climate (see e.g. Collier et al., 2001). With no particular emphasis on the licitness or otherwise of these flows, the solution mindset tended not to emphasise transparency or enforcement, nor conditions in the capital-receiving economies. Instead, the recommended responses tended to stress the need to improve the attractiveness of the home economy for investors.

Interestingly, the major volume on illicit financial flows led by African researchers addresses these perceptions head on. The various contributions to Ajayi & Ndikumana, eds. (2015) show that factors that do *not* determine their estimates include: risk-adjusted returns to investment (Ndikumana, Boyce & Ndiaye, 2015); 'orthodox' monetary policy—high interest rates in particular (Fofack & Ndikumana, 2015); macroeconomic 'fundamentals', especially the pursuit of inflation control and balance of payments sustainability (Weeks, 2015); and capital account liberalisation (Lensink & Hermes, 2015). As Weeks

(2015) sums up his findings: 'the orthodox narrative that capital flight results from unsound macro policies [is reversed]. On the contrary, capital flight may force governments into policies that work against the majority of the population.'

Evidence is also found in various contributions for the following determinants of capital flight: external debt, much of which has historically left again through the 'revolving door' (Ajayi, 2015; Murinde, Ocheng & Meng, 2015); weak rules and/or capacity, most clearly in (Arezki, Rota-Graciozi & Senbet, 2015) which addresses the impact of thin capitalisation rules in resource-rich countries; habit, and the impact of continuing impunity—including social determinants of tax compliance and the possibility of vicious circles of IFF and governance (Ayogu & Gbadebo-Smith, 2015; Kedir, 2015); and far from least, international financial secrecy (Massa, 2015; Weeks, 2015; Barry, 2015; Moshi, 2015).

While in some sense, 'capital flight' is a subset of illicit financial flows, the two should not be confused either in scale and substance or in terms of political mindset and policy implications. Nonetheless, it is inescapable that there is overlap in some of the measurement approaches and indeed in the substance, to the extent that capital flight is captured as unrecorded flows - while IFF are deliberately unrecorded.

Finally in this section, we explore further the nature of multinational companies' tax abuses and the extent of their inclusion in the definition of IFF. As noted, Raymond Baker's original work took all of the profit shifting behaviour observed—not unreasonably—to be illegal tax evasion. This allowed the NGO that Baker established, Global Financial Integrity, to include his approach in a definition of IFF requiring strict illegality of capital or its transfer. However, it is clear in inspection of Baker's analysis that much that has been labelled multinational tax *avoidance* by others would be included. Prof. Sol Picciotto (2018) has highlighted that there are in fact three categories to consider, rather than two: instead of looking at illegal evasion and legal avoidance, policy should identify illegal evasion; unlawful avoidance; and lawful (successful) avoidance, while recognising that there are likely to be grey areas between each.

Table 1.2, developed as part of the UN process to agree indicators for SDG 16.4, clarifies illicit assets as the key outcome of each illicit flow—and distinguishes types of tax avoidance following Picciotto's proposal. Since each illicit asset type is associated with harms ranging from the underlying loss of public assets, promotion of criminal activities and tax losses, this simpler approach may be less helpful for specific policy responses. It does however offer a

Table 1.2. A simpler outline of illicit financial flows

Legal category	Origin of assets	Behaviour type	Result when transferred abroad
Legal		Tax compliance	**Licit**: Legally generated, fully tax compliant and legally transferred assets abroad
		Lawful tax avoidance	**Illicit?** Lawfully tax avoiding assets abroad
Unlawful	Legally generated profits, capital gains and income	Unlawful tax avoidance	**Illicit**: Legally generated, but unlawfully tax avoiding assets abroad
		Market/regulatory abuse	**Illicit**: Circumvention of regulations via hidden (offshore) ownership for unlawfully earned profit at home/abroad
Criminal		Illicitly transferred, and/or transferred for illicit purposes	**Illicit**: Legally generated but violating regulations for cross-border transactions such as evading currency controls, or transferred to fund illegal activities (including terrorism)
		Tax evasion	**Illicit**: Legally generated, but criminally tax evading assets abroad
	Proceeds of corruption	*Bribery; Grand corruption; Illicit enrichment; Embezzlement*	**Illicit**: Corruption-related illegal assets transferred abroad
	Proceeds of theft/related crime	*Theft; Extortion; Kidnapping; Fraud; Bankruptcy*	**Illicit**: Theft-related illegal assets transferred abroad
	Proceeds of illegal markets	*Drug trafficking; Counterfeiting; Firearms trafficking; Trafficking in persons; Smuggling of migrants; Wildlife trafficking*	**Illicit**: Illegal assets (from illegal economic activities)

Source: Cobham and Janský (2017b), building on earlier outline by UNODC, from which text in italics is drawn.

broader framing which may prove helpful in allowing simpler, harm-relevant indicators to be constructed.

Picciotto's three categories make up the various forms of profit *shifting*, which must be distinguished from profit *misalignment*. Misalignment is a broader term that has gained currency since 2013, when the G20 and OECD declared that the single goal of the Base Erosion and Profit Shifting Action

Plan (BEPS) was to better align taxable profits with the location of multinationals' real economic activity. Profit misalignment can occur due to any of the three categories of profit shifting activity intended to reduce companies' tax liabilities, and also from a fourth category: misalignment that arises simply from the fact that OECD tax rules do not explicitly seek alignment, and therefore some divergence from full alignment would be expected even in the absence of tax-motivated shifting.

In addition, differences in governments' willingness to pursue their full tax base will give rise to misalignment that does not result from attempts to procure profit shifting from elsewhere. Furthermore, there are natural differences in profitability, such as different capabilities of employees, that are independent of profit shifting, but which it may not be possible to isolate from profit shifting. Figure 1.2 shows the resulting distinctions between profit misalignment; profit shifting illicit financial flows; and non-legal profit shifting (the figure is for conceptual discussion only—it does not provide scale estimates of its various parts).

The broader definition of IFF, reflecting harm rather than strict legality, is also clearly reflected in the key UN documents that precede the global, political agreement on the Sustainable Development Goals—in particular, multinational tax avoidance is repeatedly identified in the pivotal report of the UNECA High Level Panel on Illicit Financial Flows from Africa, and subsequently in the report of the High Level Panel of Eminent Persons to the UN Secretary-General.

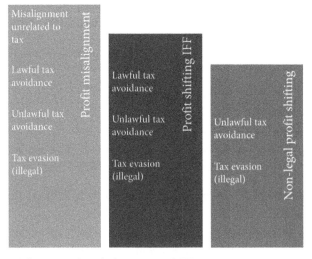

Figure 1.2. Multinational tax behaviour and IFFs.
Source: Authors.

A final, pragmatic reason to include multinational tax abuses within the scope of IFF is simply that the estimates may be of notably higher quality than for some other aspects.

1.3. Impact

One of the reasons to pursue better estimates of illicit financial flows is to support, in turn, a better understanding of the scale and nature of their impacts across a range of aspects of human development. These impacts, like the phenomena themselves, are many and varied. Figure 1.3 provides one stylisation of these, distinguishing between IFF that rely on illegal and on legal capital respectively.

Illegal capital IFF, in general, are seen as providing the greatest threat to negative security: that is, the ability of states to prevent, or to negate, insecurity at the personal, community, environmental and political levels: more specifically, the ability and willingness of states to act to reduce the risk of violence against the person, the risk of insecurity due to tensions between groups, the risk of environmental degradation and the risk of political rights violations. The state can be increasingly undermined by the growing role of criminal activity, including the trafficking of drugs, people and illegal goods from e.g. logging, fishing and mining, which may come to require or rely on the support of some state functions such as the military or customs agents; and also by the growth of crimes directly against the state, namely bribery to subvert state power for private gain (typically of multinational companies), and the effective

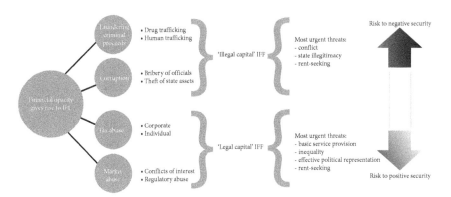

Figure 1.3. Overview of IFF and human security linkages.
Source: Cobham (2014).

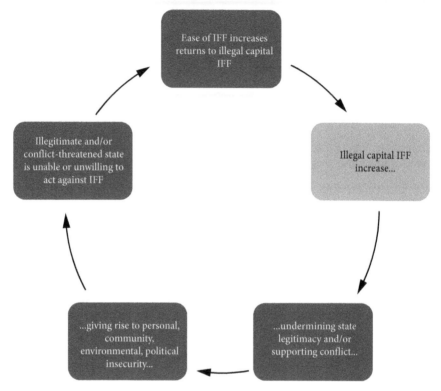

Figure 1.4. The vicious cycle of negative insecurity and illegal capital IFF.
Source: Cobham (2014).

theft by people in positions of power of state assets (or per Table 1.1, the creation of illegitimate state liabilities).

As Figure 1.4 illustrates, illegal capital IFF can give rise to a vicious cycle of negative insecurity, in which the growth of IFF further undermines the state's legitimacy and/or fuels internal conflict; weakening in turn the state's will or ability to act against IFF, and so increasing the returns to the underlying activity and the incentives to take part.

Legal capital IFF are seen as forming a similar vicious cycle with respect to positive security—that is, the ability of states to provide, to positively construct, secure conditions in which rapid human development can take place. This relates to economic opportunity and freedom from extreme economic inequality; and to the security of basic human development outcomes related to health and nutrition.

Tax is fundamental to the emergence of a State which is both able and willing to support the progressive realisation of human rights—and the relationships here go far beyond revenue. The 4Rs of tax (Cobham, 2005; 2007) provide a simple framework to consider these. Revenue is clearly crucial to States' ability to provide public services from effective administration and the rule of law to health, education and infrastructure; as redistribution is crucial to contain or eradicate both horizontal and vertical inequalities. Less obvious may be the role of taxation in re-pricing—ensuring that the true public costs and benefits of social goods (like education) and ills (such as tobacco consumption and carbon dioxide emission) are reflected in market prices.

Perhaps the most important result of tax, however, is also often overlooked: political representation. Prolonged reliance on revenues from natural resources or foreign aid tends to undermine channels of responsive government, giving rise to corruption and broader failures of accountability. The act of paying tax provides an important accountability link (Brautigam, Fjeldstad, & Moore, 2008; Broms, 2011). Empirical studies suggest the higher the share of tax in government spending, the stronger the process of improving governance and representation (Ross, 2004; and powerfully confirmed with much stronger data by Prichard, 2015); while direct tax—taxes on income, profits and capital gains—appears to play a particularly strong role (Mahon, 2005).

Figure 1.5 shows the potential vicious cycle that could arise with respect to legal capital IFF and positive (in)security. If the starting point is taken as an increase in legal capital IFF, the risks are of undermining both the available revenues to provide positive security, but also the political responsiveness to be willing to do so. The resulting insecurity and inequalities have the potential to further weaken both the capacity and the willingness of the state to fight IFF, reinforcing the cycle.

Work on health impacts in particular has indicated potentially very powerful effects of IFF. Christian Aid (2008) began the current wave of tax justice campaigning by international development NGOs with an estimate that revenue losses due to trade-based tax abuse could result in the needless deaths of nearly 1,000 children each day. More recently, O'Hare, Makuta, Bar-Zeev, Chiwaula, & Cobham (2014) use illicit flow estimates with GDP elasticities of mortality to show that of 34 sub-Saharan African countries, a curtailment of illicit flows could see substantial mortality reductions—such that 16 countries rather than 6 would have reached their MDG target by 2015.

Reeves et al. (2015) explore the underlying relationship and find that 'tax revenue was a major statistical determinant of progress towards universal health coverage' in lower-income countries, and that this is overwhelmingly driven by direct taxes on profits, income and capital gains. Using alternative revenue data, and a more robust regression approach, Carter & Cobham (2016) confirm the importance of tax generally, while adding some caveats and more

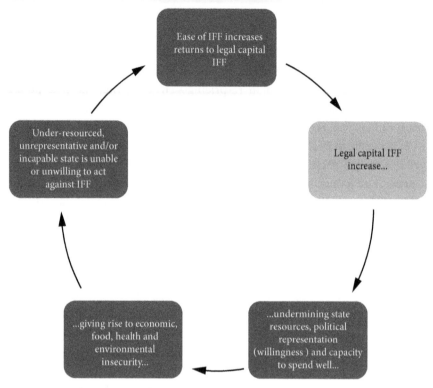

Figure 1.5. The vicious cycle of positive insecurity and legal capital IFF.
Source: Cobham (2014).

detailed findings. In particular, they find a larger statistical association between direct taxes and public health expenditure than between indirect taxes and health spending; and that countries making greater use of direct taxes tend in general to exhibit higher public health spending, broader coverage of and access to public health systems.

A growing body of work has looked at the relationship between IFF and inequality. Income and wealth inequality are increasingly recognised as an obstacle to economic growth as well as to human development (e.g. Ostry, Berg, & Tsangarides, 2014; Piketty, 2014), and explicitly targeted and tracked throughout the Sustainable Development Goals framework. Cobham, Davis, Ibrahim, & Sumner (2016) show that allowing for IFF could be sufficient in many countries to require an upward adjustment to recorded income inequality of the same order as that required in adjusting top incomes for income reporting held by tax authorities (but systematically not provided in response to the household surveys on which most income distribution data is based)—perhaps

5 points on the Gini coefficient. Alstadsaeter, Johannesen, & Zucman (forthcoming) use leaked data to show how strongly tax evasion in Scandinavia is concentrated in the top 0.01 per cent of the wealth distribution; and hence how understated inequality will be if estimates rest on household surveys and tax reporting data alone. The ability of elites to opt out of direct taxation—whether as individuals or as major companies—not only undermines the redistribution possible through given tax policies, but also contributes with lobbying to reduce the attractiveness of pursuing redistribution. In the case of corporate taxation, multinational profit shifting creates an artificial disadvantage for smaller, national businesses—which are typically responsible for the majority of employment in a country.

Illicit financial flows have, therefore, tremendous power to cause damage to states, economies and societies. The extent of that damage depends ultimately on the scale of IFF themselves. The aims of this volume therefore include supporting the selection of better estimates for future work on impacts; and supporting efficient prioritisation of approaches and data likely to lead to better estimates.

PART 2

ESTIMATES OF IFF SCALE

2

Trade Estimates

International trade plays an important role in some of the most prominent studies aimed at estimating the scale of illicit financial flows. A case in point is one of the first estimates of illicit financial flows in the book by Raymond Baker (2005), who in 2006 founded Global Financial Integrity (GFI), an NGO which is well-known for its own estimates. Mainly on the basis of around 550 interviews with corporate employees, Baker (2005) estimated that more than USD 539 billion flows out of developing and transitional economies each year due to a combination of commercial tax evasion, fraud in international trade, drug trafficking, and corruption; and that international trade abuses account for the largest part. These abuses are due both to criminal (illegal arms trade, smuggling) and illicit (mispricing between unrelated and abusive transfer pricing between related companies, and 'fake transactions') activities. On the basis of Baker (2005), Christian Aid (2008) estimates the amount of tax revenue lost to developing countries annually through these two techniques, transfer mispricing and false invoicing, at 157 billion USD.

In contrast with the pioneering estimates by Baker (2005) based partly on interviews (direct, if anecdotal, evidence), most of the more recent approaches to estimation recognise that it is not possible to observe illicit financial flows directly and estimate them indirectly. These approaches are based on the little available economic data that is available about activities potentially related to illicit financial flows. Specifically, the methodologies often focus on exploiting anomalies in the data that may arise from the process of hiding the flows (but can also arise for other reasons—a critical point to which we return when we critically evaluate the estimation methodologies).

The most prominent approaches focus on anomalies in the current account (via misreported or mispriced trade, discussed in this chapter) and in the capital account (through partially unrecorded capital movements, discussed in the next chapter). Some of the authors combine the two approaches, including GFI reports covering most developing countries, and Ndikumana and Boyce who focus on African countries (in these cases we discuss their trade and capital components in the respective chapters). Both

Estimating illicit financial flows: A critical guide to the data, methodologies and findings. Alex Cobham and Petr Janský, Oxford University Press (2020). © Alex Cobham and Petr Janský.
DOI: 10.1093/oso/9780198854418.001.0001

of these group of approaches are reviewed in the few existing reviews of illicit financial flows such as, for example, the edited volume of Reuter (2012) and Johannesen & Pirttilä (2016), who mostly use the term capital flight (a related but distinct concept, which has earlier generated quite a lot of research interest, e.g. Cuddington, 1987, Dooley, 1988, Collier, Hoeffler, & Pattillo, 2001, Beja, 2005). In these reviews and elsewhere, both of these approaches have been subjected to critical evaluations and we discuss them alongside the relevant literature.

Within the trade estimates we distinguish three broadly defined groups of approaches, roughly according to the data used, and we discuss them one by one. (This classification is not perfect with some studies fitting in more, or none, of these groups, but we believe that it does help us to enhance the discussion.) The first subchapter examines estimates based mostly on country-level data (i.e. for each country or country pair we have only one piece of information available), although some of the reviewed studies use more detailed data. The second subchapter discusses studies based on commodity-level trade data. Each of these first two subchapters deals with a specific methodological approach as well. The first subchapter focuses on so called trade mirror statistics, while the second subchapter investigates studies looking at abnormal prices. The studies discussed in these two subchapters, and in the first one in particular, have been subject to evaluation by other researchers, such as Hong & Pak (2017) or Nitsch (2017), that have pointed out the methodological weaknesses such as unrealistic assumptions in these studies (and we discuss critical observations from these evaluations below). Emerging partly as a response to these criticisms, the final subchapter discusses the most recent and, from the point of view of rigour, most promising studies. These studies rely on only recently available detailed transaction-level data. This kind of detailed data is so far available only for a limited number of countries, although their number is increasing.

We thus provide a broad classification of the existing trade data-based estimates of illicit financial flows, of which we provide an overview in Table 2.1. In addition to prevailing method and level and sources of data, Table 2.1 includes examples of recent studies as well as our brief evaluation of the reliability of methodology and availability of estimates in terms of country coverage. This is of course only a quick bird's eye view—the individual studies covered differ from each other within the subchapters and each study has its own pros and cons, including its suitability for estimation of scale of illicit financial flows or for audit purposes.

Table 2.1. Broad classification of trade data-based estimates of illicit financial flows

Sub-chapter	Prevailing level of data	Prevailing sources of data	Prevailing method	Recent examples	Reliability of the methodology	Availability and country coverage
2.1	Country (and commodity)	IMF (and UN Comtrade)	Mirror trade statistics	GFI's Spanjers & Salomon (2017)	Not recommended as estimates of scale, perhaps suitable for preliminary identification for audit purposes	Excellent and most of the world
2.2	Commodity (and transaction)	Country-specific (and UN Comtrade)	Abnormal prices	Chalendard, Raballand, & Rakotoarisoa (2019)	Not recommended as estimates of scale, perhaps suitable for preliminary identification for audit purposes	Excellent and most of the world
2.3	Transaction	Country-specific	Systematic differences between intra-firm and arm's length prices	Davies, Martin, Parenti, & Toubal (2017)	Good (estimates of scale and for audit purposes)	Limited and only a few countries

Source: Authors

2.1. Country-level Trade Estimates: Mirror trade statistics

2.1.1. Overview

The early estimates of illicit financial flows on the basis of trade data (which happen to be also some of the first estimates of illicit financial flows more generally) are based on aggregate country-level international trade data. Most of these studies capture the quantity of illicit flows by contrasting what a country claims it imported from (or exported to) the rest of the world with what the rest of the world states it exported to (or imported from) that given country. The development of this method of—what others call and we are going to call—mirror trade statistics, which compares import and export data for the same trade flow, goes back to Morgenstern (1950, 1974) and Bhagwati (1964, 1974) and was applied, for example, by Beja (2008) for China and by Berger & Nitsch (2012) for five largest importers. On the one hand, we include all of approaches using the logic of the mirror trade statistics method in this subchapter, although some of them, such as Berger & Nitsch (2012) or Ndikumana (2016), have been applied at the commodity level (and not at the country level as the name of the subchapter suggests). One the other hand, we do not discuss in detail literature related specifically to tariff evasion, as pioneered by Bhagwati (1964) and later developed, for example, by Javorcik & Narciso (2008).

We focus in our description on perhaps the two most prominent mirror trade statistics approaches. These are those by the organisation GFI, and by the duo of authors Ndikumana and Boyce. Both combine a trade-related IFF component with estimates based on capital-account data that we discuss in the next chapter. They both assume that traders deliberately misreport trade through faking invoices or other forms of mis-invoicing and we discuss these two in detail below. Before that we briefly explore various motivations why trading partners might mis-invoice the trade volumes or prices. A recent overview of these various motives is provided, for example, by Kellenberg & Levinson (2016) and Nitsch (2017) and they range from tariff evasion to tax evasion. In Table 2.2, together with Nitsch (2017), we distinguish four types of trade mis-invoicing measured along two dimensions—first whether the trade flows are exports or imports and, second, whether these flows are overinvoiced or underinvoiced. We agree with Nitsch's (2017) argument that the broad range of incentives to misreport trade provides a challenge for the empirical assessment of its scale and in the this and the following two subchapters we review how various researchers and methods have dealt with this challenge so far.

Table 2.2. Types of trade mis-invoicing

	Overinvoicing	Underinvoicing
Export	Export overinvoicing To take advantage of export subsidies—Celasun & Rodrik (1989a), Celasun & Rodrik (1989b)	Export underinvoicing To evade export restrictions, to circumvent trade restrictions (a misclassification of products or a misdeclaration of the final destination of a shipment) or to avoid product taxes—Fisman & Wei (2009), Kellenberg & Levinson (2016), Kee & Nicita (2016)
Import	Import overinvoicing To misclassify other imports (underreport some imports and thus overreport other imports)—Chalendard, Raballand, & Rakotoarisoa (2019)	Import underinvoicing To reduce the payment of customs duties or to avoid product taxes—Yang (2008), Kellenberg & Levinson (2016)

Source: Authors on the basis of Nitsch (2017) and other literature

2.1.2. Data

Both GFI's Spanjers & Salomon (2017) and Ndikumana & Boyce (2010) use IMF's Direction of Trade Statistics (DOTS). DOTS covers many countries and has been the preferred source of international trade data because of its superior coverage of countries. DOTS include imports and exports of merchandise goods only (i.e. not services) and this limitation holds also for the other often used data source, UN Comtrade. Also, in both databases imports are usually reported on a cost, insurance and freight (CIF) basis and exports are reported on a free on board (f.o.b.) basis. C.i.f. values include the transaction value of the goods, the value of services performed to deliver goods to the border of the exporting country and the value of the services performed to deliver the goods from the border of the exporting country to the border of the importing country. F.o.b. values include the transaction value of the goods and the value of services performed to deliver goods to the border of the exporting country.

DOTS includes information at country level with trade flows between country pairs available for a subgroup of countries. When available, GFI's Spanjers & Salomon (2017) use DOTS data preferably at bilateral level (around half countries in Europe and Western Hemisphere) and otherwise at aggregate level (two thirds of all countries including a vast majority of countries in Sub-Saharan Africa and most countries in Asia and other regions). They do further adjustments to their trade mis-invoicing estimates (not discussed in detail below) using data from Hong Kong, Switzerland, South Africa and Zambia with additional data for these countries. Similarly, Ndikumana & Boyce (2010) rely on the IMF's DOTS (using bilateral data for a group of industrialised countries) in trade adjustments of their estimates for trade invoicing.

Some recent research, such as Berger & Nitsch (2012), Kellenberg & Levinson (2016) and Ndikumana (2016), uses UN Comtrade. UN Comtrade data (discussed in some detail below) seem to be in some respects equivalent to IMF's DOTS data (but, importantly, the coverage of countries has been lower in UN Comtrade) and in respect of disaggregation, UN Comtrade seems to be the preferable source: data are available at a product level and for recent years, on a monthly basis. The mirror statistics approach could be applied to (rarely available) transaction-level data as well, but it is only possible if this data is available from two reporting countries so that their bilateral trade could be analysed (since in practice most of the transaction-level data that is currently available is limited to one country only, as we discuss in the final subchapter). This is in contrast with the abnormal prices methodologies discussed in the following subchapter, for which one country data source is sufficient and that might partly explain why most of the research at the frontier on the basis of the transaction-level data discussed in the third subchapter builds on ideas similar to those in the abnormal prices research (rather than mirror trade statistics).

Both IMF's DOTS and UN Comtrade, if used at country-level in particular, provide a very good international coverage in terms of a number of countries for which there is information available. However, the information is highly aggregated, giving the values of imports and exports with disaggregation by trading partner only, and any analysis on the basis of this data is naturally constrained by this aggregate data's limitations. We evaluate the methodologies critically below and it is clear that many of the limitations stem from, or are interlinked with, the nature of the data, its aggregate level in particular. Also, the IMF has expressed concerns about the use of the discrepancies in these international trade datasets. In a consultation for the SDG indicator (Inter-agency Expert Group on SDG Indicators, 2015, p. 280), the IMF argued that official estimates of trade mis-invoicing cannot be derived by transforming trade data from the IMF's DOTS or UN Comtrade either by individual data or in aggregate. Instead, the IMF representative Carol Baker argued that estimates of illicit financial flows should be based on an understanding of specific country's circumstances and on administrative data such as customs reports and we review the leading available estimate based on this type of data in the final sub-chapter.

UN Comtrade database contains the most detailed data available for global analysis of international trade. The most detailed classification of commodities (goods or products) follows the Harmonized System categorisation at the six-digit level. The UN Comtrade database collates, standardises and makes available data from national authorities (typically customs authorities) on the annual quantity, value and trade partner country of commodity trade. Complications in the data collation process mean that there are some limitations to what can be expected of the dataset.

UN Comtrade (2018) lists six limitations in particular, which we summarise as follows. First, confidentiality results in some data on detailed commodity categories not being available, although this is still captured in data on higher-level aggregates. Second, coverage is not complete; that is, while the database runs from 1961 to the present, not all countries report all of their trade for every year. Third, classifications vary—that is, different commodity classifications are used by different countries in different periods, so comparisons cannot always be exact. Fourth, conversion cannot always be precise; that is, where the database includes data that has been converted from one classification to another, these will not always map precisely one on to the other and hence imprecision may result. Fifth, consistency between reporters of the same trade is not guaranteed: that is, exporter and importer country might record the same trade differently due to various factors including valuation (e.g. imports c.i.f. versus export f.o.b.), differences in inclusions of particular commodities or timing. Sixth, country of origin rules mean that the 'partner country' recorded for imports will generally be the country of origin and need not imply a direct trading relationship. These limitations are relevant for analysis of prices as well as for mirror trade statistics. We believe that they require caution, but should not prevent careful use of the data.

2.1.3. Methodology

The trade mis-invoicing estimates by the GFI, recently reported by Spanjers & Salomon (2017), are based on the assumption that whatever exports or imports are reported by advanced economies, but not equally reported by developing countries, are illicit financial flows (either under-invoicing or over-invoicing). In addition to what they call lower bound estimate using only developing country-advanced economies relationships, their upper bound estimates are scaled up on the basis of assuming that traders mis-invoice with other developing countries at the same rate they mis-invoice with advanced economies. An earlier similar approach applied by the GFI is named the trade mispricing model, e.g. Kar & Cartwright-Smith (2009), but here we focus on the recently published version by Spanjers & Salomon (2017). (While finalising the book, we note that Global Financial Integrity (2019) just published its most recent set of estimates, for 148 countries for years 2006–2015. The most significant methodological change, according to the report, involves the use of both DOTS and Comtrade data to generate two sets of estimates. We also note the change in assumed trade costs from 10 to 6 per cent.

GFI's Spanjers & Salomon (2017) use the following series of equations to explain their 'bilateral advanced economies calculation.'

$$ID_{jp,t} = \frac{I_{j,t}}{r} - X_{p,t}$$

$$ED_{jp,t} = \frac{I_{p,t}}{r} - X_{j,t}$$

where $I_{j,t}$ are imports by the developing country j from the partner country p at time t, $I_{p,t}$ are partner country p's imports from the developing country j at time t, $X_{j,t}$ are developing country j's exports to partner country p at time t, and $X_{p,t}$ are partner country p's exports to the developing country j at time t. Through the use of r (assumed to be 1.1) they aim to make the import and export data comparable by converting import data reported as c.i.f. to an f.o.b. basis, in which export data are reported in IMF's DOTS.

Spanjers & Salomon (2017) interpret negative values of ID as import under-invoicing and illicit inflows and positive values as over-invoicing and illicit outflows. In parallel, they interpret negative values of ED as export over-invoicing and illicit inflows and positive values of ED as export under-invoicing and illicit outflows. In their interpretation, they make a number of assumptions that we discuss and, with the help of existing literature, critically evaluate below.

Furthermore, for developing countries for which the bilateral data used in the equations above are not available (almost two thirds of developing countries), Spanjers & Salomon (2017) apply what they call world aggregate calculation—substituting the individual partner countries p above with one partner, the whole world, w. Spanjers & Salomon (2017) themselves recognise a number of challenges related to this step. First, it implicitly treats developing country partner trade data as being as accurate as those of advanced economies. Second, it leads to what they call erratic swings in magnitude.

Spanjers & Salomon (2017) apply this approach to developing countries and their partner advanced economies to arrive at what they label low estimates (they scale down the world aggregate calculation to include only the share of trade with advanced economies using the partner data). For their high estimates, they extrapolate this to the world total, assuming that trade mis-invoicing is as prevalent with other developing countries as it is with advanced economies. When the scale of trade mis-invoicing is summed up across all developing countries, the high estimates are bound to double count flows between developing countries, an issue that the low estimates avoid.

In a separate, but similar stream of studies, Ndikumana & Boyce (e.g. 2010) also estimate trade mis-invoicing. Ndikumana & Boyce (2010) make the trade invoicing adjustment by comparing countries' export and import data to those of trading partners, assuming the industrialised countries data to be relatively accurate and interpreting the difference as evidence of mis-invoicing. They use equations equivalent to those of Spanjers & Salomon (2017) to arrive at values of $ID_{jp,t}$ and $ED_{jp,t}$. They then, in line with GFI's high estimates, extrapolate these estimates for industrialised countries to global totals by dividing each of $ID_{jp,t}$ and $ED_{jp,t}$ with the average shares of industrialised countries in the African country's exports and imports, respectively.

An important distinguishing feature of the Ndikumana & Boyce methodology in contrast with of GFI's Spanjers & Salomon (2017), is that for each year and each African country, the values of estimates of export discrepancies and import discrepancies are summed up to a total trade mis-invoicing (which is then added to their total estimate of capital flight). In GFI's labelling we can write the equation of Ndikumana & Boyce as:

$$Trade\ misinvoicing_{it} = ID_{jp,t} + ED_{jp,t} = \frac{\dfrac{I_{p,t}}{r} - X_{j,t}}{ICXS_i} + \frac{\dfrac{I_{j,t}}{r} - X_{p,t}}{ICMS_i}$$

where $ICXS_i$ and $ICMS_i$ are the average shares of industrialised countries in the African country's exports and imports, respectively. It implies that outflows and inflows can net out at this stage. This would lead to similar estimates to the GFI method when both export and import mis-invoicing estimates have the same sign, but to very different magnitudes where one indicates outflows and the other, inflows. Overall, Ndikumana & Boyce net off their estimates of illicit inflows to obtain a more conservative (and also more volatile) series, while the GFI argues that because 'there is no such thing as net crime', it makes sense to consider gross outflows (summing absolute values to arrive at a sum of illicit financial flows).

In practice a similar methodological approach can be applied not only at the country level, but also at the commodity level. For example, there are two pieces of research carried out in the late 2000s that consider the mirror trade statistics and aim to explain the observed gap. Fisman & Wei (2009) focus on the trade in arts and find evidence consistent with smuggling patterns. Kee & Nicita (2016) find that exporters or products that have higher ad valorem equivalents of non-tariff measures tend to have larger trade discrepancies, suggesting firms mis-declare product codes or country of origin to circumvent the cumbersome and opaque non-tariff measures. Berger & Nitsch (2012) use a similar approach for more products and argue that the reporting gaps partly represent smuggling activities.

More recently, and more explicitly focused on illicit financial flows, United Nations Economic Commission for Africa (ECA) & African Union (2015), in the report of the High Level Panel on Illicit Flows from Africa (the 'Mbeki report'), aim to assess illicit financial flows at the country and sector levels through trade mispricing using mis-invoicing. They consider their methodology similar to the trade mispricing model used earlier by GFI, e.g. Kar & Cartwright-Smith (2009), and thus similar to the most recent trade mis-invoicing estimates of Spanjers & Salomon (2017). Although the logic remains the same, the quality of the methodology increases substantially and ECA (2015) is able to address many, but not all, problems of trade mis-invoicing estimates discussed below.

ECA (2015) improves the earlier methodologies in a number of aspects. In contrast with the GFI approach, the Mbeki report by ECA (2015) uses data from UN Comtrade, which provides bilateral trade data at the product-level for more than 5000 products (GFI's preferred IMF data do not contain this detail). ECA (2015) recognises that discrepancies can occur for a number of reasons, including but not limited to illicit financial flows. In line with Ndikumana & Boyce, but in contrast with GFI, ECA (2015) net off the estimates for a given pair of countries for a given product, which helps them avoid the issue of negative illicit financial flows. Rather than assume that c.i.f. values are 10 per cent higher than f.o.b. values, as both Ndikumana & Boyce and the GFI do, ECA (2015) estimate it using the CEPII's BACI database built upon UN Comtrade. Overall, with the application of these improvements ECA (2015) likely achieves more reliable estimates of trade mispricing than the other approaches; but some other important drawbacks of this adaptation of trade mirror statistics method remain. A similar, although modified, approach has been applied by Economic Commission for Latin America and the Caribbean (2016, p. 124) and, most recently, by Kravchenko (2018) of the United Nations Economic and Social Commission for Asia and the Pacific (ESCAP).

The research of Ndikumana (2016)is similar to that of Ndikumana & Boyce, but makes use of a different level and source of data. (Despite these differences, and Ndikumana (2016) using commodity- rather than country-level trade data, we include it here—as with the Mbeki report above—because of its similarities to Ndikumana & Boyce). Ndikumana (2016), in a report prepared, and later partially updated following a critical feedback, for UNCTAD, follows a similar methodological approach as in the research by Ndikumana and Boyce discussed above, but at a more detailed, commodity level. Ndikumana (2016) estimates export mis-invoicing (DX), and import mis-invoicing (DM), for country i, product (or commodity) k, and partner j at time t:

$$DX^k_{i,j,t} = M^k_{j,i,t} - \beta \times X^k_{i,j,t}$$

$$DM^k_{i,j,t} = M^k_{i,j,t} - \beta \times X^k_{j,i,t}$$

where $M^k_{j,i,t}$ stands for imports by country j from country i in time t of commodity k, and, similarly, $X^k_{i,j,t}$ for exports by country i to country j as reported by country i, and β is the freight and insurance factor (similarly to r in the previous subchapter).

As in the research by Ndikumana and Boyce, Ndikumana (2016) argues that positive values of DX and negative value of DM provide indications of export and import underinvoicing, respectively, and negative values of DX and positive values of DM indicate export and import overinvoicing, respectively. Ndikumana (2016) applies the methodology to selected countries and commodities. Carton & Slim (2018) use a modified version of the mirror trade statistics, applied to the Comtrade data of OECD countries and supplemented by trade intensity index. The methodology of both of these recent papers is also dependent on assumptions similar to those of Ndikumana and Boyce. Most of the criticism discussed below is therefore broadly relevant—in some cases likely to a lower extent because of the more detailed data used. In addition, the critical discussion specific to Ndikumana (2016) has been documented by Forstater (2016a) and Forstater (2016b). For example, Brülhart, Kukenova, & Dihel (2015) explain the trade gap in Zambia's copper exports by the copper being traded by companies headquartered in Switzerland, but exported to other countries than Switzerland. Ponsford & Mwiinga (2019) document broader concerns using the example of the Zambian government's request for financial models from extractive companies.

While these trade-based estimates of illicit financial flows may include some trade mispricing by multinational enterprises for the purpose of shifting profits to countries with lower taxation (so called transfer mispricing), trade mis-invoicing is a more crude approach to tax reduction than most of those challenged in the OECD Base Erosion and Profit Shifting action plan, the major international attempt to curtail the problem. The survey conducted by Baker (2005), which found widespread commercial tax *evasion* through trade, relates to an earlier period; and it may be thought likely that the documented explosion in sophistication of multinational tax minimisation practices has seen non-trade-based forms of avoidance become dominant.

Instead, the anomalies now estimated through mirror trade statistics may be more likely to reveal unrelated party transactions that aim to shift part of one party's income into a different country (so called trade mispricing). As GFI, for example, now state on their website (http://www.gfinteg-rity.org/issue/trade-misinvoicing, accessed 1 June 2018)—in contrast to Baker (2005):

Because they often both involve mispricing, many aggressive tax avoidance schemes by multinational corporations can easily be confused with trade mis-invoicing. However, they should be regarded as separate policy problems with separate solutions. That said, multinational corporations can and do engage in trade mis-invoicing. This activity, however, involves the deliberate misreporting of the value of a customs transactions, and is thus illegal tax evasion, not legal tax avoidance.

In the mirror trade statistics approach, researchers use mostly country-level trade data to establish anomalies in the declared values of total exports and imports, on the basis that these reveal illicit shifts of value. On one view, these estimates are rather conservative. They are able to pick up only a share of all of trade mispricing or trade mis-invoicing. The data does not pick up, for example, trade transactions where the mis-invoicing is incorporated in the same invoice exchanged between exporter and importer. In addition the data includes only goods and their results thus exclude any scale of mis-invoicing of services and intangibles. On the other hand, the estimates are based on a number of important assumptions and are bound to include much more than trade mis-invoicing, as discussed below.

Overall, the earlier studies succeeded in highlighting the importance of tax havens and illicit financial flows and bringing these issues to wider attention, but there are difficulties with these estimates and some of the individual methods were earlier criticised by, for example, Hines (2010) or Fuest & Riedel (2012) and a number of other chapters in the book edited by Reuter

(2012). Both Forstater (2015) and Reuter (2017) consider the estimates of illicit financial flows as overestimates and as playing a misleading role in the public debate.

Some problems are common to most of the pioneering research in this area (including these trade estimates as well as the capital account estimates in the following chapter). To be able to derive any estimates, most of the methods necessarily rely on strong assumptions, for example, about what the data on trade reflects. Similarly, most of the estimates do not shed more light on specific policy measures—the results may not provide more guidance for policy other than a general recommendation to reduce illicit financial flows; or, in the worst possible case, they could suggest erroneous areas for policy priority, if the broad trade channel is over-estimated. We discuss some of these critiques in detail below.

Because the studies which are critical of the methodologies, are often important contributions in themselves we briefly review their critical points one study at a time below. For each of the selected recent studies, we briefly sum up and evaluate their main points, including their views, if any, on how to improve estimates in the future. None of the reviewed critical studies dispute the existence of trade-based illicit financial flows, but they do raise important reservations about their estimated scale and the methodologies, notably their assumptions. This is underlined by Reuter (2017) in a recent study for the World Bank, who summarises some of the criticisms of, above all, the GFI approach in particular—but importantly also draws two other conclusions. First, he acknowledges that GFI is the only organisation that has consistently studied the phenomenon. Second, he argues that whatever the criticisms of the existing estimates, there is no doubt that illicit financial flows are substantial enough to merit close attention.

One of the few recent papers explicitly aimed at reviewing the methods, Johannesen & Pirttilä (2016) highlight three important conceptual issues (again of some relevance also to estimates based on capital account data). First, these estimates are likely to capture some completely legitimate flows, which the applied methodologies are not able to distinguish. Second, the approaches of GFI as well as Ndikumana & Boyce estimate net illicit financial flows and provide some scope for outflows and inflows to neutralize each other (at transaction, commodity, or country level). Where these result in zero or negative total illicit financial flows, they will complicate interpretation of the estimates. Third, since the illicit financial flows are often estimated as residuals or discrepancies, the resulting estimates will tend to be compounded by measurement errors associated with the trade flows.

Hong & Pak (2017) are concerned that the GFI estimates overestimate how much developing countries lose due to illicit financial flows. Hong & Pak (2017) focus on a specific assumption of what they call the partner-country trade data comparison method (what we prefer to call here trade mirror statistics). They argue that the assumption of no mis-invoicing in partner countries cannot be supported and raise doubts about the reliability of the method. Hong & Pak (2017) argue that the advanced economies trade data cannot serve as a counterfactual to the developing countries' trade data.Hong & Pak (2017) convincingly show that advanced economies also likely suffer from trade mis-invoicing, and therefore that the results of the trade mirror statistics approach are biased. Unfortunately, given the data limitations, the scale of bias is hard to determine. As a more promising alternative approach to mirror trade statistics, Hong & Pak (2017) consider the abnormal prices research that we discuss in the following subchapter.

Being critical of the methodologies as well as the excessive attention trade-based illicit financial flows might receive at the cost of other types of flows for which similar estimates do not exist, Forstater (2016a) focuses on the trade mirror statistics approach, while Forstater (2018) discusses tax and development more generally; and Forstater (2015) discusses profit shifting by MNEs (and we discuss her views on this in the later chapter focused on this type of illicit financial flows). Forstater (2016a), as well as her blogs, focuses on criticising empirical methodologies of illicit financial flows and their interpretations. For example, Forstater (2016a) provides some detailed criticisms of the Ndikumana (2016) report by Ndikumana. She proposes four areas for further work—understanding domestic realities, measuring international progress, commodity value chains and the role of multinational companies. The brief paper by Forstater (2016a) is accompanied by a comment by one of the GFI economists, Matthew Salomon, who agrees that focusing only on trade mis-invoicing as representative of all illicit financial flows would be too narrow, but asserts that trade mis-invoicing is an important area of further research and that even when there are detailed administrative data available, illicit financial flows remain unobservable and assumptions are needed to estimate them.

In a series of contributions—Nitsch (2012), Nitsch (2016), and Nitsch (2017)—Nitsch discusses the limitations of the trade-based methodologies. For example, Nitsch (2016) critiques the GFI methodology, focusing in particular on deficiencies in the use of mirror trade statistics to quantify the extent of capital outflows due to trade mis-invoicing. He identifies what he believes to be arbitrary assumptions, mixed methodologies and skewed sampling to argue that their estimates have no substantive meaning. Nitsch (2017) observes that a highly disaggregated transaction-level data is usually not available to researchers and mis-invoicing behaviour is thus often identified from more aggregate trade information, which introduces two types of problems. First, at a more aggregate level, discrepancies in mirror trade statistics from mis-invoiced trade transactions may cancel each other out. Second, for the analysis of aggregate data, the set of assumptions that is used for the identification of mis-invoicing practices typically becomes even more restrictive and we discuss these assumptions below. An additional complication is that the accuracy of trade mis-invoicing estimates is unknown, since, as Nitsch (2017) argues, only an unknown fraction of all misreported trade activities is identified from official statistics.

Building on his earlier critical assessment in Nitsch (2012), Nitsch (2016) provides insights into pitfalls of mirror trade statistics and how the problems might be overcome (albeit he does not seem to be very optimistic on this topic in Nitsch (2017)). Nitsch (2017) presents similar critical points to Nitsch (2016) but makes somewhat more strident conclusions about existing methodologies ('a matter of faith') without providing much new guidance for improved methodologies in the future.

Below we focus on the discussion of assumptions by Nitsch (2016). Nitsch (2016) observes that the trade mirror statistics approach is in principle a credible methodology only if a few restrictive assumptions hold: for example, if it was applied on transaction-level data with information on the transactions from both countries, and the mis-invoicing affected only one side of the transaction. The latter is a crucial implicit assumption of the trade mirror statistics approach as applied by the GFI: the trade statistics of the two countries are assumed to be affected differently, with one a perfect reflection of reality (the transaction is recorded and is recorded correctly) while the other is deliberately mis-invoiced. While Fisman & Wei (2009) make the assumption explicit and argue why it is likely to hold in the case of antiques and cultural property, it is not clear from the GFI and other similar research how often trade mis-invoicing is carried out in this way (whether none, one, or both of the countries' statistics should be affected). Given these assumptions, not only it is hard to estimate the scale of illicit financial flows, but also hard to know the accuracy of these estimates.

Focusing on the deficiencies of the mirror trade statistics approach as applied by GFI in particular, Nitsch (2016) identifies four crucial assumptions of the GFI approach and some of these relate to other applications of mirror trade statistics. First, GFI assumes that the differences between export and import values are homogeneous across countries at the rate of 10 per cent of transportation costs. He documents the sensitivity of this assumption as well as that it is not consistent with the observed values. A similar robustness check has been recently carried out by Erskine (2018), who shows systematic differences in mis-invoicing for landlocked and coastal African countries (a good proxy for a relative scale of transportation costs), providing further support for country-specific approach, as exemplified by ECA (2015). Second, all discrepancies in countries' trade statistics (other than these transportation costs) are assumed to be a result of trade mis-invoicing and thus illicit financial flows—which seems bound to lead to overestimates.

This assumption has been addressed by GFI to a degree. Since 2013, following a critical analysis by Kessler & Borst (2013), GFI take into account the transit trade of Hong Kong, which is important for China in particular, and this should make the estimates somewhat more realistic. They also made a few similar adjustments for other countries. But there are a number of countries that serve as transit jurisdictions and their role in trade might cause trade gaps ('Rotterdam and Antwerp effect'), as argued, for example, by Herrigan, Kochen, & Williams (2005).

Third, only discrepancies that lead to (positive) outflows out of developing countries are considered. A number of assumptions could explain this methodological position—either there are only outflows out of developing countries or only outflows are worth their focus or the method works well when outflows are estimates and not so well when inflows are estimates. At least one form of this assumption seems to be reflected in that GFI adds a particular flow to the overall sum only if it is an outflow from developing countries (any estimates that might indicate an inflow to developing countries are set at zero). And in a more recent report by GFI, Spanjers & Salomon (2017) also provide the estimated inflows in developing countries.

The fourth assumption, identified by Nitsch (2016), is that GFI assumes that countries' aggregate trade with the world is representative about trade mis-invoicing of country's partners. This aggregation enables the inflows and outflows to cancel out each other and thus the estimates based on comparison with the world are lower-bound estimates. This fourth assumption applies only to a part of GFI estimates since 2013, when they started using bilateral data for a share of the developing countries. GFI still partly, in their high estimates, relies on extrapolation, or scaling up, on a sample of advanced economies partners for the whole trade of developing countries—if advanced economies are likely to be the destination of more illicit financial flows than other countries, this extrapolation biases the estimates upwards.

There is another reason why this extrapolation likely leads to upwards bias. Any use of trade mirror statistics faces the challenge of attributing observed discrepancies to one of the partners since import overinvoicing in one country is equivalent to export underinvoicing in its trading partner. Without any decision, both of these were counted and thus double counted in the total. GFI solves this by focusing on outflows from developing countries. However, by this extrapolation, estimated trade mis-invoicing related to the trade among developing countries is counted twice. Furthermore, Kellenberg & Levinson (2016) find evidence of trade misreporting in both developing and developed countries, with only a few detected differences, andHong & Pak (2017) make a similar point. Given the importance of these assumptions and changes in methodology, it is perhaps not surprising that the estimates published by the GFI are not very consistent over time. Also, Nitsch (2017) notes that the country-level estimates for some countries vary by orders of magnitude over the years.

Among his other, perhaps more minor, comments, Nitsch (2016) notes that although GFI has been transparent about the use of the data and methodologies, the fact that they often make changes in their methodologies makes any subsequent analysis difficult. He also observes that in GFI's first report on illicit financial flows out of developing countries, Kar & Cartwright-Smith (2008) start combining trade and capital-account data based estimates, but that they do not sufficiently discuss how the two overlap or complement each other.

Overall, Nitsch (2016) acknowledges that given the nature of illicit financial flows and data available, there is no first-best solution and he provides suggestions for a more nuanced approach in three areas. His first call for more micro evidence—perhaps focused on a small number of trading relationships important for a given country—is partly already being answered, as we review the recent research in our third subchapter. He hopes that this could shed more light on the relative importance of trade mis-invoicing in illicit financial flows. Second, for a global estimate he suggests to focus on a few large countries responsible for a majority of illicit financial flows. Third, he sees a potential in the use of the trade mirror statistics approach, especially at the product level and when institutional knowledge about practices of trade mis-invoicing is absent.

2.1.4. Results

It is necessary to consider the results with a high degree of caution in the light of the critical evaluation of the methodologies above. This includes the results estimated by the GFI. In the most recent GFI analysis of illicit financial flows to and from developing countries between 2005 and 2014, Spanjers & Salomon (2017) estimate the illicit financial flows (or outflows) from developing countries in 2014 at between $620 billion and $970 billion. In this report they publish such a range for the first time. Also for the first time, they put equal emphasis on inflows and estimate them in 2014 at between $1.4 and $2.5 trillion. These and earlier estimates of the GFI had arguably had an impact on media and public debate, with, for instance, The Economist (2014) using their results and linking them, among other examples, with money laundering through trade mis-invoicing by Mexican drug gangs. Focusing on trade-based money-laundering, Gara, Giammatteo, & Tosti (2018) provide a recent application of the method for Italy. Nitsch (2016) looks at the estimates of the GFI reports over time and observes two patterns: the estimated illicit financial flows increase over time, while estimates at the beginning of the sample period have been mostly revised downwards. He also points out the high variance of some of GFI's country-level estimates over the years, with some country estimates differing substantially from year to year (in some cases due to changes in methodology).

In the most recent report, GFI still combine capital-account and trade approaches to estimating illicit financial flows (we describe the former in the next chapter). In their lower bound estimates of outflows, trade mis-invoicing is responsible for two thirds of the total, while what they call unrecorded balance of payments flows (using net errors and omissions from the capital account as a proxy for these, which we discuss in detail in the next chapter) accounts for the remaining third. They estimate that sub-Saharan Africa suffers most in terms of illicit outflows. Sub-Saharan Africa is also the focus of the series of papers by Ndikumana & Boyce (e.g. 2010). Ndikumana & Boyce tend to publish only overall estimates of capital flight including trade mis-invoicing, and we thus cannot discuss their estimates here in detail. Instead, we discuss their overall estimates in the following chapter that focuses on estimates using capital account data.

In a section devoted to estimates of trade mispricing, United Nations Economic Commission for Africa (ECA) & African Union (2015) estimate these trade-based illicit financial outflows from Africa at $242 billion for a period between 2000 and 2008. Making use of their product-level data, ECA (2015) estimate that around 56 per cent of these outflows come from oil, precious metals and minerals, ores, iron and steel, and copper. They highlight the most affected countries (such as Nigeria and Algeria for oil, Zambia for copper) as well as the trading partners involved. In an update to ECA (2015), Economic Commission for Africa (2018a) estimate that net IFFs between Africa and the rest of the world averaged $73 billion per year during the period 2000–2015 from trade reinvoicing alone. Economic Commission for Latin America and the Caribbean (2016) estimates that outflows from countries in Latin America and the Caribbean through international trade price manipulation have increased in the last decade, representing 1.8 per cent of regional GDP (totalling US$765 billion in the period 2004–2013). In 2013, illicit outflows climbed to US$101.6 billion and the associated tax losses stood at about US$31 billion (0.5 percentage points of GDP) as a result of foreign trade price manipulation. This amount represents between 10 per cent and 15 per cent of the actual corporate income tax take. Mexico and Costa Rica are estimated to be among the most severely affected.

Taking a similar, but somewhat more general approach, Kellenberg & Levinson (2016) observe the differences in mirror trade statistics and find that gaps between importer- and exporter-reported trade at the country level vary systematically with GDP, tariffs and taxes, auditing standards, corruption, and trade agreements, suggesting that firms intentionally misreport trade data. Using the example of Cameroon, Raballand, Cantens, & Arenas (2012) present the use of mirror trade statistics as a useful tool to help identify customs fraud. Similarly, for Madagascar, Chalendard, Raballand, & Rakotoarisoa (2019) use mirror trade statistics at the individual transaction level to identify discrepancies and then products and importers in which customs fraud seems to be likely.

2.1.5. Conclusions

The influential illicit financial flows estimates by the GFI and Ndikumana and Boyce are based on country-level trade data, and are subject to well-argued critical evaluations of their methodology and results. The GFI estimates in particular have had their share of both media attention and criticism, and the latter remains largely relevant despite some methodological revisions over time. These limitations, coupled with the increasing availability of commodity-level trade data for a number of developing countries (e.g. through the UN Comtrade database), indicate a gap in research that could result into more reliable trade-based estimates. We investigate how existing research has made use of the advantages (as well the disadvantages) of these possibilities in the next subchapter, before turning to the state of the art studies based on transaction-level data in the final subchapter.

2.2. Commodity-level Trade Estimates: Abnormal prices

2.2.1. Overview

Having discussed misreported trade volumes in the previous subchapter on the mirror trade statistics approach, we now turn to a discussion of misreported trade prices. The relevant studies here are based on trade data that allow identification of 'abnormal' prices at the commodity level. As the previous subchapter documents, some of the early trade data approaches in the literature on illicit financial flows use international trade data and the more recent study often used data at commodity (or product) level to study trade mispricing. Trade mispricing occurs when transactions between both related and unrelated parties are mispriced to avoid tariffs, taxes or achieve similar, illicit or other, objectives (in contrast to a more narrowly defined transfer mispricing that describes only transactions between related parties within a multinational corporation). In other words, trade mispricing (among unrelated trade partners) and transfer mispricing (among related partners such as affiliates of the same MNE), consist of inflating (or deflating) prices in order to shift income or profits from one country to another to take advantage of tax or other differences. For illicit financial outflows, trade mispricing enables shifting income or profits out of countries mainly either through import overinvoicing or export underinvoicing, although there are some plausible motivations for import underinvoicing or import overinvoicing, as summed up in Table 3 above.

In this subchapter we focus on studies making use of abnormal prices. These studies usually examine the normality or extremeness of trade prices, which are most often derived as unit values by dividing trading amount in currency with the corresponding amount of trade—weight in kilograms. The prices can be estimated as unit values only with these more detailed, commodity-level, data, rather than the country-level data used often in the studies based on trade mirror statistics approach. Already some of the above discussed research uses commodity level trade data, but its focus is on trade mirror statistics and thus trade that is not being recorded by one of the trade partners. In this subchapter we focus on trade mispricing and thus illicit financial flows that are being observed in the data.

2.2.2. Data

Much of the research by Simon Pak, John Zdanowicz and colleagues, such as de Boyrie, Pak, & Zdanowicz (2005), uses data from the United States Merchandise Trade Data Base of the United States Department of Commerce, Bureau of Census, which is a reliable source of detailed data, but only for one country's trading relationships, the United States. The US trade data is available on a monthly basis since 1989. Some studies combine this data source with other data sources—for example, Christian Aid (2009) also uses monthly Eurostat data for EU countries, which dates back to 1988. For both data sets used by Christian Aid (2009), even when some products have no defined measure of units and are thus not included in the analysis, the total number of observations per year is in millions (more than 10 million for the US during 2005–2007 period, while over 80 million observations for the EU in 2007). Some of this work uses the United Nations UN Comtrade database, discussed—including its limitations—in the previous subchapter.

2.2.3. Methodology

A number of studies have used trade data to study abnormal prices in order to estimate the scale of capital flight or illicit financial flows, with a duo of authors Pak and Zdanowicz carrying out pioneering work in this area (Christensen, Kapoor, Murphy, Pak, & Spencer, 2007; Zdanowicz, 2009) with their early study from 1994 (Simon J. Pak & Zdanowicz, 1994) and with perhaps a latest similar study published in 2018 (Cathey, Hong, & Pak, 2018). A number of these studies, such as de Boyrie et al. (2005), Zdanowicz, Pak, & Sullivan (1999), Pak, Zanakis, & Zdanowicz (2003) use detailed transactions data from the United States Merchandise Trade Data Base of the United States Department of Commerce, Bureau of Census. Cathey, Hong, & Pak (2018), Pak in a report for Christian Aid (2009) and Pak (2012) use Eurostat data for EU countries in addition for the US data.

All of these and a number of other papers make use of a price filter approach or some variation of it and we describe it below. The objective of this method is to construct a price matrix from which normal prices are derived and compared with the actual prices to identify 'abnormal' prices and thus estimate the scale of related capital flows. The prices are constructed as unit values by dividing the financial amounts by physical weights. This approach reflects a hypothesised assumption that unit values for a given product category should vary only within a relatively narrow interval. It implies that any outliers, abnormal prices, might suggest mis-invoicing and we discuss critical assumptions below.

In the detailed description of methodology, we focus on one of the papers, de Boyrie, Pak, & Zdanowicz (2005), in which they estimate the magnitude of abnormal pricing in international trade between the US and Russia. They use transactions data for over 15 thousand import harmonized commodity codes and over 8 thousand export harmonized commodity codes with detail over 18 million import transactions and 13 million export transactions per year for the period between 1995 and 1999. The fact that they focus on one country, Russia, enables the authors to provide detailed overview of the relevant literature, with Tikhomirov (1997) identifying Cyprus, the UK, Switzerland, the Netherlands, Germany and Denmark as the countries, additional to the US focus by de Boyrie, Pak, & Zdanowicz (2005), used to export capital from Russia.

Their price filter analysis relies on determining some transaction prices as abnormal. Importantly, they consider Russia-US transaction prices normal only when they are within the inter-quartile range of prices of (i) transactions between Russia and the US, or, alternatively, (ii) transactions between the US and all countries in the world. We capture this approach in the following equation for an example of capital flight resulting from over-invoiced exports from Russia to the US in year t for a commodity k:

$$KF^k_{i,j,t} = \left(P^k_{i,j,t} - lower\ quartile\ of\ P^k_{world,j,t} \right) \times X^k_{j,i,t}$$

where i is Russia, j is the US, t is a year, k is a selected commodity. The equation for under-invoiced imports would follow a similar logic (using upper quartile instead of lower quartile), and similarly in alternative specifications with the use of $P^k_{Russia,j,t}$ instead of $P^k_{world,j,t}$ and median price instead of quartiles. For each alternative benchmark prices (i.e. world-US or Russia-US, quartile or median), they arrive at estimates of total capital flight by summing over-invoiced exports and under-invoiced imports together and across all commodities. In addition to estimating the scale of capital flight, they use econometric models by Cuddington (1987) to test whether the capital flight is due to money laundering, tax evasion or portfolio consideration.

Pak has adjusted this methodology for a larger set of countries for Christian Aid (2009). It uses the same data source for the US, and the detailed Eurostat data of 27 then members of the EU. As in de Boyrie, Pak, & Zdanowicz (2005), Pak in Christian Aid (2009) assumes that the price range between an upper quartile price and a lower quartile price for the most detailed product classification is the arm's length price range. In contrast with de Boyrie, Pak, & Zdanowicz (2005), the trade data used are grouped at product level classification which is likely to result—with some overpriced and some underpriced transactions—into underestimation of the amount of mispricing. Also, Christian Aid (2009) notes that the fact that partner data from other countries are not used in this analysis and that large transactions that are only slightly mispriced might go undetected and contribute to underestimation. Other reasons, such as the product homogeneity assumption discussed above or the volatility of prices during the studied time periods (years used for the price quartiles), could support overestimation.

Using the example of Madagascar, an African country with one of the lowest income per capita and lowest shares of taxes per GDP, Chalendard, Raballand, & Rakotoarisoa (2019) use detailed statistical data from both Madagascar confidential database and UN Comtrade. Chalendard, Raballand, & Rakotoarisoa (2019) used the abnormal prices approach to indicate product misclassification. Specifically, they used inconsistent unit value as indicative of customs fraud—unit values of rice and fertilizers (products exempted from value added tax) were much higher than corresponding world prices.

Naturally, there are limitations to this methodological approach, some of which are common to trade mirror statistics discussed in the previous subchapter and some of which are new. For example, when deliberate trade mispricing does occur, it might be possible to detect it only when the mispricing is extreme and almost impossible when the mispricing is only slight. As The Economist (2014) argues, money launderers, who curb their greed and invoice goods up or down by, say, 10 per cent only, will probably continue to get away with it. We discuss the limitations, including the assumptions that determine price abnormality, below, and we focus here on the critical evaluation of the main Pak and Zdanowicz price filter approach, e.g. Carbonnier & Zweynert de Cadena (2015) and Nitsch (2012).

One important set of assumptions is about the role of prices used in the estimation. For such estimation of mispricing, one would ideally like to have a measure of what the price was if it was an arm's length transaction. This approach to estimating trade mispricing is similar to what recent studies at the frontier of research are estimating, but here the lack of persuasive counterfactual normal prices is substituted with quartile range thresholds. This most often used interquartile price range is endogenous and does not seem to be an objective basis for an arms' length price range. In addition, when product categories are used since transaction- or product-level data are not usually available, each category includes goods with a different degree of heterogeneity. Pak & Zdanowicz (1994) argue that the use of inter-quartile range is supported by US regulation on transfer prices in international trade and they use two versions (US-Russia trade and US-world trade) and median prices as alternative benchmarks of normal prices. Still, these thresholds are understandably criticised, e.g. by Johannesen & Pirttilä (2016), as arbitrary. Pak in Christian Aid (2009) acknowledges it, actually using the same word (page 52). In addition to the arbitrariness of setting the interquartile range as the norm, Nitsch (2012) highlights that implementation of such a definition is sensitive to the number of observations—with a small number of relevant data points, as is often the case, potentially leading to biased results. In addition, variations in prices might be caused by (unobserved) differences in the timing of carrying out and/or recording trade transactions.

The required assumption of this approach is that there is a way to determine which prices are abnormal, but in reality the available data do not provide other options than the inevitably arbitrary statistical definitions such as interquartile ranges. Generally, there is no reliable guidance on what price is normal or not. As a potential remedy, in addition to average or other statistical distributions of unit values being used as the control prices or proxies for arms' length prices (in the inter-quartile method by Pak & Zdanowicz, 1994), also prices available from the markets can be used, as in the pioneering research by Hong, Pak, & Pak (2014), in which the authors use the import price of bananas reported by UNCTAD almost on a monthly basis. However, the market prices for many goods and product categories are not readily available, and some data sources might be actually subject to the similar challenges as the international trade unit values.

Nitsch (2012) points out that the data usually used are for product categories rather than products and that information is limited in respect of homogeneity of these product categories, including in quality, that might lie behind some observed differences in unit values. He argues that many of the product categories (around half) are catch-all with the word 'other' in their names.

It follows that one important assumption of this approach, which is partly shared even with the more recent studies in the following chapter, is that the products within the identified detailed product-level categories are homogenous. This homogeneity assumption enables the authors to make abnormality responsible for the deviation from the prevailing prices of the product category defined by inter-quartile price range or median price. In the case of de Boyrie, Pak, & Zdanowicz (2005), they use harmonized commodity codes in the international price matrix, which are specific product classifications more detailed and arguably more useful than industry classifications (such as standard industrial classification codes). These harmonized commodity codes are arguably the most detailed publicly available trade classification (the more confidential sources of more detailed data are discussed in the next subchapter). Still, if this assumption does not hold, for example in the case of quality differences, the method is to overestimate the extent of mispricing. An additional complication is that the identification of abnormal prices through unit values assumes that trade mis-invoicing is occurring exclusively via abnormal prices rather than weight, in case of which the identification of abnormal prices is inaccurate and, furthermore, the extent of this inaccuracy is unknown.

Partly to counter similar critique, de Boyrie, Pak, & Zdanowicz (2005) in the discussion of their results emphasise that their analysis identifies only potentially abnormally priced trades (for example, to help investigators pre-select cases for auditing) rather than proving that they are abnormal. They acknowledge that when the number of transactions is small for a certain commodity, their identification may not be reliable. Given the discussed assumptions, also other researchers using this approach argue for its use not for estimation of scale of trade mis-invoicing, but as a tool for detecting suspicious transactions from detailed trade data, for example, for auditing purposes by tax and legal authorities (Hong & Pak, 2017). Indeed, this is similar to what some economists at the research frontier do as we discuss in the following subchapter on studies using transaction-level data.

Relatedly, the World Customs Organisation (2018) presented its study report on IFFs and trade mis-invoicing to the Development Working Group of the G20 in July 2018. The multi-co-authored report argues that estimates of both partner country trade statistics and price filter methods are not sufficiently robust and should not be understood as a reliable quantitative measurement of the scale of IFFs, but rather as a risk indicator, which can be useful in comparing the risk of IFFs across commodities, countries and over a longer time period. The World Customs Organisation (2018) also makes the important point that rather than disputing the accuracy of individual assessment mechanisms, attention should instead focus on actions to combat IFFs, the existence of which is indisputable; the estimates of which, however, are dependent on the methodologies used.

2.2.4. Results

Academic studies have used trade data to study trade mispricing (Pak, 2007; Zdanowicz, 2009), and these types of methods have been also often applied by non-governmental organisations such Tax Justice Network (2007), Hogg et al. (2009), or Hogg et al. (2010). They all broadly support the view that tax indeed motivates trade pricing decisions. However, the important assumptions needed and the partially aggregated nature of the data pose methodological limitations that lead us to interpret these results with caution.

The one study of Pak, Zdanowicz et al that we describe in the methodology section in detail, de Boyrie, Pak, & Zdanowicz (2005), attributes flows through trade mispricing to money laundering and tax evasion. For US-Russia trade data, they estimate the amount of capital shifted through abnormal prices from Russia in 1995 at 3 per cent and 6 per cent of total trade for exports and imports, respectively. They estimate annual capital flight from Russia to the US to range from a low of 0.2 billion USD in 1997 to a high of 0.6 billion USD in 1999 when compared to US-Russia transactions, and, alternatively, to range from a low of 1 billion USD in 1998 to a high of 5 billion USD in 1999 when compared to the US-world trade.

In a combination of mirror trade statistics and mispricing methods, Chalendard, Raballand, & Rakotoarisoa (2019) estimate for Madagascar that undervaluation and product misclassification, each roughly accounting for a half of the total, are responsible for potential revenue losses of almost 100 million USD, which represented 30 per cent of total non-oil revenues collected by customs in 2014. Clothing and telephones are most often under-valued, while fertilizers and rice are often misclassified.

Interestingly, Hong, Pak, & Pak, (2014) apply the abnormal pricing method with market prices for their main results, but compare it with estimates based on the interquartile price filter as well as trade mirror statistics. They show that imports are undervalued by 54 per cent on average between 2000 and 2009 using market prices as a benchmark in the case of US banana imports from Latin American and Caribbean countries; while using the other two, more common methods they find little evidence of either under- or over-valuation of US banana imports—suggesting, perhaps, that the methodological limitations of the common methods may tend to bias results *against* uncover-ing illicit activity in commodity-level data. Most recently, in a working paper of a Swiss-based research network focused on Laos and Ghana, Carbonnier & Mehrotra (2019) discuss results indicating economically significant estimates of abnormal pricing in Swiss commodity imports.

2.2.5. Conclusions

The existing evidence based on commodity level data is useful in highlighting the specific commodities and countries most vulnerable to trade mispricing, but the results are of limited reliability for estimating the scale and are super-seded in their credibility by estimates based on transaction-level data.

One area of promising future research could be to use compare the results achieved with the relatively detailed commodity-level data reviewed in this subchapter with the results using the methods at the frontier of research discussed in the following subchapter. It might be possible to calibrate estimates using UN Comtrade, on the basis of more reliable transaction-level data for countries for which both are available. This would provide evidence of not only the scale of potential bias of UN Comtrade-based commodity-level studies, but also indicate whether and to what extent UN Comtrade can be relied upon when there are no transaction-level trade data available.

2.3. Transaction-level Trade Estimates: Research frontier

2.3.1. Overview

There is an increasing number of research papers that use detailed trade data at the level of transactions and, with this, methodologies that deliver more credible results. Their most obvious disadvantage in contrast with the studies discussed in the previous two subchapters is that they are limited in geographical coverage, usually focusing on one country only (namely, the source of the unique data). Most of the existing evidence is for major, high income economies such as the United States, France or the United Kingdom, but there are also recent preliminary results for South Africa by Wier (2017)—a first study using such detailed data and providing evidence for transfer mispricing for a developing country, and future research is likely to provide evidence for smaller and lower-income countries. The current difficulties in obtaining consistent, high-quality data of this type mean that the leading global estimates at present rely instead on national-level data—and serious criticisms, including of the GFI approach discussed above, have been raised and we discussed them above. While most of the studies below do not explicitly mention illicit financial flows, they are natural follow-ups to the previous two subchapters in estimating the scale of transfer and trade mispricing.

Below we discuss the earlier evidence for the US by Clausing (2003) and Bernard, Jensen, & Schott (2006), two influential empirical research papers on transfer mispricing for the US from the 2000s. Clausing (2003) provides one of the first empirical pieces of evidence consistent with theoretical predictions regarding tax-motivated income shifting behaviour. Bernard,

Jensen, & Schott (2006), in their well-cited working paper, developed a new method for identifying transfer mispricing and applied it to detailed data of US-based MNEs. There is also more recent evidence for the United States by Flaaen (2017), who uses transaction-level data to find profit-shifting behaviour by US MNEs via the strategic transfer pricing of intra-firm trade.

We also discuss the perhaps most persuasive recent evidence by Davies, Martin, Parenti, & Toubal (2017) as well as by Vicard (2015), both of which rely on detailed data for France. Vicard (2015), in a Banque de France working paper, provides evidence of transfer pricing and its increasing role for France over time. Using similar French data to Vicard (2015) but for one, earlier year only (1999), Davies, Martin, Parenti, & Toubal (2017) arrive at a somewhat lower estimate, most of which is driven by the exports of 450 firms to ten tax havens. We also discuss recent research for Denmark, in which Cristea and Nguyen (2016) use firm-level panel data on Danish exports to find evidence of profit shifting by MNEs through transfer pricing. We note that there is also recent evidence for the United Kingdom, although similarly to Wier (2017) for South Africa, we do not discuss below these recent research contributions. Liu, Schmidt-Eisenlohr, & Guo (2017) use detailed data on export transactions and corporate tax returns of UK MNEs, and conclude that firms manipulate their transfer prices to shift profits to lower-taxed destinations.

2.3.2. Data

This research area, which has been intensively developing in the last few years, uses data that are typically at the transaction level, and are confidential but sometimes made available through a collaboration with the country-specific source responsible for collection of the data and for its use for research purposes.

In one of the earliest contributions to this literature, rather than transaction-level data, Clausing (2003) uses monthly data on import and export product prices collected by the Bureau of Labor Statistics from 1997 to 1999 that differentiate between intrafirm and arm's-length transactions (in total, 425,000 observations of monthly prices 33 per cent of these for exports and 38 per cent for intrafirm trade). Bernard, Jensen, & Schott (2006) use the Linked/ Longitudinal Firm Trade Transaction Database which links individual trade transactions to specific firms in the United States. It contains detailed foreign trade data, including whether the transaction takes place at arm's length or between related parties, assembled by the U.S. Census Bureau and the

U.S. Customs Bureau which captures all U.S. international trade transactions between 1993 and 2000.

There are two recent papers using transaction-level data. Vicard (2015) uses detailed firm level export and import data by origin, destination and product to estimate revenue impact of profit shifting through transfer pricing. He exploits the panel dimension of data and provides estimates for years 2000–2014. Also using French firm-level data, Davies, Martin, Parenti, & Toubal (2017) make use of 1999 information on the prices of products and whether they are arm's length or intrafirm transactions. They also employ the data to estimate the counterfactual arm's length prices of an intra-firm transaction. Furthermore, they argue that France's relatively simple exemption system of international corporate income taxation provides a more suitable system for studying tax-motivated transfer mispricing than the more complicated US system that aimed then to tax worldwide income of MNEs resident there. Similarly to Davies, Martin, Parenti, & Toubal (2017) for France, Cristea and Nguyen (2016) argue that Denmark is an interesting case study because of its territorial taxation system, in which only income earned from activities performed by Danish residents gets taxed. Cristea and Nguyen (2016) use a firm-level dataset of exports from Denmark between 1999 and 2006.

2.3.3. Methodology

To indicate whether there is evidence of tax-motivated transfer pricing in US intrafirm trade prices, Clausing (2003) applies a regression analysis to observe the relationship between export or import prices with tax rate, and includes a dummy variable to indicate when trade is intrafirm. Other similarly indirect evidence to Clausing (2003) that we do not discuss below includes Swenson (2001), who used firm-product level data to show that variations in the reported customs values of US imports from five major economies during the 1980s are consistent with the transfer pricing incentives created by taxes and tariffs. Also for the US, Neiman (2010) uses transaction-level data to show that intra-firm prices are less sticky and have a greater exchange rate pass through than arm's length prices. For the value added manufacturing data from across the OECD countries, Bartelsman & Beetsma (2003) disentangle the income shifting effects from the effects of tax rates on real activity and find evidence consistent with transfer pricing. Similarly, Overesch (2006) uses German MNEs' data to show that intra-firm sales are related to corporate tax rates.

The research discussed below with truly transaction-level data estimates the extent of transfer mispricing as the difference between the so called comparable uncontrolled prices and the actual MNEs' prices multiplied by the quantity traded:

$$\text{IFF by transfer mispricing} = (\text{Comparable uncontrolled prices} - \text{Actual MNEs' prices}) \times \text{Quantity traded}$$

Most of the research below uses this equation implicitly or explicitly in one form or another, but varies substantially with regard to details and especially how they estimate the prices and what control groups or variations in tax rates and other variables they make use of in their empirical strategies.

Bernard, Jensen, & Schott (2006) use a theoretical model to show that the difference between arm's-length and related-party prices depends on firm, product and country characteristics. In their empirical part, they estimate arm's-length-related-party price wedge as the difference between the log comparable uncontrolled price (a proxy for arm's-length price that they estimate on the basis of detailed data at the country, firm, month and transport mode level) and the log related-party price (which they directly observe). They regress firms' price wedges on destination-country tax rates and destination-country product-level import tariff rates as well as proxies of product differentiation and firm market power.

In his empirical strategy, Vicard (2015) uses the price wedge between arm's length and related party trade on a market (defined by destination country and product) and its correlation with the corporate income tax rate of each partner country compared to France as a systematic evidence of transfer mispricing.

In their theoretical framework, Davies, Martin, Parenti, & Toubal (2017) show that due to the concealment costs of transfer mispricing, only some MNEs might choose to do it, with the probability increasing with the tax differential between home and host countries and the amount of exports. In their framework, Davies, Martin, Parenti, & Toubal (2017) also recognise that intra-firm prices could systematically deviate from arm's length prices not only because of tax avoidance stressed by most of the other literature, but also because of pricing to market behaviour (which implies that exporters adjust their prices to the prices that prevail in the export markets). In their empirical approach, they control for pricing-to-market determinants (transport costs, tariffs, GDP per capita) to capture only the tax avoidance effects. In contrast with existing literature, the methodology and data of Davies, Martin, Parenti, &

Toubal (2017) provide evidence of the impact of tax rates and tax havens on transfer prices themselves rather than evidence suggestive of transfer pricing more generally. Furthermore, they use the somewhat ad hoc and outdated classification of tax havens proposed by Hines & Rice (1994), which results in ten tax havens indicated in their data sample: the Bahamas, Bermuda, the Cayman Islands, Cyprus, Hong Kong, Ireland, Luxembourg, Malta, Singapore, and Switzerland.

For the Danish export data, Cristea and Nguyen (2016) use triple differ-ence estimations to exploit the response of export unit values to acquisitions of foreign affiliates and to changes in corporate tax rates. They estimate the extent to which MNEs manipulate both transfer prices to affiliates and arm's length prices to unrelated firms in order to reduce their global tax payments. They further argue that by ignoring the MNEs' manipulation of arm's length prices and using these as comparable uncontrolled prices, tax authorities and researches underestimate the extent to which the MNEs manipulate prices in order to shift profits.

2.3.4. Results

For the US trade data Clausing (2003) finds a strong relationship between countries' tax rates and the prices of intrafirm transactions. Controlling for other variables that affect trade prices, as country tax rates are lower, US intrafirm export prices are lower, and US intrafirm import prices are higher. Her results indicate that a 1 per cent drop in taxes abroad reduces US export prices between related parties by 0.9 to 1.8 per cent. This finding is consistent with theoretical predictions regarding tax-motivated income shifting behav-iour. Bernard, Jensen, & Schott (2006) find that the prices exporters set for their arm's-length customers are substantially larger than the prices recorded for related-parties. The difference is smaller for commodities than for differ-entiated goods, is increasing in firm size and firm export share, and is greater for goods sent to countries with lower corporate tax rates and higher tariffs.

For French trading companies Vicard (2015) shows that the price wedge between arm's length and related party transactions varies systematically with the corporate tax rate differential between France and its trading partner. He estimates that this profit shifting decreased France's corporate tax base by 8 billion USD in 2008, and that the related missing tax revenues amount to 10 per cent of the corporate tax paid by multinational groups located in France that trade with a related party. He also finds that the scale is increasing over time. He estimates the semi-elasticity of corporate profits to tax differentials at 0.5: that is, a 10-percentage point increase in tax differential would increase the pre-tax income reported by the affiliate by 5 per cent. This is based on transfer pricing in goods trade only and is thus relatively high in relation to other estimates on balance sheet data, which he challenges.

Estimates of Davies, Martin, Parenti, & Toubal (2017) suggest that export prices decrease with corporate tax rate only for intra-firm transactions, and only for countries with very low tax rates and especially tax havens (which they consider to combine low tax rates with other characteristics including banking secrecy). Davies, Martin, Parenti, & Toubal (2017) arrive at a somewhat lower estimate than Vicard (2015), most of which is driven by the exports of 450 firms to ten tax havens. Indeed, they find no evidence of tax avoidance once they disregard tax haven destinations. Still, they consider their estimates of tax avoidance through transfer pricing—at 1 per cent of total corporate tax revenues in France—as economically sizable.

Looking at the sensitivity of exports to tax rates, Cristea and Nguyen (2016) estimate that Danish MNEs reduce their export prices by 6 per cent in response to a 10 percentage point decrease in the tax rate of a country with lower rates than Denmark, which corresponds to a tax revenue loss of around 3 per cent of Danish MNEs tax returns. The responses in export prices are higher for differentiated goods (7 per cent) and for MNEs who establish new affiliates during the sample period (9 per cent).

2.3.5. Conclusions

The expanding number of research papers providing evidence consistent with trade or transfer mispricing in an increasing number of countries suggest that this is a universal phenomenon. One implication might be that it warrants global solutions. One such solution, for multinationals at least, would be the abandonment of the arm's length principle in favour of a unitary taxation approach (as is now under consideration at the OECD). Before any reform happens, it should be beneficial to see similar empirical analyses for other countries, if only to provide a preliminary basis for potential detailed audits by tax authorities or guidance on the type of regulation that is needed to limit tax avoidance, or to increase awareness and pressures for a reform.

These studies derive their credibility from and build on detailed, country-specific data and, therefore, cross-country estimates are usually not available. The shift in data availability that would allow comparable cross-country analysis with substantial worldwide coverage, would be dramatic—however desirable—and feels distant at best. For the time being, the low number of countries with similar analysis and the diversity of data available and thus methodologies applied, do not enable a credible comparison of results across countries or the estimation of the global scale of the mispricing.

2.4. Conclusions on Trade Estimates

We end this chapter on trade estimates with conclusions drawn from our understanding of the large body of research and policy literature summarised in the preceding sub-chapters. First, international trade is an active channel for illicit financial flows and the research leading to trade estimates has been useful in a number of respects. From numerous case studies as well as indicatively from a number of aggregate studies reviewed here we learn about the use of trade mispricing to transfer funds illicitly across borders. The trade estimates have been helpful in shedding light on international trade data discrepancies. Also, many of the relevant studies have proven useful for customs officials in highlighting cases suitable for more detailed audit, and for policy makers in underlying areas of potential concern. We consider most of the recent transaction-level studies credible for estimation of the scale of trade-based illicit flows. In contrast, the estimates based on the trade mirror statistics approach and country-level data might have been helpful in the past for raising awareness about these issues, but we do not consider them sufficiently credible to inform us about the scale of illicit financial flows over time. We consider some of the abnormal pricing estimates useful as indicators for audit and other purposes, but we would not rely on them for estimates of overall scale.

Second, we observe improvements in the methodology applied by the GFI and other researchers in their quest to provide more reliable trade data-based estimates of illicit financial flows. Despite the related research usefulness in other respects and its recent advances, the employment of trade estimates for the SDG target is not straightforward. We recognise that much research has been carried out recently on trade mis-invoicing and on trade as a channel of illicit financial flows for many countries, and that there is an argument for its inclusion in the indicator of the target as discussed by, among others, the United Nations Economic Commission for Africa (ECA) (2015), Economic Commission for Latin America and the Caribbean (2016) and, most recently, by Kravchenko (2018) of the United Nations Economic and Social Commission for Asia and the Pacific (ESCAP). However, we find that their estimates are still not of sufficient reliability, and allow for a wider interpretation than illicit financial flows. In addition, an increasing number of trade estimates from the frontier of research reach strong conclusions based on relatively high-quality data and methods. We judge the quality of these frontier estimates as sufficient, but their country coverage is poor and it does not seem feasible to extend them to many more countries in the near future. Indeed, there seems to be a trade-off for the trade estimates—either they are available for many countries but less credible, or they are of relatively high quality but available only for few countries (and, furthermore, it is presently difficult to compare the estimates across the few countries). There remains a gap to be bridged between the two subgroups of trade estimates, to achieve both sufficient quality and coverage. Clearly, more research in this area is required. For the time being, no indicator from the group of trade estimates seems to be workable as the indicator of the SDG target.

Third, while we identify a number of promising areas of further research, none seem sufficiently promising in the medium term to enable their inclusion as the SDG target indicator. One option is to improve the current methods, either at the country level—as exemplified by GFI's recent changes or Kellenberg & Levinson (2016)—or at more detailed, commodity-level such as ECA (2015). Another promising area of future policy-relevant research is extending the current transaction-level methods to more countries, while making sure that they are comparable, ideally, across both countries and years. Even more reliable than the current one-country, one-data-source studies would be estimates based on customs data from both countries of the trading pair involved in any given transaction examined for illicitness. Before transactions-level data are available in most countries, to reach near-global coverage it might be worth trying to adapt these methodologies for trade data sets with less detailed data but better country coverage, as Kellenberg & Levinson (2016) have done with the trade mirror statistics method and UN Comtrade data. But so far, given the data limitations, a better country coverage can be attained to some extent only at the expense of methodological rigor.

3

Capital and Wealth Estimates

Having examined anomalies in the current account (trade mispricing) in the previous chapter, we now turn to approaches to estimation of illicit financial flows (as some of the authors do, we also use the term illicit financial flows and capital flight interchangeably) that make use of anomalies in the capital account (unrecorded capital movements). We address three capital account-based approaches: of GFI; of Ndikumana and Boyce; and of Henry, the first two of which combine trade-based and capital account components. Additionally, we assess here estimates of offshore wealth that partly—for example, in the case of Henry—overlap with capital estimates.

While GFI and Ndikumana and Boyce estimate illicit financial flows, Henry's estimates focus on the stock of wealth held offshore and to that aim he aggregates the estimates of flows. Indeed, how much wealth is held offshore and how much of it is illicit is another research question related to estimates of scale of illicit financial flows. Other than Henry's estimates of offshore wealth (in 2012 in particular), Zucman, in 2013 and in his follow up estimates with co-authors, Alstadsaeter, Johannesen, & Zucman (2018), has produced influential estimates of wealth held in tax havens. Although methodologically different, we include these offshore wealth estimates in this chapter—also because Henry's estimates methodologically overlap with the GFI and Ndikumana and Boyce.

Before Henry (2012) and Zucman (2013), some related research with the ambition to provide global estimates of offshore wealth or illicit financial flows was linked with development implications of tax havens and motivated by tax revenues not collected due to illicit activities that might be used to invest in social policy programmes in poor countries. A number of studies, mostly by non-governmental organizations and some academics, emerged around the year 2000 and provided some of the first estimates of assets held offshore and associated illicit financial flows and government tax revenue losses relevant for poor countries, using various methodologies. Oxfam (2000) estimated that poor countries suffered a yearly loss of around USD 50 billion due to tax havens, whereas Transparency International (2004) estimated that corrupt heads of states are responsible for billions of dollars in illicit financial flows out of their countries.

Estimating illicit financial flows: A critical guide to the data, methodologies and findings. Alex Cobham and Petr Janský, Oxford University Press (2020). © Alex Cobham and Petr Janský.
DOI: 10.1093/oso/9780198854418.001.0001

Quite a few other studies focus on what assets might be illegally already held abroad and could be recovered. Tax Justice Network (2005) estimated that the value of assets held offshore lay in the range of USD 11—12 trillion and suggested that the global revenue loss resulting from wealthy individuals holding their assets untaxed offshore may be as much as USD 255 billion annually. Cobham (2005), on the basis of shadow economy estimates of Schneider (2005) and the results of Tax Justice Network (2005), derived a loss to poor countries of around USD 100 billion a year. Henry for Oxfam (2009) estimated that at least USD 6 trillion of poor country wealth is held offshore by individuals, depriving poor countries' governments of annual tax receipts of between USD 64 and 124 billion and, in a similar way, Henry (2012) estimated that a global super-rich elite had at least USD 21 trillion hidden in tax havens by the end of 2010 and that poor countries could be losing USD 189 billion in associated tax revenue every year. These studies were mostly first of their kind and put the related topics on the policy agenda. More recent research may offer greater rigor also. We discuss the studies of Henry (2012) and Zucman (2013) in this chapter after first considering the capital account-based IFF estimates of Ndikumana and Boyce and of GFI.

3.1. Capital Flight: Ndikumana and Boyce

3.1.1. Overview

There have been a number of approaches to estimation of illicit financial flows on the basis of capital account data, with Erbe (1985) and World Bank (1985) being among the first to estimate the scale of capital flight, but most recent ones aim to estimate the difference between capital inflows and capital outflows. Capital inflows include net increases in external debt and net foreign direct investment. Capital outflows consist of the current account deficit and net additions to reserves.

As discussed in chapter 1, the older literature on capital flight tended to address a specific element of current illicit flow estimates, i.e. the element passing through the capital account. In addition, much of the policy discussion was framed around flight as a legitimate portfolio investment response to (lower-income country) problems of investment climate (see e.g. Collier et al., 2001). Ndikumana and Boyce, however, and the wider IFF literature, focus instead on the tax and regulation-circumvention motives.

In fact, the various contributions to Ajayi & Ndikumana, eds. (2015) show that factors that do *not* determine their estimates include risk-adjusted returns, 'orthodox' monetary policy (high interest rates in particular), macro 'fundamentals' (especially the pursuit of inflation control and balance of payments sustainability), and capital account liberalisation. As Weeks (2015) puts it, 'the orthodox narrative that capital flight results from unsound macro policies [is reversed]. On the contrary, capital flight may force governments into policies that work against the majority of the population.'

3.1.2. Data

The Hot Money 'Narrow' Method (HMN) uses only balance of payments data, usually from the International Monetary Fund, and is thus equivalent to the net errors and omissions reported there. This is the preferred method by the GFI.

Others, including the duo of Ndikumana and Boyce, prefer to use other data sources. For example, Ndikumana & Boyce (1998) argue that the World Bank's data on debt provide more accurate estimates of the change in external debt.

Ndikumana & Boyce (2010) rely on data mostly from the IMF, specifically its International Financial Statistics, Balance of Payments Statistics, DOTS as well as IMF's various country online information in selected issues and statistical appendix. Importantly, Ndikumana & Boyce (2010) also use the data from the World Bank's Global Development Finance and World Development Indicators.

3.1.3. Methodology

Ndikumana & Boyce (1998) thus measure the capital flight, KF_{it}, in a year t for a country i as, using a simplified version of their notation:

$$KF_{it} = \Delta DEBT_{it} + FDI_{it} - \left(CA_{it} + RES_{it}\right)$$

where $\Delta DEBT_{it}$ and, FDI_{it} is net foreign direct investment, CA_{it} is the current account balance, and RES_{it} is net additions to the stock of foreign reserves.

In a number of papers Ndikumana & Boyce (1998, 2003, 2010, 2011) have provided a number of estimates on the basis of this methodology, with a range of additional adjustments aimed at refining these estimates. For example, Ndikumana & Boyce (2010) make four adjustments: for trade mis-invoicing, exchange rate fluctuations, debt write-offs and underreporting of remittances. The trade mis-invoicing estimate is discussed in detail in the previous chapter

(Ndikumana & Boyce (2010) make the trade invoicing adjustment by comparing countries' export and import data to those of its trading partners, assuming the high-income countries data to be relatively accurate and they interpret the difference as evidence of trade mis-invoicing.) Ndikumana & Boyce (2010) make these adjustments, but do not highlight the scale of these individual adjustments, only the resulting overall estimates of capital flight.

3.1.4. Results

In contrast with the other approaches survyed in this chapter, Ndikumana and Boyce do not aim to provide global results and focus on sub-Saharan African countries instead. Also, as mentioned above, their results do not disentangle the various adjustments they make. For example, Ndikumana & Boyce (2010) estimate that total capital flight from 33 sub-Saharan African countries between 1970 and 2004 amounted to 443 billion US dollars (and 640 billion US dollars when imputed interest earnings are included). Ndikumana & Boyce (2010) highlight that these estimates exceed these countries' external debts (which in 2004 amounted to 193 billion US dollars).

3.1.5. Conclusions

Over the past two decades, Ndikumana and Boyce have provided the most prominent estimates of capital flight from sub-Saharan African countries. While these estimates have proved useful in raising awareness about the illicit financial flows, they do have methodological constraints. These are mostly shared with the other similar approaches discussed below and so we discuss them together in the following sub-chapter on the approach of GFI.

3.2. Capital Account Anomalies: Global Financial Integrity (GFI)

3.2.1. Overview

For capital account anomalies, the two most commonly used methods are the World Bank Residual Method (WBR) and the Hot Money 'Narrow' Method (HMN).

While most of these estimates in recent years have been prepared by GFI or Ndikumana and Boyce discussed above, UNDP commissioned a report by a lead author of the GFI estimates, Kar (2011).

3.2.2. Data

GFI uses the balance of payments data published by the IMF as the only source for their estimates of balance of payments leakages (Spanjers & Salomon, 2017).

3.2.3. Methodology

The World Bank residual model subtracts the total of funds actually used by a country from the total of funds entering that country and, if there are more funds coming in than funds being used, the resulting shortfall is considered to be illicit flows. The hot money model considers all errors in a country's external accounts as illicit flows. Both these methods rely on anomalies in the Balance of Payment (BoP) identity, as expressed in a notation by World Bank's Claessens & Naude (1993) and followed by Kar & Freitas (2012) and others:

$$A + B + C + D + E + F + G + H = 0$$

Where:
A: current account balance
B: net equity flows (including net FDI and FPI)
C: other short-term capital of other sectors
D: FPI involving other bonds
E: change in deposit-money banks' foreign assets
F: change in reserves of the central bank
G: net errors and omissions (NEO)
H: change in external debt

The WBR method captures the difference between recorded inflows and recorded uses, which is given by the (negative) sum of the current account balance, net equity flows, change in reserves of the central bank and change in external debt. By the BoP identity:

$$-(A + B + F + H) = C + D + E + G$$

Of the components on the right-hand side, however, C+D+E are licit: composed of other short-term capital of other sectors, FPI involving other bonds, and the change in deposit-money banks' foreign assets. As such, the WBR method is likely to exhibit a substantial upwards bias as an estimator of IFF. Similarly, Fontana (2010) summarizes the World Bank residual method by the following equation: Illicit flows = (increase in foreign debt + increase in FDI)—(financing of the current account deficit + additions to the country's reserves).

The main alternative, the HMN method, is given by the remaining right-hand side component, G: net errors and omissions. G is simply the balancing residual constructed to maintain the BoP identity, and so serves as an indicator of error—and possibly of illicitness—in the overall capital account. Again, Fontana (2010) summarizes the Hot Money model by the following equation: Illicit flow = all funds coming in (credit)—all funds going out (debt). Recently, this method, labelled as net errors and omissions (NEO) has been used by Novokmet, Piketty, & Zucman (2018) to provide estimates of offshore wealth for Russia, which are three times higher than those estimated by another methodology by Alstadsaeter, Johannesen, & Zucman (2018). The longest-standing series of estimates, although published for African countries only, are those of Ndikumana & Boyce (e.g. 2008), discussed in the previous subchapter (they also contrast sources and uses of foreign exchange in the capital account and make a number of adjustments for exchange rate fluctuations on the value of external debt, for debt write offs and for under-reported remittances).

Likely the most well-known estimates are those produced by GFI. In 2012, GFI shifted from using the WBR method (e.g. Kar, Cartwright-Smith, & Hollingshead, 2010) to the HMN (e.g. Spanjers & Salomon, 2017, who label this method as balance of payments leakages). This change has naturally led to some inconsistencies in the results series over time (as well as the apparent increased role of trade mis-invoicing in illicit financial flows), as discussed in some detail by Nitsch (2016). GFI combines these capital account estimates with trade estimates, discussed in the previous chapter.

While illicit inflows could be considered to counteract detrimental effects of illicit outflows by increasing available capital resources, this position is questionable (see ECA(2015) for a more detailed discussion) because the damage of IFF to governance may be more important than the net resource effect. The benefits to the economy of illicit financial inflows to the economy may well be less than those of licit inflows, since the illicit inflows may themselves be going to fund the illicit economy (e.g. repatriation of profits by transnational organized criminal organizations may be used to fund expansion of activities in the country in question; the flows could also represent financing of terrorism); or be circumventing regulation or taxation designed to ensure fair competition. For our purposes, illicit financial inflows seem just as likely as illicit outflows to be distributed as or more unequally than funds in the licit economy, and so our primary interest is in estimates that do not 'net out' illicit financial inflows.

3.2.4. Results

Having reviewed both capital account and trade approaches, it is also possible to combine these two types of models, capital-account and trade, and we discuss the results achieved by this combination. Most notably, the research by GFI uses the World Bank residual and hot money models and further makes adjustments for trade mis-invoicing. Their hot money-based model estimates that the developing world lost USD 859 billion in illicit outflows in 2010 (significantly more than the USD 129 billion in aid by OECD countries in 2010). Their estimates, Kar & Freitas (2012), suggest that bribery, kickbacks, and the proceeds of corruption continued to be the primary driver of illicit financial flows from the Middle East and North Africa, while trade mispricing was the primary driver of illicit financial flows in the other regions. On the basis of this kind of estimates, Hollingshead (2010) uses national corporate income tax rates to estimate the tax revenue loss from trade mispricing in poor countries between USD 98 billion and USD 106 billion annually over the years 2002 to 2006.

In the most recent 2017 GFI analysis of illicit financial flows to and from developing countries between 2005 and 2014, Spanjers & Salomon (2017) estimate the illicit financial flows (or outflows) from developing countries in 2014 at between $620 billion and $970 billion. In this report they publish such a range for the first time and they also put equal emphasis on inflows and estimate them in 2014 at between $1.4 and $2.5 trillion. In this most recent report, they still combine capital-account and trade approaches to estimating illicit financial flows. In their lower bound estimates of outflows, trade mis-invoicing is responsible for two thirds of the total, while what they call unrecorded balance of payments flows (using net errors and omissions as a proxy for these) accounts for the remaining third. They estimate that Sub-Saharan Africa suffers most in terms of illicit outflows.

Cobham & Gibson (2016) show (in Figure 5) a comparison for estimates of total African IFF, between GFI methodology with WBR and HMN—Kar & Cartwright-Smith (2010), and Kar & Freitas (2012), respectively—and the Ndikumana & Boyce approach. Differences between the series frequently exceed the total value of the lowest estimate. Ndikumana & Boyce demonstrates greater volatility, as would be expected given in particular their use of net rather than gross trade mispricing. At the aggregate level, GFI's updated (HMN) methodology tends to produce the more conservative estimates. These differences provide an important illustration of the sensitivity of estimates to assumptions. Note, too, that these are shown at the aggregate level; disaggregated, there are examples of quite different country patterns over time.

3.2.5. Conclusions

These capital account anomalies are of two types examined in this group of approaches. They either include changes in foreign portfolio investment, private and central banks' foreign assets or they include only net errors and omissions. The limitations are obvious: the first is clearly not only anomalies and the latter is only anomalies, but not necessarily only illicit financial flows.

There are two main reasons to consider additional approaches. First, anomaly-based estimates inevitably attract criticism over the possibility that they may confuse 'innocent' anomalies including data errors and mismatches due to timing and rounding errors with evidence of illicitness, and the sensitivity to some of the assumptions made—see for example the various views expressed in five chapters of the World Bank's illicit flows volume (Reuter, 2012: chapters by Eden; Fuest & Riedel; Leite; Murphy; and Nitsch). As such, while the range of estimates have established the scale of the issue in terms of the broad order of magnitude, the degree of confidence in the estimates may be less suited to specific policy analysis at the level of countries and IFF types. The second concern relates to the bluntness of the leading estimates. While it is useful to compare the component attributable to trade with that attributable to the capital account, and to separate out some individual and corporate tax abuses, greater specificity of the channels of IFF would be valuable to support policy prioritisation. Underlying these issues is the simple fact that flows that are hidden by design do not lend themselves to measurement.

From the point of view of the creators, the advantages of using the estimates of illicit financial flows by GFI or of a similar type are obvious from their relative media and policy success—they provide clear figures that many people can relate to, and that the media as well as researchers and policy makers can reference.

The drawbacks might be less obvious, but are more important. These estimates indicate the possible aggregate extent of flows, rather than necessarily providing an accurate guide to prioritise specific policy efforts. The models rely on official statistics that are sometimes of poor quality, especially in lower-income countries. They do not take into account flows resulting from illicit activities, such as smuggling or black market activity, because proceeds from such activities are not captured in national accounts; nor a range of multinational tax abuses that do not generate anomalies in the series in question. Due to data publication time lags, GFI results—in common with most we evaluate—have a near two-year delay in publication of its estimates. Additionally, GFI provide results for individual lower-income countries, but not for their higher-income counterparts; although these results could possibly be arranged with GFI or estimated independently.

3.3. Offshore Capital and Wealth: Henry's Estimates

3.3.1. Overview

Ndikumana and Boyce have generally focused more on the stock of capital held outside African countries, than on the annual outflows. Similarly, Henry (2012), in a report for Tax Justice Network (TJN), produces global estimates with a largely common methodology, scaling up from outflows to estimates stocks of capital held offshore. The alternative approach here is to use data on international asset and liability positions in order to establish anomalies in the position of particular jurisdictions.

Henry (2012) states his objective as measuring long-term unrecorded cross-border private financial capital flows and stocks or unrecorded capital flows and stocks, with a focus on developing countries in particular. He also identifies a relatively wide scope of estimates, although not all relevant economic activity is included and, for example, he omits some types of non-financial wealth. In addition to new empirical estimates, Henry (2012) provides an overview of some earlier estimates and discusses other relevant evidence such as on transfer mispricing.

3.3.2. Data

Henry (2012) uses a number of various data sources, including the World Bank, the IMF, central banks and countries' national accounts. Each method uses different set of data sources, for example, for the unrecorded capital flow method he uses in most cases data from the WB's World Development Indicators. Henry's (2012) analysis of private banking assets uses a wide variety data sources including banks' annual reports and interviews with private banking industry experts. Henry (2012) uses data for the period 1970–2010 and presents the results for the year end of 2010, while his 2016 updated estimates are for the year end of 2014 (Henry, 2016).

3.3.3. Methodology

To describe methodology, we base our description on Henry (2012) and the available documentation of his methodology (his 2016 updated estimates seem to be applying the same or similar methodological approach, (Henry, 2016)). He combines four methods. While the first method is comparable to the capital account-based methods used by the GFI and Ndikumana and Boyce (in his words, unrecorded capital flows: 'sources-and-uses'), the other three are based on an accumulated offshore wealth model, an analysis of private banking assets and an offshore investor portfolio model. These multiple methods are used to explore consistency. We describe the methods one by one below.

With the sources-and-uses method Henry (2012) aims to model unrecorded capital flows. To that objective he uses an adjusted version of the World Bank Residual (WBR) method which we describe in detail in the previous two subchapters and which estimates unrecorded capital outflows as the difference between recorded sources of foreign capital and uses of foreign capital. Henry applied a similar methodology in a report for Oxfam (2009). Similarly to Ndikumana and Boyce, Henry makes several adjustments. He follows their practice of exchange rate adjustments. He also deducts exceptional financing from the debt stock series, uses adjusted debt stock rather than debt flows and incorporated debt reschedulings and change in arrears. He applies his method for period 1970–2010 for each of 139 countries (the selection of which might be discussed in more detail) that Henry considers key capital source countries and that are mostly low-middle income countries. For 2010 his sample of countries covered most of the world's population and a half of global GDP.

The accumulated offshore wealth model builds on the sources-and-uses method and aims to estimate how much the capital outflows are worth over time. Henry (2012) assumes that most (he writes '50 to 75 percent, on average') of the flows offshore are reinvested there and the resulting offshore earnings are neither repatriated nor subject to any taxes. He assumes that the capital outflows are invested offshore at 'a modest CD [certificate of deposit] rate'. Henry (2012) shows that China (and round-tripping via Hong Kong) is a counter example to the assumptions of this methodology and he argues that an adjustment for round-tripping is in place—17 per cent in the case of China, but perhaps in the case of other countries as an upper bound as well. In his analysis of private banking assets, Henry (2012) focused on cross-border private banking assets under management at the top 50 international private banks for the period 2005–2010.

Henry's (2012) headline estimates are based on an offshore investor port-folio model, a version of which was developed and applied by Tax Justice Network (2005). Henry (2012) builds upon and at the same time critically reviews the work of (Tax Justice Network, 2005), which he argues tended to underestimate the offshore financial wealth, which (Tax Justice Network, 2005) put at 9.5 trillion USD (and an additional 2 trillion USD in non-residential offshore real estate). The model takes data from the Bank for International Settlements (BIS) on cross-border deposits and other asset holdings by non-bank investors and scales them up (a multiplier of 3, which he considers conservative and provides references for values around 4) to arrive at total financial assets.

While the logical reasoning behind the four methodological approaches is clear, the relative lack of details (such as a detailed presentation of results or individual data sources) makes it challenging to evaluate the methods com-prehensively. We tend to consider the accumulated offshore wealth model as an important reminder that outflows can be invested and multiplied over time (but in this specific method the assumptions play a crucial role and the estimates are by definition based on estimates from a different method and this might multiply some of the inaccuracies), while the analysis of private banking assets serves as a reality double check and indeed serves as a triangu-lation point (but it is, for example, not clear from the available data how much of the assets are held offshore or onshore).

The other two methods are the core of Henry (2012). While a critical evalu-ation of the sources-and-uses method (a version of the WBR method) is already included in the previous two subchapters, we briefly discuss the off-shore investor portfolio model here. There is the crucial assumption of the multiplier, which directly influences the estimated offshore wealth and while they are estimates of this multiplier, it does not seem possible to judge its accuracy beyond interviews with experts and the like. Additionally, there are now newer estimates of the multiplier as well as much broader range of the BIS data (including bilateral information on deposits) available and it might be interesting to revisit the estimates of Henry (2012) and to evaluate the method's estimates empirically with this improved data.

3.3.4. Results

Henry (2012) estimates that the offshore financial assets of high net worth individuals are in a range from 21.02 trillion USD to 31.53 trillion USD in 2010. Henry (2016) published updated estimates and the range has increased to 24–34 trillion USD and from 9 trillion USD to 12 trillion USD for developing countries. Henry's (2012) 9 trillion USD estimate for developing countries derives from the application of the sources-and-uses method (an adjusted World Bank Residual method) that he applied to 139 countries and results into a range of 7.3 to 9.3 trillion USD. Equivalent estimates by Henry for Oxfam (2009) are a lower bound of 6.2 trillion USD by 2007 and they imply 150–200 billion USD annual outflows out of developing countries and we might expect similar figures in later years, although Henry (2012) does not provide this (outflow) form of presentation of the estimates. The accumulated offshore wealth model of Henry (2012) may add as much as 3.7 trillion USD to global total unrecorded capital outflows.

Henry's (2012) headline range of 21–32 trillion USD comes from the offshore investor portfolio model and includes financial offshore wealth only (the range is a result of assuming the multiplier is either 3 or 4.5). Henry's (2012) analysis of private banking assets finds that at the end of 2010 the top 50 international private banks managed more than 12.06 trillion USD in cross-border invested assets from private clients (including through trusts and foundations) and he considers this to be consistent with the results of the offshore investor portfolio model. He also observes that the top ten banks in his group are stable and grew even faster than the top 50 as a whole (20 per cent in comparison with 16 per cent per year on average between 2005 and 2010). Henry (2012) argues that the multiple estimates are consistent with each other (for example the results of sources-and-uses model for developing countries seem consistent with the combination of the offshore investor portfolio model and of the assumption of 25–30 per cent share of developing countries in offshore wealth). Furthermore, Henry (2012) compares his overall estimates with the 2011 Credit Suisse Global Wealth Report, which puts global wealth at 231 trillion US dollars, and argues that it makes his estimates seem reasonable and conservative.

3.3.5. Conclusions

Overall, the Tax Justice Network report of Henry (2012) made a significant contribution to the study of wealth held offshore, and it provided one of the first and most elaborate empirical estimates of this phenomenon, helping to bring public and researchers' attention to it. The contribution is especially valuable if one considers it as an 'open challenge to the IMF and the World Bank—to all comers, in fact—to see if they can come up with better estimates' (Henry, 2012, p. 4). The international organisations have not responded yet with their estimates, although they do now devote themselves more to some related research and policy than in the past. The following subchapter presents a formidable response to this challenge, coming instead from academic research.

3.4. Wealth in Tax Havens: Zucman's, and Alstadsaeter, Johannesen, & Zucman's Estimates

3.4.1. Overview

In an original contribution, Zucman (2013) estimated how much undeclared wealth held might be hidden in tax havens using detailed data on financial wealth managed by Swiss banks on behalf of foreigners that he further updated and presented (Zucman, 2014, 2015). In a recent follow-up study with co-authors, Alstadsaeter, Johannesen, & Zucman (2018) disaggregate the earlier estimates of offshore wealth by Zucman (2013) by country. Alstadsaeter, Johannesen, & Zucman (2018) still uses the detailed Swiss data but enrich it with other international sources, including the recently disseminated bilateral data from the Bank for International Settlements (BIS) on deposits in a number of tax havens by foreigners. This enables them to present how much wealth various countries' citizens hold in tax havens (or offshore, two terms that we use here interchangeably, but more detailed specification is provided by Alstadsaeter, Johannesen, & Zucman, 2018, p. 7).

In this subchapter, we present research by both Zucman (2013) and Alstadsaeter, Johannesen, & Zucman (2018), but focus on the latter that include country-by-country estimates, which are in line with this book's objectives of having country-level indicators that enable tracking over time. Zucman (2013) and Alstadsaeter, Johannesen, & Zucman (2018) provide methods and estimates that likely provide the currently most reliable estimates of wealth in tax havens, although better data in the future should enable further research to improve on them in a number of areas that we discuss below (for example, they do not capture non-financial wealth and they provide estimates of only financial wealth).

3.4.2. Data

Alstadsaeter, Johannesen, & Zucman (2018) use three main data sources. First, they use detailed statistics from the central bank of Switzerland on the bank deposits, portfolios of equities, bonds, and mutual fund shares managed by Swiss banks on behalf of foreigners. This is data described in detail and first exploited for estimates of offshore wealth by Zucman (2013). In addition to having this data by definition of its source only for the Swiss banks' operations in Switzerland, the crucial limitation of this data, acknowledged and dealt with by the authors, is that a large share of wealth owned by foreigners in Switzerland belong on paper to shell companies and other legal entities such as trusts and foundations that disguise the country of the beneficial owner.

Second, they use bilateral data on deposits in a number of tax havens by foreigners disseminated by the BIS since 2016. Until then the BIS published only the country-level data and it was thus not available when Zucman (2013) did his original analysis. The BIS data allows to exclude interbank deposits (deposits between banks that do not involve households), which Alstadsaeter, Johannesen, & Zucman (2018) do. The main limitation of this data is that, in contrast with the Swiss data, they do not include information on portfolio securities, which is the largest form of offshore wealth in the Swiss data.

Third, they use the IMF's balance of payments and international investment position data to quantify the discrepancy in international investment positions. The equities, bonds and mutual fund shares owned by households on foreign accounts are recorded on the liability side, but not on their asset side (due to tax havens not reporting assets owned by foreigners).

They further use data from central banks, discussed by (Johannesen & Zucman, 2014), to exclude cross-border bank deposits by corporations and to keep only those by households.

3.4.3. Methodology

Alstadsaeter, Johannesen, & Zucman (2018) first estimate the global offshore wealth using the discrepancy in international investment positions, in this following the approach of Zucman (2013).

Zucman (2013) observes differences in the securities assets and securities liabilities of all countries in the world: at the end of 2008 there are more liabilities (40 trillion USD) than assets (35.5 trillion USD), because, as he argues, tax havens are responsible for this difference and they usually do not report about assets owned by foreigners. An exception is Switzerland, on which data Zucman (2013) draws. He makes a number of assumptions (such as assuming that 25 per cent of household offshore wealth worldwide takes the form of deposits and 75 per cent of securities, as is the case in Switzerland), which are described in detail in his paper and are mostly needed due to data gaps, to arrive at an estimated 8 per cent of total wealth worldwide held in tax havens. Alstadsaeter, Johannesen, & Zucman (2018) make similar assumptions as Zucman (2013), for example, they also assume on the basis of data from central banks that a given share of cross-border bank deposits belong to corporations and keep only those that belong to households.

Once Alstadsaeter, Johannesen, & Zucman (2018) estimate global offshore wealth using the same approach of Zucman (2013) and more recent data (they put it at around 10 per cent of world GDP and 5.6 trillion in 2007), they proceed in three steps to allocate it according to who owns the wealth: they start with who owns wealth in Switzerland, then proceed who owns wealth in the other tax havens, and, lastly, they combine the estimates from the two previous steps. The main obstacle they need to overcome in the first step is that most owners of Swiss offshore wealth is hidden behind anonymity, which has markedly increased after an EU regulation known as the Saving Tax Directive was introduced in 2005. This thus enables them to use data from 2003–2004 about the countries of owners as likely proxy for the owners of the shell companies in later years. Specifically, they assume that a country's share of wealth not owned via shell companies in 2003–2004, it also owns the same per centage of the wealth owned via such shells. They support this assumption with consistent evidence from the leaked data of the Swiss subsidiary of the banking giant HSBC discussed in a related paper by the same authors (Alstadsaeter et al., 2017).

Similar to the Swiss central bank, most other tax havens' authorities also collect data on who owns wealth in their banks, but they publish them through the BIS only since 2016 (although the data are retrospective until 2000s or earlier) and in a less detailed form. At the time of their research (August 2017), Guernsey, Hong Kong, the Isle of Man, Jersey, Luxembourg, Macao, and Switzerland reported the data, while other important tax havens did not—the Bahamas, Singapore, and the Cayman Islands. However, for these latter tax havens they estimate the deposits owned in them by other countries as a residual. Crucially, the BIS data include information about deposits only, not about other offshore wealth. They thus make an important assumption that the distribution of deposits is the same as that of offshore wealth. In essence, to estimate the amount of offshore wealth in each tax haven using the BIS data, Alstadsaeter, Johannesen, & Zucman (2018) thus assume that the ratio of deposits to portfolio securities is the same in every tax haven (as in Switzerland), an assumption already made by Zucman (2013). They acknowledge that this might lead to potential biases (e.g. US corporations may own most of the bank deposits in Cayman Islands, but US households might own only a small share of the total offshore wealth in the Cayman Islands), but they argue, and we agree, that with the current data it is difficult to control for or quantify the size of the potential biases. What further research should investigate in detail even with the currently available data is the sensitivity of the estimated offshore wealth to this and other important assumptions.

Then, in the third step, Alstadsaeter, Johannesen, & Zucman (2018) sum the estimates of wealth held by other countries in Switzerland and in the other tax havens to arrive at their final country-by-country estimates of offshore wealth. Overall, the methodological approach to country-by-country estimates of wealth in tax havens of Alstadsaeter, Johannesen, & Zucman (2018) can be roughly summarised as their estimated offshore wealth for country i and year t:

$$
\begin{aligned}
&\textit{Offshore wealth}_{it} \\
&= \textit{Global offshore wealth} \left(\textit{derived from the IMF's international investment positions} \right)_t \\
&\quad \times \frac{\textit{Wealth in Switzerland} \left(\textit{Swiss central bank} \right)_{it} + \textit{Wealth in the other tax havens} \left(BIS \right)_{it}}{\textit{Wealth in Switzerland} \left(\textit{Swiss central bank} \right)_t + \textit{Wealth in the other tax havens} \left(BIS \right)_t}
\end{aligned}
$$

Alstadsaeter, Johannesen, & Zucman (2018) then proceed to show implications of offshore wealth for distribution of wealth for ten countries, but we do not discuss these here in detail because they are not sufficiently relevant to our main objective of illicit financial flows.

We consider the methodologies and estimates of Zucman (2013) and Alstadsaeter, Johannesen, & Zucman (2018) as the most reliable estimates of offshore wealth available, in terms of the country breakdown in particular. Still, these research papers naturally have their limitations. Both of these inevitably focus exclusively on financial wealth and their estimates are thus underestimates because they ignore non-financial wealth such as real estate, gold, works of art etc. Also, Alstadsaeter, Johannesen, & Zucman (2018) present main results for 2007 and argue that the more recent period is contaminated by the use of shell companies. So there is obviously a scope for detailing the development in recent years, which might be important, as they acknowledge, for example in the case of China.

3.4.4. Results

Using the discrepancy in international investment positions similarly to Zucman (2013), Alstadsaeter, Johannesen, & Zucman (2018) observe the scale of offshore wealth over time since 2001. They find that it remained equal to about 10 per cent of world GDP (5.6 trillion USD in their benchmark year 2007). This is slightly lower and similar in trends to interview-based estimates by (Boston Consulting Group, 2017). Other companies and researchers also usually arrive at higher estimates, including Henry (2012) above, and they thus consider their estimates conservative. According to the detailed Swiss data, a large share of this estimated offshore wealth is held in Switzerland, but it is declining in recent years (30 per cent in the recent years, compared to 40–50 per cent in the 2000s). In contrast, Asian tax havens are on the rise; Hong Kong in particular experienced a steep increase in recent years and is now the second most important tax haven after Switzerland according to their estimates.

From the Swiss data Alstadsaeter, Johannesen, & Zucman (2018) estimate that some countries own more wealth in Switzerland relative to their GDP (Saudi Arabia, United Arab Emirates, Spain, France, Argentina, Egypt), while other countries less (Denmark, Norway, Sweden, Japan, India, China). Overall, they do not observe clear patterns. From the other tax havens' BIS data, they find that in 2007 Singapore, Luxembourg, Jersey and the Cayman Islands were most important. Asian countries seem less represented in Switzerland and more in other countries (Singapore in particular, and, likely, in later years in

Honk Kong after its increase in importance). Russia seems to have a lot of wealth in Switzerland and elsewhere, especially in Cyprus. While many European countries favour both Switzerland and other tax havens (including Luxembourg and Jersey) almost equally, Middle-Eastern countries favour Switzerland.

From the sum of these two estimates, they learn that while an equivalent of 10 per cent of world GDP is held in tax havens globally, there are important differences across countries: a few per cent in Scandinavian countries, around 15 per cent in Europe and up to 60 per cent in Russia, Gulf countries and some countries in Latin America. They do not find a relationship between the scale and tax, financial or institutional characteristics, but do find that geography (such as proximity to Switzerland and reliance on natural resources) and history (such as instability since the Second World War), which is consistent with recent findings of Andersen, Johannesen, Lassen, & Paltseva (2017) that flows to tax havens are related with oil prices and political shocks. As a robustness check, Alstadsaeter, Johannesen, & Zucman (2018) show that their estimated offshore wealth is mostly very well correlated with how many shell companies a country created as indicated by the so called Panama Papers (the main exception being China, for which they do not estimate much offshore wealth, but for which many shell companies were created). In the remainder of the paper that we do not discuss here, Alstadsaeter, Johannesen, & Zucman (2018) show that taking into account the estimated offshore wealth increases the top 0.01 per cent wealth share substantially in Europe and in Russia.

3.4.5. Conclusions

The reviewed research by Zucman (2013) and Alstadsaeter, Johannesen, & Zucman (2018) may be considered to provide the most reliable, current estimates of offshore financial wealth hidden in tax havens. Alstadsaeter, Johannesen, & Zucman (2018) estimate offshore wealth at 10 per cent of world GDP. Switzerland is the top tax haven in terms of offshore wealth, but its role is declining over time, with Honk Kong and other Asian tax havens becoming more important. They find quite a lot heterogeneity as to which countries own more or less wealth in Switzerland and in other tax havens. Overall, we learn a lot from their results, but better data in the future should enable further research to improve on them.

Despite recent progress in research on the scale of offshore wealth, best exemplified by Alstadsaeter, Johannesen, & Zucman (2018), there is still a long way to go to have reliable estimates of offshore wealth. The main limitation seems to be the available data, despite improvements in recent years, including the publication of the BIS bilateral data. Still, Switzerland is the only tax haven that publishes comprehensive statistics on the amount of foreign wealth managed by its banks. We thus join Alstadsaeter, Johannesen, & Zucman (2018) in calling for improving statistics.

3.5. Conclusions on Capital and Offshore Wealth

To conclude this chapter on capital and offshore wealth, we draw the main lessons from the extensive and still expanding academic and policy litera-ture reviewed in detail above. While the capital estimates enable a good coverage of countries and years and are feasible (possibly why we have seen them used as perhaps the most prominent estimates so far), they lack the required quality and are not reliable indicators of illicit financial flows and, increasingly, not seen as such. Capital estimates can be useful in specific cases, as exemplified by Novokmet, Piketty, & Zucman (2018), but at the moment these do not seem promising as a basis for an indicator of the SDG target. Therefore, we mostly discuss in these conclusions the other part of this chapter, offshore wealth.

First, offshore wealth estimates are and should be an integral part of the mission to estimate the scale of illicit financial flows. Wealth held in tax havens is a direct consequence of some of the illicit financial flows heading from onshore to offshore. The Panama Papers and other offshore leaks have highlighted the importance of financial secrecy and offshore wealth. A country should be clearly better off when a lower share of country's wealth is held offshore and vice versa. Illicit financial flows that result into offshore wealth should be reduced and this should contribute to sustainable development.

Second, offshore wealth is clearly important and the scale seems to be substantial. The recent estimates of Alstadsaeter, Johannesen, & Zucman (2018) put the scale of financial offshore wealth at 10 per cent of world GDP, with some countries much more vulnerable. This is supported by other estimates, including the capital estimates, that usually arrive at even higher estimates of offshore wealth. Some current estimates are not based on official data or require crucial assumptions to arrive at specific-country estimates. Some other current estimates—namely capital estimates on the basis of balance of payments data—are not so reliable. From the point of view of the SDG target indicator, it would be useful if these strengths were combined in one reliable indicator—based on official statistical data without the need for important assumptions.

Third, undeclared offshore wealth can be reduced and this makes it policy-relevant as a basis for the SDG target indicator. Offshore wealth estimates vary a lot across countries and tax havens. On the one hand, there is a lot of hetero-geneity among countries having wealth in tax havens. On the other hand, the role of Switzerland seems to be declining which might be due to changes in international regulations influencing offshore wealth, such as exchange of information, to which Switzerland, in the end, agreed. Furthermore, recent research has shown that a focus by tax authorities on wealth held by individuals offshore might bring the wealth onshore. For example, Johannesen, Langetieg, Reck, Risch, & Slemrod (2018) find that the US Internal Revenue Service's enforcement efforts initiated in 2008 caused approximately 60 thousand people to disclose offshore accounts with a combined value of around $120 billion. Overall, a reduction in undeclared offshore wealth seems a suitable policy target.

Fourth, the SDG target is set in terms of illicit financial flows, while offshore wealth is usually estimated as a stock. This creates a potential technical chal-lenge in harmonising the expectations of the target and the actual estimates. One potential solution is to estimate the income streams (perhaps comparable to the notion of illicit financial flows) that may accrue on offshore assets. For example, Johannesen & Pirttilä (2016) provide a comparison of these: both Henry (2012) and Zucman (2013) estimate an offshore income stream of around $190 billion annually (Henry assumes a much more cautious rate of his return, on his much higher estimated stock). However, the additional extrapolations (from outflows to stocks, and then to potential income streams) inevitably add a higher degree of uncertainty.

Fifth and overall, the offshore wealth estimates are promising with respect to the indicator of the SDG target with some of the leading estimates—Alstadsaeter, Johannesen, & Zucman (2018)—being of notably high quality. Although the offshore wealth estimates are not so strong in the coverage of countries and years, it might be feasible to extend them given the expected improvement in the availability of the relevant data, and we discuss these opportunities in our proposal for new indicators. Indeed, partly because data availability is increasing and the related research is relatively advanced in this group of estimates, we return to offshore wealth in chapter 6.

4

International Corporate Tax Avoidance

We start with the introduction to international corporate tax avoidance as illicit financial flows and then discuss empirical findings in two stages. First, we discuss an estimation framework used frequently by economists and we show the results, often available for specific channels or selected countries. Second, in a series of sub-chapters we discuss the methodologies and results of the few studies that provide global estimates of profit shifting scale.

Tax avoidance by multinational companies is the most widely recognised tax 'injustice'. The tax affairs of technology companies such as Google and Facebook, or commodity companies such as Glencore and Chevron, have sparked both popular anger and policy responses from Italy to Indonesia, and from Australia to Zambia. The related revenue losses for lower-income countries have been a particular target for tax justice activists, development advocates and researchers at international organisations.

A clear conclusion emerges from the existing research that the international tax system provides MNEs with opportunities to decrease their taxes through intra-company transfer prices, strategic management of the location of intangible assets or distortion of the corporate debt structure. The research confirms that many MNEs do often make use of these opportunities and do shift income to tax havens (Clausing, 2003; Hines & Rice, 1994; Huizinga & Laeven, 2008). However, until recently at least, the literature has been less conclusive in respect of scale of profit shifting flows and revenue implications.

This is, nonetheless, an aspect of illicit financial flows where the evidence for stronger impacts on lower-income countries is relatively compelling—and hence there is a strong case for its inclusion in the Sustainable Development Goals' target to curtail illicit financial flows. But lobbying and arguments based on the (wrongly) presumed lawfulness of corporate tax avoidance, coupled with an insistence on interpreting 'illicit' as synonymous with 'illegal', has led to disagreement.

Such an insistence appears to overlook the fact that many avoidance schemes are found to be unlawful, without reaching the point of criminality. Are these illicit? Equating 'illicit' with 'illegal' is often taken to bring a clarity and a technical neutrality to the illicit financial flows discussion—but in practice would

Stepping Westward: Writing the Highland Tour c.1720–1830. Nigel Leask, Oxford University Press (2019). © Nigel Leask.
DOI: 10.1093/oso/9780198850021.001.0001

introduce a systematic bias against lower-income countries. Legal findings of criminal tax evasion, or unlawful avoidance, depend on a range of factors. These include whether the underlying legislation is clear and up-to-date; whether the tax authority has both the resources and the political independence and/or support to prosecute a multinational; and whether the legal system is sufficiently well resourced and independent to try such a case well and fairly. By and large, each of these factors is less likely to be met in a low-income country as opposed to a high-income country—and so considering only proven illegal tax behaviour by multinationals will result in estimates that are systematically biased against finding illicit financial flows in lower-income countries, *even assuming* that multinationals' tax behaviour does not vary between countries.

In this section we proceed on the basis of the wider definition of illicit, as set out above, including cross-border flows which are deliberately hidden. The main focus is on the evaluation of the scale of multinationals' profit shifting (and the corresponding corporate income tax revenue losses). We use the term 'profit shifting' in order to abstract from the questions of legality and criminality that can be assessed only for individual transactions within a given multinational, and instead to cover the range of underlying phenomena that result in profit misalignment. We view this as in line with (i) the dictionary definition of 'illicit', covering socially unacceptable behaviour as well as proven illegality; and (ii) the international consensus, expressed in the G20/OECD Base Erosion and Profit Shifting (BEPS) project, that multinationals' profit misalignment should be curtailed. This consensus is expressed most clearly in the single aim of the BEPS Action Plan: 'The G20 finance ministers called on the OECD to develop an action plan to address BEPS issues in a co-ordinated and comprehensive manner. Specifically, this Action Plan should provide countries with domestic and international instruments that will *better align rights to tax with economic activity*' (OECD, 2013a, p.11, emphasis added). Those involved in other policy processes, such as the indicator setting for the SDGs, will necessarily take their own view.

As with the other aspects of illicit financial flows, assessments of the individual channels that give rise to profit shifting largely reflect the evaluation of deviations from some expected 'normal' pattern of data. A specific channel by which multinationals seek to achieve profit misalignment, the mispricing of commodity trade, is assessed in a subchapter on trade mispricing below; but in the preceding subchapters we largely focus on other profit shifting channels and the overall degree of misalignment eventually achieved discussed and estimated for many countries in the studies covered in a subchapter below. The studies covered there are mostly aiming for a global coverage of countries and obtain estimates of country-level scale of profit shifting. Still, before moving to these studies, in the following subchapter we survey the detailed profit shifting studies that have over the past years and recent decades developed into a vast body of literature.

There are three main recognised profit shifting channels: debt shifting through loans within one MNE group, location of intangible assets and intellectual property, and strategic transfer pricing. Table 4.1 sums up these three main channels of profit shifting and provides a few examples of related studies. All three are motivated mostly by the MNEs' desire to lower their taxes by transferring their profits to countries where they pay lower taxes. In the case of debt shifting, this transfer is achieved through loans at high interest rates from one MNE unit located in a country with low taxes to a profitable affiliate in a country with high taxes. In the case of location of intangible assets, intellectual property such as brands or research and development is located artificially at an MNE's subsidiary in a tax haven, to which high service fees are then paid by other affiliates of the MNE. In the case of strategic manipulation of transfer prices, profits are shifted by increasing or decreasing the prices of goods or services being transferred between the various foreign parts of a MNE in such a way as to minimise the tax burden faced in all the countries put together. In addition to these three main channels MNEs engage in other profit shifting strategies that might also result into illicit financial flows. As discussed in the following subchapter below, the common feature to most channels is the manipulation of prices for intra-group transactions. Since these are prices for which data are not typically available publicly, we briefly survey the key findings in this area, but focus primarily on estimates that relate to the achieved scale of profit shifting, ideally with comparable estimates for many countries.

To this end, there are three main types of data on which researchers have drawn. First, and generally preferable, are data on the reporting of individual

Table 4.1. The main profit shifting channels of MNEs

The main profit shifting channels	Examples of relevant studies
Debt shifting	Fuest, Hebous, & Riedel (2011), Buettner & Wamser (2013)
Location of intangible assets and intellectual property	Dischinger & Riedel (2011), Evers, Miller, & Spengel (2015)
Strategic transfer pricing	Clausing (2003), Davies, Martin, Parenti, & Toubal (2017)

Source: Authors

multinationals. At present, the available datasets of this type tend to have major limitations; but the results can also be the most compelling for the partial activity they refer to, based on deviations in reported profit from the location of reported activity. Second, estimates can be based on deviations in jurisdictions' apparent efficiency in raising corporate tax revenues, using national-level data on revenue and activity. Third, falling between the first two in terms of the aggregate level of data and analysis, estimates can be based on deviations in the reported national-level profitability of foreign direct investment (FDI) in each jurisdiction.

The following section 4.1 summarises research findings which do not generally aim to provide a global scale, but rather to establish particular patterns of multinational tax behaviour that give rise to the overall issue, i.e. individual channels of profit misalignment. This section also surveys some key research that provides partial scale estimates. The remaining sections 4.2 to 4.7 deal with what we consider the main currently available global estimates. Finally, we identify main conclusions from the existing research, and proceed to offer policy recommendations and to identify key areas that would benefit from improvements in methodology and in the availability of data. On the last question, the most obvious recommendation is for large multinationals' reporting under the new OECD standard for country-by-country reporting to be made public—which at a stroke, and with near-zero cost, would radically change what is known about these leading global economic actors and the associated illicit financial flows.

4.1. Empirical Findings on International Corporate Tax Avoidance

4.1.1. Overview

We begin with reviewing briefly some relevant research into the phenomenon which is more closely focused than to yield directly any estimates of profit shifting scale or tax revenue loss for more than one country.

4.1.2. Data

The bulk of the analysis here has been concerned with microeconomic responses, through various channels, to tax rate differentials between jurisdictions. Typically, authors have relied on company balance sheet data—often taken from Bureau van Dijk's Orbis or Amadeus data bases. Orbis, has been used intensively by other profit shifting studies as recently reviewed by Dharmapala (2014). Some of the recent studies include Johannesen et al. (2017) and OECD's Johansson et al. (2017). Still, the OECD (2015, p. 27) in its BEPS report stresses the limitations of this data for analysing profit shifting.

Although Orbis is likely the most frequently and one of the most suitable used data set in papers looking at profit shifting, the latter being a reason why we use it in this paper, Orbis has its limitations. They are discussed at some length by Cobham and Loretz (2014), Clausing (2016), and recently acknowledged by Schimanski (2017) and Garcia-Bernardo et al. (2017). One of the most relevant limitation for the reviewed area of research is that the Orbis data is biased against tax havens (and developing countries), i.e. the group of countries that we aim to study. Perhaps even more importantly, Tørsløv, Wier, & Zucman (2018) show that most of some MNEs' profits are not included in the Orbis data. Specifically, they show that only a weighted average of 17 per cent of global profits is included in Orbis.

Partly in response to these limitations of Orbis, other data have been used to examine profit shifting. For example, tax revenue data are the basis for the estimations of IMF's Crivelli et al. (2016) and Cobham and Janský (2017a). Another alternative to Orbis are datasets that exist for a few countries with information on MNEs headquartered there. The data of the United States Bureau of Economic Analysis has been used recently by Zucman (2014), Zucman (2015), Clausing (2016) and Cobham and Janský (2017b), while Germany's MiDi data has been employed, for example, by Weichenrieder (2009), Hebous & Johannesen (2015) and Gumpert et al. (2016). Similar foreign affiliate statistics for OECD countries is exploited by Tørsløv, Wier, & Zucman (2018). Perhaps even more promising is the use of confidential corporate tax returns, as done by Dowd et al. (2017) for the United States, Bilicka (forthcoming) for the United Kingdom or Reynolds & Wier (2016) for South Africa, which brings us to a discussion of profit shifting studies in these countries.

A number of countries, including Germany, Japan, the United Kingdom and the United States, provide limited public, or more extensive private access to researchers to datasets on the activities of multinationals to which they are either home, or host economies (or both). This has given rise to studies which, while not global in scope, do provide the basis for assessments of the scale of profit-shifting. In addition, they can offer complementary evidence in respect of particular channels. We survey the key contributions here.

4.1.3. Methodology

Economists often study the sensitivity of reported income to differences in tax rates and so there are a number of studies providing evidence of profit shifting, especially on how tax rate differentials affect reported pre-tax profits and on which strategies MNEs employ to reallocate profits within the group. Since the related literature is voluminous and growing, we refer to recent review articles by Dharmapala (2014) and Beer, Mooij, & Liu (2019) and other more recent articles, such as Clausing (2016) or Dowd, Landefeld, & Moore (2017), for additional details.

Dharmapala (2014) reviews the literature on how the reported income changes with respect to tax rates differences across countries, represented by Hines Jr & Rice (1994) and Huizinga & Laeven (2008). For example, Dharmapala (2014) defends the prevailing use of statutory tax rates as more exogenous than effective tax rates (the actual tax rates faced by an affiliate), which might differ widely from the statutory ones due to deductions that in part reflect endogenous choices made by the firm, such as its decisions about the use of debt. Additionally, although Dharmapala (2014) considers the economists' approach more rigorous, he also points to the accountants' related research (Collins, Kemsley, & Lang, 1998; Dyreng & Markle, 2013; Klassen & Laplante, 2012).

The Hines–Rice approach modified for panel data, in the words and notations of Dharmapala (2014), can be simplified as:

$$\log \pi_{it} = \beta_1 \tau_{it} + \beta_2 \log K_{it} + \beta_3 \log L_{it} + \gamma X_{it} + \mu_i + \delta_t + \varepsilon_{it}$$

where π_{it} is the profit of affiliate i in year t, τ_{it} is the tax rate difference between the parent and the affiliate, K_{it} is capital input, L_{it} is labour input, X_{it} are additional affiliate-level controls, μ_i is an affiliate fixed effect (which controls for the unobserved characteristics of affiliate i that do not change over time), δ_t is a year fixed effect (which controls for unobserved common changes in the profitability of all affiliates in a given year), and ε_{it} is the error term. The main coefficient of interest is β_1 and reflects the extent to which the multinational shifts profits into or out of affiliate i. It is a marginal effect, i.e. the change in reported profits associated with a small change in the difference between the tax rates in the parent and affiliate economies, holding all else constant.

This original basic framework has been extended over the past decades in a few areas, for example, by moving from aggregate country-level analysis to the micro-level analysis of the behaviour of individual multinational affiliates and by relying on panel data (both already included in the version described by the equation above) or by using other indicators than fixed tangible assets and employment compensation for capital and labour inputs, respectively. Further innovations have been introduced more recently. For example, Huizinga & Laeven (2008) used the overall pattern of tax rates faced by all affiliates of the MNE rather than only the difference between the parent and the affiliate, Dharmapala & Riedel (2013) included a variable for arguably exogenous profit shocks, and Dowd, Landefeld & Moore (2017) allow for non-linear semi-elasticity with respect to the tax rates.

Some of the most convincing empirical evidence is on specific profit shifting channels with pioneering estimates for Europe by Huizinga & Laeven (2008). Some similar approaches with applications to lower-income countries have been developed by Fuest & Riedel (2012) and Johannesen, Tørsløv, & Wier (forthcoming). Both indicate the importance of profit shifting for lower-income countries, but their methodological approaches do not extent to evaluate the scale of profit shifting or the associated tax revenue losses. Recently, in an unpublished draft, Nicolay, Nusser, & Pfeiffer (2016) review the literature on the effectiveness of anti-avoidance legislation and use a sample of European multinationals to test whether firms substitute between profit shifting strategies and whether this implies interdependence between different anti-avoidance regulations in place. Their empirical results, further strengthened by exploiting a reform of thin capitalization rules in France in a difference-in-difference approach, suggest that substitution between profit shifting channels takes place and that thin capitalization rules are not effective in reducing total profit shifting if no strict transfer pricing rules are present.

Riedel (2015) reviews the related literature and concludes that existing results at the lower (upper) end suggest that MNEs transfer less than 5 per cent (30 per cent or more) of their income earned at high-tax affiliates to lower-tax entities. Neither Riedel (2015) nor most other academics develop their estimates of profit shifting into estimates of revenue impacts. Together with Fuest, Spengel, Finke, Heckemeyer, & Nusser (2013) we observe that empirical studies scarcely extrapolate their estimates to profit shifting volumes. An early exception is Huizinga & Laeven (2008) with estimates of profit shifting scale and related tax revenue losses for 21 European countries (with losses largely concentrated in Germany) that has been rarely followed with respect to these country-level estimates.

There are other exceptions and, even more optimistically, their number as well as reliability seem to be increasing with time. In addition to the mostly global estimates discussed in the sections below, there are two other exceptions—Clausing (2009) and Zucman (2014) with their estimates for the United States. The following section looks at these and other country-specific assessments, before we move to global findings.

Their as well as most other estimation methodologies can be summarised as:

$$CIT\ revenues\ lost\ from\ BEPS = (applicable\ tax\ rate) \times$$
$$(a\ hypothetical\ counterfactual\ (without\ BEPS)\ CIT\ base - current\ CIT\ base).$$

where CIT stands for corporate income tax and, of course, one of the difficulties in estimating the scale of the profit shifting problem is the limited data that are available, as well as the difficulty associated with establishing the counterfactual levels of profit in each country absent profit shifting incentives and the applicable tax rate. Indeed, a counterfactual tax base and a relevant tax rate are needed in most of the similar estimations. The problem with a counterfactual is that firms' true economic profit before profit shifting is not observable, but we need a reasonable estimate of it for any estimates of the revenue implications. Additionally, whether we have data on taxes paid according to financial or tax accounting is important. The problem with a tax rate is that an applicable rate is seldom known, it might be the statutory rate, an estimated effective tax rate or some other rate.

4.1.4. Results

According to survey of the recent literature by Heckemeyer & Overesch (2017), who follow the earlier meta-analysis by Mooij & Ederveen (2008) and suggest that transfer pricing and licensing are the dominant profit-shifting channels, a semi-elasticity of reported income with respect to the tax rate differential across countries amounts to 0.8. In Dharmapala's (2014) example this entails that a 10 per centage point increase in the tax rate difference between an affiliate and its parent (e.g. because the tax rate in the affiliate's country falls from 35 per cent to 25 per cent) would increase the pre-tax income reported by the affiliate by 8 per cent (for example, from $100,000 to $108,000).) Dharmapala's (2014) observes that the estimated magnitude of BEPS is typically much smaller than that found in earlier studies and that the magnitude, at least as estimated by the semi-elasticity, has been decreasing over time. However, the data used usually suffer by important issues discussed, for example, by Keightley & Stupak (2015), and the methodology, for example, does not allow for non-linearity of the semi-elasticity with respect to the size of tax rates Dowd, Landefeld, & Moore (2017).

Even when ignoring the various downsides of the estimates, an important dilemma ensues, which Dharmapala (2014) describes in the following way. He considers the semi-elasticity relatively small and in contrast to a widespread policy discourse that points to descriptive statistics regarding the fraction of income reported by MNEs in tax havens as indicating that international corporate tax avoidance is large in magnitude and importance. The kind of estimates reviewed by Dharmapala (2014) capture, however, marginal effects (i.e. the change in reported profits associated with a small change in tax rates, holding all else constant), and therefore, as Miller (2014) sums up, are not necessarily inconsistent with evidence that large amounts of income have been shifted offshore. Also, Dharmapala (2014) addresses this question directly and he ponders whether the large fraction of the net book income of MNCs reported in havens might reflect 'inframarginal' income shifting that empirical analysis focused on semi-elasticity cannot detect or it has some other explanation. He argues that in the policy discourse it would be common to point to the reporting of 40 per cent of the MNEs' income (which he observes on the basis of Bureau of Economic Analysis data) constituting BEPS activity, whereas he argues that it might be termed an 'inframarginal' phenomenon that is difficult to explain using the estimated elasticities. He argues that a semi-elasticity in the range of 0.4 to 0.8 would (if it were possible to extrapolate from small changes in the tax rate) imply that 10–20 per cent of income (rather than 40 per cent) would be shifted to havens. Furthermore, similar analyses do not take into account the finding of Kawano & Slemrod (2015) that countries tend to implement policies that both lower the corporate tax rate and broaden the corporate tax base, and this might bias the estimates of semi-elasticity, as they show using the replications of Clausing (2007) and Devereux (2007).

This heterogeneous group of recent estimates includes further research than we have space for in this review, since our priority is the estimated impact of international corporate tax avoidance on government tax revenues. Therefore, in the remainder we focus on recent research that generates specific estimates in terms of revenue loss in dollars, tax or percentages of GDP.

4.1.5. United States

Two of the exceptions are Clausing (2009) and Zucman (2014) with their estimates for the United States. Zucman (2014) on page 130 assumes that profits reported in tax havens are taxed negligibly in tax havens and mostly untaxed in the headquarters' or owners' countries and estimates:

$$CIT \text{ revenues lost from BEPS} =$$
$$Share \text{ of profits reported in tax havens} \times corporate \text{ tax base}$$

On the basis of this formula and available data, he concludes that profit-shifting to low-tax jurisdictions reduces the tax bill of US-owned companies by about 20 per cent. In another estimate on page 131, Zucman (2014) assumes that AETRs decrease due to BEPS, mostly (the other effects can be taken into account and the BEPS is responsible for the rest) and estimates:

$$CIT \text{ revenues lost from BEPS} =$$
$$AETR \text{ historical decrease (due to BEPS)} \times corporate \text{ tax base}$$

He observes that the effective tax rate paid by US-owned firms has been reduced by a third, from 30 to 20 per cent, between 1998 and 2013. Using the formula he argues that these companies would have, all else equal, paid $200 billion in additional taxes in 2013 if it had stayed constant.

Clausing (2009) estimates the tax responsiveness or semi-elasticity of gross profits reported by United States MNE entities in foreign countries to effective tax rate differentials between foreign affiliates and their United States parent, based on Bureau of Economic Analysis survey data on foreign activities of United States MNEs aggregated at the country level. She then uses this result to calculate, in five steps, how much government revenue would differ in the United States without profit shifting and arrives at USD 60 billion lost from profit shifting from United States MNEs in 2004, which represents 35 per cent of United States federal corporate income tax collections. Subsequently, Clausing's (2011) best estimate of the revenue loss associated with the income shifting of multinational firms in 2008 is approximately $90 billion, or about 30 per cent of U.S. government corporate tax revenues. More recently, Clausing (2016) uses the BEA data to estimate the US government revenue losses implied by BEPS and extends, speculatively, as she says, these estimates to the world and that is why we include it below together with other global estimates, in the following subchapter.

Guvenen, Mataloni Jr, Rassier, & Ruhl (2017) identify the scale of profit shifting as being responsible for a part of mismeasurement in official statistics for US GDP and productivity. They estimate that from 2008 to 2014, domestic business-sector value added in the United States, on average, is understated by slightly more than 2 per cent or about $280 billion per year. A large part of these earnings should be reattributed from the Netherlands ($73 billion in 2012), Bermuda ($32 billion), Ireland ($29 billion), and Luxembourg ($24 billion). The profit shifting adjustments are large in particular in industries that are intensive in research and development and are most likely to produce intangible assets that are easy to move across borders.

A number of other studies also focus on the United States. Keightley & Stupak (2015) review the data relevant for BEPS estimates. United States Joint Committee on Taxation (2014) calibrate the level of current profit shifting at about 20 per cent of the corporate tax base in 2013 and OECD (2015) derive that the effect on corporate taxes would be larger than the 20 per cent (or USD 70 billion), because tax collections are not proportional to the tax base due to tax credits. Its staff members, Dowd et al. (2017), estimate that reported profits in Bermuda, the Cayman Islands, Ireland, Luxembourg, the Netherlands, and Switzerland would decline by more than $100 billion in 2010 had these countries had statutory tax rates of 29 per cent and average tax rates of 17 per cent. Importantly, they observe that the effect on profits reported in a foreign subsidiary of a 1 per centage point increase in the net of tax rate (that is, a tax decrease in a foreign country) depends crucially on whether the country has a low rate or a high rate. Under the quadratic specification, a change in the tax rate from 5 per cent to 4 per cent results in a 4.7 per cent increase in profits, while a change from 30 per cent to 29 per cent results in a 0.7 per cent increase in profits (in contrast with a 1.4 per cent increase when the traditional linear specification is used).

4.1.6. Europe

In a related area of research, governments around the world are concerned with a tax gap as the difference between the true amount of tax legally due and what taxpayers actually pay. A recent report by FISCALIS Tax Gap Project Group (2018) reviews much of the important corporate income tax gap literature and argues that it is too early to identify a consensus methodology, which could be applied across countries. It also argues that providing an overview of methods, as the report as well as this chapter does, is a first step to an emergence of such consensus methodology. It stresses that the focus should be on the trend of the results rather than on the absolute values. It observes that as of June 2017 about ten EU member states have taken steps of already estimate a CIT gap: three member states (Ireland, France and United Kingdom) did not reply to their questionnaire, six member states use or intend to use bottom-up methods (Belgium, Bulgaria, Denmark, Italy, Finland and Sweden), either based on risk-based audits or on random audits and three member states use top-down methods (Italy, Romania and Slovakia) with national accounting methods as a basis for the calculation. While the Netherlands uses a bottom-up approach on its programme for small and medium enterprises, four member states (Czech Republic, Portugal, Latvia and Lithuania) have indicated that they are planning to undertake CIT gap estimates in the future. Overall, only three countries publish their results (Denmark, Italy and Slovakia).

We discuss this concept only briefly and focus on results for Germany, as an example of a big EU member state with a range of relevant research. The efforts of the EU's Tax Gap Project Group resulted in a report by European Commission (2016b) that discusses the concept of tax gaps generally and focuses on VAT gap estimations across a number of EU states. Some tax gap estimates include international corporate tax avoidance and are thus relevant here (Bloomquist, Hamilton, & Pope, 2014). According to European Commission (2016b), only Germany seems to carry out and publish estimates of corporate income tax gaps, namely using a top-down approach by Bach (2013) and a bottom-up one by Finke (2014). There is also a lively discussion in the United Kingdom—in somewhat contrasting contributions, Murphy (2012) and Oxford University Centre for Business Taxation (2012) discuss the corporate tax gap by UK corporations.

In an unpublished draft, Finke (2014) used propensity-score matching to account for missing counterfactual of MNEs' profit before profit shifting. Her results suggest that MNEs in Germany on average pay 600,000 EUR (about 27 per cent) less profit taxes than a German domestic standalone, taken as the counterfactual. When extrapolated to the full sample, this implies a revenue loss of about 8.6 bn Euro. She finds that the effect exists only for MNE with at least one subsidiary in a low-tax jurisdiction, and that a 2008 reform substantially reduced the difference in tax payments between MNEs and domestic control group.

In another important German-focused study, Weichenrieder (2009) uses the MiDi database of the Deutsche Bundesbank on German inbound and outbound FDI to find an empirical correlation between the home country tax rate of a parent and the net of tax profitability of its German affiliate, consistent with profit shifting behaviour. Using the same data as well as another German data set on services, Hebous & Johannesen (2015) document that the service trade of tax havens partly reflects genuine specialization in service industries and partly profit shifting, and argue that the loss of government revenue resulting from this type of corporate tax behaviour is likely to be modest.

Looking more broadly, Murphy (2012) provides annual estimates of 150 and 850 billion euros for total EU tax avoidance and evasion, respectively (the latter being based mostly on the shadow economy estimates of Schneider, Buehn, & Montenegro (2010).

Recently, European Commission's Alvarez-Martinez et al. (2018) used a computable general equilibrium model, designed specifically for corporate taxation and multinationals, to estimate the size and macroeconomic effects of base erosion and profit shifting. Their central estimate of corporate tax losses for the EU amounts to €36 billion annually or 7.7 per cent of total corporate tax revenues. As they acknowledge, their central estimate hides a large range of estimates reflecting the range of tax rates elasticities available in the empirical economic literature. For instance, the net losses in tax revenues for the EU may range between €9.7 and €71.6 billion depending on the elasticities of tax shifting used in the calibration of the model. The USA and Japan also appear to lose tax revenues respectively of €101 and €24 billion per year or 10.7 per cent of corporate tax revenues in both cases. The authors argue that these estimates are consistent with gaps in bilateral multinationals' activities reported by creditor and debtor countries using official statistics for the EU. Furthermore, their results suggest that by increasing the cost of capital, eliminating profit shifting would slightly reduce investment and GDP and raise corporate tax revenues thanks to enhanced domestic production, which could in turn reduce other taxes and increase welfare. Unfortunately, they are able to estimate these results only for 28 EU member states and the United States and Japan.

4.2. Estimates for the World, and Low- and Middle-income Countries in Particular

To estimate global illicit financial flows, data with global coverage is clearly preferable. In practice, however, there exists at present no public data source on the economic activities of multinationals which does not suffer from grave and systematic weaknesses in coverage. In terms of methodology, the results could in most cases be strengthened by allowing for the tax and/or secrecy behaviour of counter-party jurisdictions; and by modelling profit-shifting as a response to actual tax rates paid, rather than statutory rates or other often misleading proxies. However, these are also areas in which data is typically lacking and, especially in the case of lower income countries, useful information emerges more often from case studies such as Economic Commission for Africa (2018b). Ultimately, in terms of global coverage of countries and with specific estimates of scale of profit shifting, the best currently available estimates are those summarised in Table 4.2 and studied in more detail in subchapters below.

Table 4.2 sums up the following research contributions to estimating the scale of profit shifting for many countries: IMF's Crivelli et al. (2016) and a follow-up study by Cobham & Janský (2018), UNCTAD (2015) and a follow-up study by Janský & Palanský (forthcoming), OECD (2015b), Clausing (2016), Cobham & Janský (2019), IMF (2014), and, very recently, Tørsløv, Wier, & Zucman (2018). We focus on these studies because most of them have been influential in the policy debate, all include an answer to what is the scale of profit shifting and how much tax revenue governments lose, in most cases providing estimates for many countries worldwide. We list these studies in an approximate order of perceived credibility and relevance of their estimates (and the most recent preliminary study as the last one). We discuss them in detail below.

IMF's Crivelli et al. (2016) estimate losses due to profit shifting related to tax havens by looking at a counterfactual if the tax havens' tax rates were not lower than in other countries. UNCTAD (2015) estimate tax revenue losses due to tax avoidance schemes that exploit a direct investment relationship on the basis of lower reported rate of return for investment from offshore hubs (tax havens). OECD (2015b) combines estimates of revenue losses due to both profit shifting related to tax rate differentials (differences in tax rates across countries) and differences in average effective tax rates for large affiliates of MNEs and domestic companies. Both Clausing (2016) and Cobham & Janský (2019) use data focused on US-headquartered multinationals only. While Clausing (2016) estimates profit shifting scale from derived semi-elasticities, Cobham & Janský (2019) quantify the extent of misalignment between reported profits and indicators of economic activity.

IMF (2014) for the world, and EPRS (2015) with a slightly different methodology for European countries, estimate corporate income tax revenues related to differences in countries' corporate income tax efficiency ratio (using gross and net operating surplus, respectively) relative to the average ratio in the other countries. One of the studies itself, OECD (2015b), argues that given the many uncertainties associated with global estimates of the scale and economic impacts of BEPS, no single empirical estimate can be definitive, but they add that such estimates are generally of more value for policymakers than extrapolating from more narrow studies involving a limited number of companies or countries. On a similar note, EPRS (2015) observe that most economists concede that estimating aggregate tax revenue losses due to tax avoidance and evasion remains elusive. Still, it is not an objective of this paper to provide their full evaluation and quite likely in due time (most of the studies were only relatively recently published) these studies are bound to receive their share of criticism, if only because some of the earlier studies' problems preserve: a number of strong assumptions, a lack of direct implications for policy and a lack of counterfactual.

Both Clausing (2016) and Cobham & Janský (2019) use data focused on US-headquartered multinationals only. While Clausing (2016) estimates profit shifting scale from derived semi-elasticities, Cobham & Janský (2019) quantify the extent of misalignment between reported profits and indicators of economic activity. IMF (2014) for the world, and EPRS (2015) with a slightly different methodology for European countries, estimate corporate income tax revenues related to differences in countries' corporate income tax efficiency ratio (using gross and net operating surplus, respectively) relative to the average ratio in the other countries. As we explain in detail below, this methodology's results, similarly to Cobham & Janský (2019), provide a comparatively wide scope for other interpretations than international corporate tax avoidance. Most recently, Tørsløv, Wier, & Zucman (2018) provide perhaps the most persuasive evidence of the global scale of profit shifting, drawing on national accounts and other data.

We focus here and on estimates of scale of this corporate tax avoidance with a worldwide coverage. Table 4.2 below provides an overview of seven such studies and we discuss them in some detail below. Each sub-chapter provides an overview of the data, methodology and results of each of seven leading approaches to the estimation of global profit shifting by multinational companies.

The difficulty of assessing realistic counterfactuals (i.e. what the tax base would be in the absence of profit shifting) is a particular problem. The studies usually aim to estimate how the actual amount of corporate tax paid differs from the counterfactual of a world without (any) international corporate tax avoidance. Assessing even the actual tax paid is not straightforward due to data limitations and as shown, for example, in a review of research in

Table 4.2. Summary of estimates of global profit shifting and associated tax revenue losses

Reference	Annual corporate income tax revenue loss estimates	International corporate tax avoidance estimated	More details on methodology	Published in an academic journal	Country-level estimates
IMF's Crivelli et al. (2016), Cobham & Janský (2018)	Long-run approximate estimates are $400 billion for OECD countries (1 per cent of their GDP) and $200 billion for lower-income countries (1.3 per cent) of their GDP.	BEPS related to tax havens.	BEPS related to tax havens by looking at a counterfactual if the tax havens' tax rates were not lower than for other countries.	Yes	Yes (by a later study of Cobham & Janský (2018))
UNCTAD (2015), Janský & Palanský (forthcoming)	Around 8 per cent of CIT, USD 200 billion in 2012 globally and USD 90 billion for lower-income countries.	BEPS through tax avoidance schemes that exploit a direct investment relationship.	Tax revenue losses due to tax avoidance schemes that exploit a direct investment relationship on the basis of lower reported rate of return for investment from offshore hubs.	No	Yes (by a later study of Janský & Palanský (forthcoming))
OECD (2015b), Johansson et al. (2017)	USD 100–240 billion, or anywhere from 4–10 per cent of global corporate income tax (CIT) revenues in 2014. It ranges from 7.5 to 14 per cent of lower-income countries' CIT revenue.	BEPS due to tax rate differentials and differences in average effective tax rates for large affiliates due to mismatches between tax systems and tax preferences.	BEPS related to tax rate differentials and differences in average effective tax rates for large affiliates of MNEs and domestic companies.	No	No
Clausing (2016)	Between $77 billion and $111 billion in corporate tax revenue losses of US government due to profit shifting by 2012. Revenue loses total $279 billion for a group of selected countries, 20 per cent of their total corporate tax revenues.	Profit shifting due to tax rate differentials.	Profit shifting scale from derived semi-elasticities	Yes	Yes

Cobham & Janský (2019)	As much as a quarter of the global profits of US multinationals may be shifted to locations other than where the underlying real activity takes place. This estimate amounts to some $660 billion in 2012, or almost 1 per cent of world GDP.	Misalignment between the location of US multinationals' economic activity versus the location of their profits.	They quantify the extent of misalignment between reported profits and indicators of economic activity.	Yes	Yes
IMF (2014)	5% of CIT in OECD and almost 13 per cent in non-OECD countries in 2012.	Corporate income tax efficiency, the spillover effects of profit shifting.	Corporate income tax revenues related to differences in countries' corporate income tax efficiency ratio (using gross operating surplus) relative to the average ratio in the other countries.	No	Yes
Tørsløv, Wier, & Zucman (2018)	They find that 40 per cent of multinationals' profits are artificially shifted to tax havens, i.e. more than 600 billion USD in 2015. They also estimate global corporate tax revenue loss around 200 billion USD per year (around 10 per cent of global corporate tax revenue).	Profit shifting to tax havens	They argue that relative to compensation of employees, firms in tax havens are abnormally profitable. They then show, using foreign affiliate statistics, that all of the abnormal profitability in tax havens can be explained by foreign subsidiaries operating in tax havens. They assume that all profitability in tax havens above profitability of local firms reflects inward profit-shifting.	No	Yes

Source: Authors on the basis of the cited literature

accounting for income taxes by Graham, Raedy, & Shackelford (2012). The second part is, as any counterfactual, intrinsically hard to estimate. The main approach is to estimate it indirectly by estimating the extent of international corporate tax avoidance and adding the implied revenue to the tax paid now. An alternative would be to assume that the counterfactual would be consistent with a full or partial alignment of economic activity with reported incomes generated by this activity across countries (Cobham & Janský, 2017d; Cobham & Loretz, 2014). A further step would be to produce a dynamic estimate, recognising that higher effectiveness of the current tax regime would produce potentially large incentives for reorganisation of business.

It is naturally, therefore, quite difficult to quantify what the corporate tax base would be in the absence of profit shifting. Some studies, however, seem not to consider this as an objective. This is discussed by Finke (2014), in terms of research on treatment effects. She argues that, indeed, the main problem in measuring the volume of tax avoidance through profit shifting is that the true profit before profit shifting is itself not observable as a reference point.

While the studies surveyed may struggle to capture the current scale of international corporate tax avoidance, they are less suited to be informative about the future prospects, especially in the view of ongoing policy changes. They also mostly focus only on corporate income tax (rather than capital gains and withholding or other tax) and leave out other tax revenues and other potentially dynamic effects of international corporate tax avoidance.

Furthermore, most of the studies use statutory rather than effective tax rates and they should employ the latter at least as a robustness check. On the one hand, average effective tax rates (AETRs) seem generally more suitable for these estimates than nominal tax rates since AETRs reflect better than the statutory rates the actual tax paid on average, which is what is usually relevant for the estimates. AETRs can differ substantially from nominal tax rates. On the other hand, there is less consensus on how to estimate AETRs and less information on AETRs across years and countries. Furthermore, differences in AETRs may be due to reasons such as R&D tax credits, i.e. other than international corporate tax avoidance, and thus might be partly misleading. Overall, good practice might be to report results using both nominal tax rates and AETRs as done by Crivelli et al. (2016) or Cobham & Janský (2018).

These estimates are only indicative or illustrative estimates, largely because currently available data do not enable estimates of substantially higher quality. Some of the estimates suffer unnecessarily from methodology weaknesses or from interpretations that are unclear or overambitious, but the field as a whole adds substantial value—both in terms of the specific results and by advancing understanding of these phenomena. Their research approaches can be refined in the future, by adjusting the methodologies as well as applying newer data and methodologies. Notwithstanding data and methodology limitations, they are in part expert estimates in the sense that they reflect the authors' informed perspective on how large the scale might be; and we therefore interpret the estimates loosely as meaning that they are all more or less in the range that these experts expect them to be.

We would likely be too optimistic to claim that there seems to be agreement on the order of scale of profit shifting and related tax revenue losses in absolute numbers. There is certainly disagreement on whether these particular numbers should be considered small or big. Dharmapala (2014) addresses, but does not fully settle this question, and provides some possible explanations as well as suggestions for future research. Hines (2014) discusses various estimates, and explains why some of may overstate the potential tax revenue to be had by eradicating BEPS. In a similar way to Dharmapala (2014), Hines (2014) discusses the relatively low values of semi-elasticities and argues that estimates of even 2 or 4 per cent may overstate the potential revenue, and would make an extremely modest contribution to the government finances of most countries. However, Hines (2014) focuses on OECD countries and as in Hines (2010) relies on a narrow and somewhat arbitrary definition of 'tax havens' to consider likely losses,. More importantly, Hines' (2014) empirical puzzle is why there is not more tax avoidance than appears to be the case— raising the possibility that better analysis, aligned with those priors, might indeed find avoidance to be larger. In contrast, Forstater (2015) expresses scepticism about what she sees as a popular narrative that a large 'pot of gold' exists to fund development efforts, which could be released by cracking down on the questionable tax practices of multinational enterprises. Lobbyists for multinational companies have made a similar argument within the UN process on SDG 16.4, and have encouraged lower-income countries to focus on alternative revenue sources.

Standing back from policy debates, the research literature can be viewed in different ways. On the one hand, it seems inevitable that attempts to estimate what is deliberately hidden will produce imperfect results—and there is certainly no perfect analysis yet. On the other hand, none of the estimates discussed suggest that the revenues at risk are not substantial in absolute terms. This is especially the case for lower-income countries, where corporate tax revenues are relatively large and overall tax revenues relatively small (Prichard, Cobham, & Goodall, 2014)), and where estimated losses tend systematically to account for a larger share of current tax revenues. Differences across countries should continue to be the subject of further research.

Overall, conclusions about the scale of any IFFs—including those related to multinational profit shifting—must be drawn on the basis of a range of methodologies and data that are all, necessarily, flawed. Nonetheless, the range of data and applied methodologies in respect of profit shifting give rise to a broadly higher degree of confidence in the findings in this area.

There are three areas of particular convergence. First, in terms of the contours of the problem, the findings indicate that only a small number of jurisdictions are consistently the recipients of disproportionate volumes of profit related to economic activity elsewhere. Second, the scale of shifted profits and revenue losses are widely distributed across other jurisdictions, with the highest values in high-income countries but the most intense losses—in relation to GDP and especially to tax revenues - in lower-income countries. Third, the overall scale of multinationals' profit shifting may reach the level of being a material distortion to global economic accounts; and the worldwide revenue losses are likely to lie in a range between $100 billion and $650 billion annually.

4.3. IMF's Crivelli et al. (2016)

4.3.1. Overview

IMF researchers Crivelli et al. (2016) focus on estimating BEPS in developing countries. The preliminary version of these estimates was first published as a part of IMF (2014) in another appendix (III, rather than appendix IV which is discussed below as IMF (2014)). Crivelli et al. (2016) estimate cross-border fiscal externalities of two types. Base spillover is the impact of one country's tax policy on the tax bases of other countries through either shifting of real activities or only reported profits. Strategic rate spillover is the impact on a country's policy choices of tax changes abroad, or the so called tax competition in its broadest sense. In terms of base spillovers, Crivelli et al. (2016) estimate worldwide losses of corporate tax base erosion and profit shifting related to tax havens at approximately 600 billion US dollars. While Crivelli et al. (2016) do not present country-level results, Cobham & Janský (2019) re-estimate their results and present the estimates for all the countries for which data are available.

4.3.2. Data

Crivelli et al. (2016) use data on corporate income tax (CIT) revenues and statutory tax rates from the private dataset of the IMF's Fiscal Affairs Department. They argue that using such country-level data is a major limitation, but they at that time saw no other way to explore these issues for a large set of developing countries.

The recent creation of the ICTD–WIDER Government Revenue Database (GRD), which combines data from several major international databases and a new compilation from IMF Article IV and country staff reports, provides a potential alternative. A further data issue relates to the definition and treatment of 'tax havens', upon which the main results rest. Cobham & Janský (2019) provide robustness checks with ICTD-WIDER revenue data, alternative tax haven lists and effective tax rates instead of statutory tax rates.

4.3.3. Methodology

They estimate an equation with base spillovers as the dependent variable with an average of corporate tax rates by tax havens (as selected by Gravelle (2013)) as one of the independent varizables. As the authors Crivelli et al (2016) note, those avoidance effects operating through tax havens can in principle be assessed by simply 'turning off' the effects on tax bases operating through that channel, calculating the implied changes in tax bases, and multiplying by the applicable CIT rate.

Crivelli et al. (2016) estimate the long term revenue (in per cent of GDP) lost by country i in period t as a consequence of profit shifting through tax havens as:

$$Long\ run\ revenue\ cost\ of\ BEPS_{it} = \tau_{it}\hat{\varphi}(\tau_{it} - W^h\tau_{-it})/(1-\hat{\lambda})$$

where τ_{it} is the domestic corporate income tax rate, $\hat{\varphi}$ is the estimated coefficient on the tax term (imposing the restriction of equality of coefficients on own and spillover effects, separately for OECD and non-OECD groups), $W^h\tau_{-it}$ denotes the haven-weighted average tax rate (this is the short run effect) and $\hat{\lambda}$ is the estimated coefficient on the lagged corporate income tax base (again imposing the restriction), used to transform it from a short run to a long run estimate. According to Crivelli et al (2016), the estimated loss can be thought of as answering the question of how much revenue would a country gain if opportunities for profit shifting were to be eliminated by raising the average rate in tax havens to the level of its own.

The basic logic behind their estimates of the revenue cost of BEPS could also be written in the following way:

> *The revenue cost of BEPS (in percent of GDP)*
> *= The applicable CIT rate*
> *× The change in corporate tax bases implied*
> *by an increase in tax havens' tax rates*

Interestingly, this estimate seems to be independent of corporate income tax revenue of a given country in a given year—it depends only on corporate income tax rate for relative estimates (in per cent of GDP) or on GDP as well (in case we are interested in dollar values). The implied change in corporate tax bases depends for each country and year on the value of corporate income tax rate relative to the haven-weighted average. This relative value is also what is likely to drive the value of the estimates over time. One of other critical comments on this earlier version of the research was presented in International Bureau of Fiscal Documentation (IBFD)'s (2015) analysis of possible effects of the Irish tax system on developing economies (pages 67–72).

4.3.4. Results

Crivelli et al. (2016) present their illustrative revenue loss calculations only in a graph that distinguishes between OECD and non-OECD members. OECD members have estimated annual losses of around 1 per cent GDP or around 400 billion USD. Non-OECD countries have higher estimated losses relative to GDP at 1.3 per cent, but lower in terms of dollars at around 200 billion USD. They argue that this is a significant amount, especially relative to their lower levels of overall tax revenue.

Cobham & Janský (2019) provide country-level estimates, as well as robustness checks with some different data sources and methodological choices. Their headline estimate of revenue losses of around US$500 billion globally is slightly lower than nearly US$650 billion in Crivelli et al. (2016), with the majority of the reduction in the total estimate relating to OECD countries. They find an even greater differential in the intensity of losses suffered by lower-income countries. In terms of tax revenue losses, their headline estimates show that Sub-Saharan Africa, Latin America and the Caribbean, and South Asia, and lower middle-income and, above all, low-income countries suffer relatively intense losses.

4.3.5. Conclusions

Crivelli et al (2016) is perhaps the most credible peer-reviewed analysis of profit shifting for multiple countries. Cobham & Janský (2019) check the robustness of their results and extend their analysis to shed light on country heterogeneity.

4.4. UNCTAD (2015)

4.4.1. Overview

UNCTAD (2015) in its World Investment Report estimate tax revenue losses related to inward investment stocks as directly linked to offshore hubs with the focus on developing countries. They aim to develop and estimate a foreign direct investment-driven approach to measuring the scale and economic impact of BEPS. Their methodology puts the spotlight on the role of offshore investment hubs (tax havens and special-purpose entities in other countries) as major global investment players and enables the estimation of the magnitude. UNCTAD (2015) estimates that some 30 per cent of cross-border corporate investment stocks have been routed through offshore hubs before reaching their destination as productive assets. Their preferred estimate of annual revenue losses for developing countries, a focus of their study, is 90 billion USD; extending the estimates globally results into 8 per cent of CIT and USD 200 billion in 2012.

Janský & Palanský (forthcoming) re-estimate their methodology, extend it in a number of ways and present for the first time the related country-level estimates.

4.4.2. Data

The methodology relies on country-level foreign direct investment data. They use data on FDI stocks on a bilateral level from the IMF's Coordinated Direct Investment Survey (CDIS), which contains data for around 100 countries between the years 2009 and 2012. For stocks of direct inward investment, they use the inward direct investment positions from the same data source. In a small number of cases, they use UNCTAD's unilateral FDI database for its better coverage of countries.

4.4.3. Methodology

UNCTAD's (2015) estimation approach, first of all, establishes the fiscal contribution of multinational enterprises and especially the corporate tax paid by their foreign affiliates, which creates the baseline from which corporate tax is avoided. They estimate that around 3 per cent of total tax revenues in developing countries is derived from MNEs' corporate income tax. Then, they identify 42 jurisdictions as sources of investment as either tax havens or special-purpose entities and show that over time, corporate investment flows from these offshore hubs to developing countries increased to a 2010–2012 average of 26 per cent. For the United States, using the Bureau of Economic Analysis data, they show that foreign affiliates of US MNEs based in this group of countries are paying comparatively small amounts of taxes (2 and 3 per cent as a share of pre-tax net income) compared with affiliates based in other locations (17 per cent).

UNCTAD (2015) then estimates, using regression analysis, that an additional 10 per cent share of inward investment stock originating from offshore investment hubs is associated with a decrease in the rate of return of 1–1.5 percentage point. UNCTAD (2015) estimates the tax revenue losses through assumptions on the profitability gap (how much foreign direct investment income is missing due to investments from offshore investment hubs; the amount of corporate profits shifted from developing economies is about $450 billion) and on the average corporate tax rate (a weighted average effective tax rate across developing countries at 20 per cent).

UNCTAD's (2015) estimation approach can be summarized and simplified as follows (with their headline numbers for developing countries in brackets):

CIT revenues lost from profit shifting for developing countries =
average offshore hub exposure of total inward FDI stock (46%) ×
responsiveness of reported rate of return to offshore investment (11.5%) ×
reported FDI stock (USD 5000 billion) × *transforming the after* –
tax values to pre – *tax values* (1.25) ×
weighted average effective tax rate (20%) = USD 91 billion

Their estimates of the relationship between reported rate of return and offshore investment seem rigorous, but it is not clear that what they estimate is actually profit shifting. To be clear, we are not disputing that an additional 10 per cent share of inward investment stock originating from offshore investment hubs is associated with a decrease in the rate of return of 1–1.5 per centage point and the role of offshore hubs does seem to be distinct, but we do not see what the likely channels of profit shifting associated with the lower returns might be and this research lacks detail and persuasiveness in this respect. Potentially, due to its methodology, UNCTAD's (2015) approach might be estimating avoidance of capital gains and withholding tax or tax treaty shopping rather than corporate income tax avoidance, but in that case the estimates for developing countries seem large and should not be derived from the amount of corporate income tax revenue. Relatedly, UNCTAD (2015) does acknowledge on page 201 that its estimates do not include the full effects of international corporate tax avoidance; their profit shifting and tax revenue estimates are mostly confined to those associated with tax avoidance schemes that exploit a direct investment relationship through equity or debt. For example, trade mispricing does not require a direct investment link, since MNEs can shift profits between any two affiliates based in jurisdictions with different tax rates.

4.4.4. Results

UNCTAD's (2015) estimates for developing countries amount to annual tax revenue losses of some $90 billion (which is almost half of the tax actually paid; with sensitivity analysis' results ranging from $70 to $120 billion). The impact on developed countries is relatively smaller; UNCTAD (2015) estimates it in the order of $100 billion.

Country-level results with extended methodology are provided by Janský & Palanský (forthcoming). They find that on average OECD countries lose least and middle-income countries most corporate tax revenue relative to the size of their economies (and to their corporate tax revenues and tax revenues).

4.4.5. Conclusions

This approach to a particular channel of profit shifting is innovative and valuable. While the use of aggregate FDI data in the UNCTAD's (2015) approach enables it to cover many diverse countries, it might be further defined by combining it with more granular FDI data such as those from Orbis, BEA and other similar sources.

4.5. OECD (2015b)

4.5.1. Overview

OECD (2015b) finds that tax planning is widespread among MNEs and entails tax revenue losses. They estimate revenue losses from BEPS conservatively at USD 100–240 billion annually, or anywhere from 4 to 10 per cent of global corporate income tax (CIT) revenues. Given developing countries' greater reliance on CIT revenues as a percentage of tax revenue, they derive that the impact of BEPS on these countries is particularly significant. The underlying paper has been recently revised as a working paper—Johansson, Skeie, Sorbe, & Menon (2017)—but there do not seem to be fundamental differences with the initial version discussed here as OECD (2015b).

4.5.2. Data

The analysis is based on 1.2 million records between 2000 and 2010, so the data is relatively outdated. The data come from the firm-level Bureau van Dijk's Orbis database, which is considered to provide the best available cross-country firm-level information, but does have significant limitations in representativeness for some countries and is based upon financial accounts rather than tax returns. Importantly, their coverage of countries is not global, with the OECD's final sample covering 46 countries: all OECD and G20 countries, Colombia, Latvia, Malaysia and Singapore. More recent analyses using this data looked at a much higher number of countries although the coverage of firms is still far from unbiased and global (Cobham & Loretz, 2014; Garcia-Bernardo, Fichtner, Heemskerk, & Takes, 2017; Johannesen et al., 2017).

4.5.3. Methodology

In OECD's (2015b) methodology the revenue loss arises from two effects. The first one is profit shifting due to tax rate differentials, the second one differences in average effective tax rates for large affiliates due to mismatches between tax systems and tax preferences. They are documented in their following two findings. First, their analysis estimates the average semi-elasticity of reported profits to tax rate differentials between unconsolidated affiliates' statutory headline tax rates and their MNE group average tax rate (taking the unweighted average of the other affiliates' statutory tax rate) at about −1.0. Second, the effective tax rate (ETR) of large MNE entities (with more than 250 employees) is estimated to be lower on average by 4 to 8.5 percentage points compared to similarly-situated domestic-only affiliates as a result of profit shifting, mismatches between tax systems and relative use of domestic tax preferences (based on 2.0 million records; this differential is even higher among very large firms and MNEs with patents). The combination of the two effects results into the overall revenue loss estimate. The estimates are based on a number of crucial assumptions and various sources (mostly Orbis) detailed in their Annex 3.A1.

Due to the data limitations in representativeness and coverage in a number of countries, OECD (2015b) produces only a global estimate based on global parameters, so no country-level estimates are available and should be a subject of future research.

4.5.4. Results

First, profit shifting due to tax rate differentials is estimated as (and we include OECD's (2015b) estimates in brackets):

> *CIT revenues lost from profit shifting due to tax rate differentials*
> *= A worldwide responsiveness of profit to asset ratio to tax rate*
> *differentials* (0.1) × *average asset profit ratio* (16.13 *derived from*
> *the average profit to asset ratio* (6.2%)) × *average tax rate*
> *differential* (3.6%) × *MNEs' average share of total profits* (59%)
> × *estimated global CIT revenue* (USD 2.3 trillion) = USD 99 billion

Second, differences in average effective tax rates for large affiliates due to mismatches between tax systems and tax preferences are estimated as (we again include OECD's (2015b) estimates in brackets):

> *CIT revenue lost from MNE mismatches between tax systems and*
> *preferential tax treatment = Average ETR difference between large*
> *MNE entities and comparable domestic entities* (3.25%) × *MNEs' share*
> *of total profits* (59%) × *Share of large MNEs* (93%) × *estimated global*
> *CIT revenues* (USD 2.3 trillion) × *upward adjustment of actual corporate*
> *tax collections after tax credits* (23%) = USD 50 billion

Table 4.3. OECD (2015b) estimates of the revenue loss due to BEPS

	Profit shifting due to tax rate differentials	Mismatches between tax systems and tax preferences	Total	Total minus two standard errors	Total plus two standard errors	Total plus two standard errors (see notes)
% of global CIT revenue	4.21 per cent	2.19 per cent	6.41 per cent	3.80 per cent	9.01 per cent	10.46%
USD billion	96.92	50.45	147.37	87.40	207.34	240.52

Notes: The final column assumes that firms not in the sample have 50 per cent higher tax planning intensity

Source: OECD (2015) and author on the basis of OECD (2015b)

The sums in these equations as well as numbers in Table 4.3 below are ours, recomputed on the basis of details from OECD (2015b). OECD (2015b) adjusts upward actual corporate tax collections after tax credits by 23 per cent to more accurately reflect the taxable income base affected by profit shifting for the fiscal estimate. The often-reported range from 4 per cent to 10 per cent of CIT revenues takes into account a 95 per cent confidence interval around the tax sensitivity estimates and the upper bound assumes that firms outside the sample have a 50 per cent higher tax planning intensity than firms in the sample. Table 4.3 shows the resulting estimates after these adjustments in terms of share of global CIT revenue as well as in billion dollars.

Currently, country-level results can only be derived by applying the global estimates to country-level data as done by EPRS (2016). EPRS (2016) extrapolated the OECD's estimates of a 4–10 per cent increase in corporation tax receipts using Eurostat data. Specifically, they consider corporate income tax revenue for all 28 EU members of 335.3 billion euro in 2013 and this results in an estimated gain of between 13.4 and 33.5 billion euro per annum of corporate tax that could be, in the words of EPRS (2016), recovered from cost-effective regulation.

4.5.5. Conclusions

The estimates by OECD (2015b) have been some of the most influential estimates of profit shifting scale in the policy debate, but are yet to undergo a peer-review process or, perhaps more importantly, to be published with the country-level results. The weaknesses of the Orbis data—especially to examine profit shifting sensitivity, due to the under-representation of both lower-income countries and secrecy jurisdictions—are increasingly well known. Perhaps unsurprisingly, then, in its work to fulfil BEPS Action 11 which requires ongoing monitoring of the scale of the problem, the OECD has set aside this approach and is now working on a quite different analysis using country-by-country reporting data (see the data discussion in section 6.1).

4.6. Profit Shifting of US Multinationals Worldwide (Clausing, 2016)

4.6.1. Overview

Clausing (2016) estimates the effect of profit shifting for the United States as well as other countries using the Bureau of Economic Analysis (BEA) survey data on US multinationals during 1983 to 2012. She finds that profit shifting is likely costing the US government between $77 billion and $111 billion in corporate tax revenue by 2012, and these revenue losses have increased substantially in recent years. She extends the methodology with additional assumptions to other countries and she finds that profit shifting is likely a large problem in countries without low tax rates. Her estimates of revenue losses total $279 billion for high-tax countries, around 20 per cent of their total corporate tax revenues.

4.6.2. Data

Clausing (2016) uses the annual survey of all US multinational groups carried out by the Bureau of Economic Analysis (BEA). In addition to data on gross profits (which are net income with foreign income tax payments added), she uses data direct investment earnings, also from the BEA, as a. This series excludes all income from equity investments—and thus avoids some double-counting, but also some income that might be indicative of profit shifting.

For her extension to the world, she further uses the Forbes Global 2000 data of the world's largest corporations, which indicate the location of corporate headquarters and the overall level of worldwide profits for the world's biggest corporations.

4.6.3. Methodology

Clausing (2016) uses the BEA survey data to estimate semi-elasticity (her average estimate is −2.92), which then help her to calculate what profits would be in the countries of operation of US affiliates absent differences in tax rates between foreign countries and the United States. She then attributes a fraction of the lower foreign profits (of low tax countries) to the United States tax base—38.7 per cent as the share of intrafirm transactions that occur between affiliates abroad and the parent firm in the United States, relative to all intrafirm transactions undertaken by affiliates abroad (with both the parent and affiliates in other foreign countries). She then multiplies the difference between these simulated profits and the current profits by her assumed US tax rate (the mostly 35 per cent lowered by 5 percentage points, presumably, to allow for some degree of tax base narrowing, to make it more realistic). Finally, she scales the estimate up, under the assumption that foreign multinational firms also engage in income shifting out of the United States, by the ratio of the sales of affiliates of foreign-based multinational firms in the United States (a proxy for the ability of foreign multinational firms to shift income away from the United States) to the sales of affiliates of U.S. based multinational firms abroad (a proxy for the ability of U.S. multinational firms to shift income away from the United States).

The revenues lost from profit shifting can be specified as:

US CIT revenues lost from profit shifting =
(US statutory tax rate (mostly 35%) – 5%) ×
(profits in the absence of tax rate differences
between the US and foreign countries – current profits)

Clausing (2016) then extends her estimates for US MNEs to most of the global economy (but not the whole world) that she considers only indicative of approximate magnitudes. She uses the Forbes Global 2000 data of the world's largest corporations, which indicate the location of corporate headquarters and the overall level of worldwide profits for the world's biggest corporations (25 countries are home to 95 per cent of the profits earned by this group of firms). She assumes that share of income of the Global 2000 firms booked in low-tax countries, defined as those with effective tax rates that are less than 15 per cent (she identifies 17 such countries), is proportionate to the share of U.S. multinational firm foreign income that is booked in low-tax countries (it is $800 for the US). She applies her earlier US-based estimate of semi-elasticity to calculate what profits would be in low-tax countries and the likely magnitude of profit shifting to low tax countries. Her estimates suggest that $545 billion for the US (of the $800 billion booked in the low-tax countries) and $1,076 billion for the group of big headquarters countries that are not low-tax countries (including the United States) would not be booked in such countries absent the tax rate difference. She then attributes this total to the tax bases of higher-tax headquarters countries based on their share of GDP for this higher-tax group of countries. To arrive at the revenue estimate, she multiplies it with a country-specific tax rate, which she assumes to be five percentage points less than their statutory rates, as in the US case.

The revenues lost from profit shifting can be specified as:

CIT revenues lost from BEPS = (Statutory tax rate – 5%) ×
(profits in the absence of tax rate differences between the US and
foreign countries – current profits)

4.6.4. Results

Clausing estimates the revenue cost of income shifting behaviour for the US at $111 billion in 2012. She applies the same methodology using an alternative, more conservative BEA direct investment earnings series, which avoids some double-counting, but also some profit-shifting, and arrives at an estimate of $77 billion in 2012. She highlights seven tax haven countries (Netherlands, Ireland, Luxembourg, Bermuda, Switzerland, Singapore, and UK Islands) that account together for 50 per cent of all foreign profits and 52 per cent of all direct investment earnings.

Overall, the estimates of revenue losses total $279 billion for high-tax countries, 20 per cent of their total corporate tax revenues. For example, for the US, revenue loss of $94 billion is estimated for 2012, in between the upper and lower estimates of the author's more detailed US-focused methodology discussed above. Clausing (2016) discusses various sources of uncertainties and, especially for the worldwide estimate admits that is an approximate estimate.

4.6.5. Conclusions

Clausing (2016) provides careful estimates, perhaps the most rigorous ones together with those of Zucman (2014) and Dowd et al. (2017), for the biggest economy in the world, the United States. The extension of her estimates for the US to the world is, as she says, only indicative of approximate magnitudes, but even that is currently valuable. Perhaps other data might be employed for this extension and be thus informative for an even wider range of countries, including lower-income ones.

4.7. Misalignment of Profits and Economic Activity of US Multinationals Worldwide (Cobham & Janský, 2019)

4.7.1. Overview

Cobham & Janský (2019) show that as much as a quarter of the global profits of US multinationals may be shifted to locations other than where the underlying economic activity takes place. Their estimate amounts to some $660 billion in 2012, or almost 1 per cent of world GDP. They find that countries at all income levels are losing out to profit shifting, compared to the taxable profits they could expect, given the current pattern of economic activity and a scenario in which the OECD BEPS aim of aligning profits with economic activity were actually to be achieved.

4.7.2. Data

Similarly to Clausing (2016), Cobham & Janský (2019) use the annual survey of all US multinational groups carried out by the BEA. Also the limitations presented by the data are similar to those by Clausing (2016). The publicly-available data are aggregated to country- and/or industry-level and are by definition for multinational groups from just a single country of headquarters, the United States.

4.7.3. Methodology

First, Cobham & Janský (2019) use a correlation estimate to measure a relative intensity of misalignment. Their second measure reflects the scale of the distortion: in effect, how much taxable profit is in the wrong place. This can be calculated as the sum of either the (positive) excess profits recorded in countries where there is not concomitant economic activity; or equivalently the sum of the (negative) missing profits from countries with economic activity. The following formula shows how they estimate the misaligned profit for a country—if the result is negative, they call it excess profit (since alignment would require its removal); if the result is positive, they call it missing profits.

*Estimated profit = Share of economic activity * Total global gross profit – Actual gross profit*

With these indicators, they develop one possible way to operationalise what the OECD literally said when it launched its BEPS initiative in 2013 with the specific aim of reforming international corporate tax rules so that they 'better align rights to tax with economic activity' (OECD 2013a: 11). Cobham & Janský (2019) provide simulation results of what the profits were in case they were distributed in line with indicators of economic activity, considering the formula proposed by European Commission (2011) for the Common Consolidated Corporate Tax Base (CCCTB) as the main scenario, which is weighted one-third tangible assets, one-third sales, and one-third split equally between compensation costs and (number of) employees (this part stays the same in the more recent proposal by European Commission (2016a)).

Ultimately, they do measure what they call misalignment of the location of profits and economic activity as approximated by the various indicators. However, with the current data and methodology, they are not able to attribute the extent of misalignment to the various reasons. Similar research is yet to decompose the scale misalignment according to various reasons including the profit shifting or a higher capital intensity of operations in some countries or industries.

4.7.4. Results

Cobham & Janský (2019) show that misalignment as recently as the mid-1990s is relatively contained—suggesting that it is only in the last two decades that BEPS has become a significant problem. The extent of deviation from perfect correlation appears small, on any measure, even if the post-crisis level and trend are above those of the pre-crisis period (around 0.2 in 2008 and around 0.03 in the subsequent years). They show the sum of excess profits, i.e. the profits estimated by the above formula for which a perfect alignment would require their transfer to another country. In other words, it shows the total value of US MNEs' profits that would need to be declared in other jurisdictions in order for the profits to be perfectly aligned with their economic activity. Misalignment by this measure grows over the period from roughly 5–10 per cent of total gross profit in the 1990s, to around 15–25 per cent in the 2000s pre-crisis, through an artificial maximum of around 50 per cent during the sharp profit fall in 2008, and broadly in the range of 25–30 per cent since 2009. In other words, the crisis, and measures taken in the immediate years after it, does not appear to have reversed the sharp growth in misalignment since the 1990s.

Their estimates of excess tax revenue received in 2012 range from $25 bn to nearly $80 bn; the estimate of missing tax revenue is of course higher, ranging from around $80 bn to $160 bn. The difference between the two ranges—i.e. roughly $50 bn to $80 bn—is the implied revenue gain of US multinationals and their shareholders, at the expense primarily of missing-profit jurisdictions worldwide. The revenue gains of excess-profit jurisdictions can be thought of as providing an estimate of the cost of bribing these excess-profit jurisdictions by the other jurisdictions into cooperative behaviour.

Also some other research studies the misalignment between reported profits and economic activity. There seems to be a policy consensus (OECD, 2013b) on the need to apply corporate taxation where a given value was created, with two sets of estimates provided by Cobham & Loretz (2014), who use company-level balance sheet data retrieved from the Orbis database provided by Bureau van Dijk, and Cobham & Janský (2015), who estimate the misalignment of economic activity using the US data provided by the government Bureau of Economic Analysis. Relatedly, Riedel, Zinn, & Hofmann (2015) find that the tightening of transfer pricing rules raises reported operating profits of high-tax affiliates, and vice versa for low-tax ones, and reduces the sensitivity of affiliates' pre-tax profits to corporate tax rate changes, and they therefore suggest the effectiveness of the regulations in limiting tax-motivated profit shifting behaviour. In another similar analysis, MSCI (2015) identify 243 companies (out of 1,093 companies within their MSCI World Index constituents; health care and IT companies stood out) paying an average rate of 17.7 per cent, versus 34.0 per cent, if these companies were paying taxes in the jurisdictions where they generate revenues, i.e. equivalent to comparing the location of reported profits and sales (the total difference amounts to USD 82 billion per year).

4.7.5. Conclusions

With the same data source, but very different methodological approach, the scale estimated by Cobham & Janský (2019) is comparable to Clausing (2016).

While the methodological approach is one of the most indirect estimates from the studies reviewed here (in this respect similar to the corporate income tax efficiency estimates in the following section) and thus not to be considered precise in terms of the specific scale of profit shifting, its value might be in providing indicative guidance on cross-country heterogeneity and trends over time. The results show countries at all levels of development suffering from under-reporting of profit reported compared to the economic activity located there; and this scale of misalignment to have increased sharply from the 1990s until at least 2012, when the decision was taken to initiate the OECD Base Erosion and Profit Shifting process.

4.8. Corporate Income Tax Efficiency Estimates (IMF (2014), EPRS (2015))

4.8.1. Overview

IMF (2014) estimated the spillover effects of profit shifting in what they call a very preliminary exercise. The calculation is based on differences in countries' corporate income tax (CIT) efficiency ratio relative to the average ratio in the other countries and a similar methodology is applied also by EPRS (2015), covered also below. Both studies argue that they capture profit shifting, whereas what they really attempt to capture empirically is CIT efficiency. Of course, profit shifting is likely to be partially responsible for a lack of CIT efficiency, but only in part, definitely not in full, since there are a number of other factors from compliance to policy. The studies, however, do not provide any credible disentangling of profit shifting from these various factors, but the authors, nonetheless, argue that they provide approximate estimates of profit shifting.

4.8.2. Data

IMF (2014) use data for corporate income tax revenue and rate from the IMF's Fiscal Affairs Department tax and revenue database and data for the Gross Operating Surplus (GOS) of corporations from the national accounts from the UN Statistics Division. EPRS (2015) uses data sources specific for the European Union (Eurostat and the European Commission's publications on taxation trends in the EU). The recently created ICTD–WIDER Government Revenue Database (GRD), which combines data from several major international databases and a new compilation from IMF Article IV and country staff reports, provides a potential alternative for future research.

4.8.3. Methodology

IMF (2014)
The methodology is described in the IMF (2014) staff paper's Appendix IV (this is different than another analysis in Appendix III, which we discuss above as a later version published as Crivelli et al. (2016)). IMF (2014) define

CIT efficiency in country i, E_i, as the ratio of actual CIT revenue (R_i) to some reference level of CIT revenue, with the latter computed as the standard CIT rate (τ_i) multiplied by a reference tax base (G_i):

$$E_i = \frac{R_i}{\tau_i G_i}$$

IMF (2014) use data for R_i and τ_i from the IMF's Fiscal Affairs Department tax and revenue database. Data for G_i, the Gross Operating Surplus (GOS) of corporations from the national accounts, is taken from the UN Statistics Division, and this benchmark is of crucial importance in their estimates. According to IMF (2014), GOS provides a proxy to what the base would be if profits were allocated on something broadly similar to a 'source' basis (interest income received from foreign operations or the tax base that a residence country operating a worldwide tax system would derive from foreign source income) and is close to the accounting concept of EBITDA (Earnings Before Interest, Tax, Depreciation and Amortization). GOS is broader than the standard CIT base because of loss carry forwards and because depreciation allowances, interest and other specific provisions are not subtracted, and therefore IMF (2014) would expect the values of E_i to be lower than one. The values of E_i higher than one indicate a very efficient corporate income tax system and vice versa. The values can differ across countries because of differences in tax compliance or policies, such as the generosity of tax deductions for depreciation and interest, or of special tax incentives such as tax holiday and patent box or too generous tax rulings as in the case of Luxleaks (Huesecken & Overesch, 2015). IMF (2014) hypothesise that the values might also be affected by behavioural responses, such as profit shifting, which cause the actual CIT base to deviate from its reference. Importantly, however, the value of GOS itself is likely affected by any profit shifting taking place and therefore does not work well as the counterfactual value of corporate tax base without profit shifting.

With their results estimated, they find a strong negative correlation between E_i and τ_i, which they interpret as suggesting strong profit shifting. With this correlation they support their crucial assumption (they call it a somewhat heroic assumption) that all of the variation in cross-country CIT efficiency ratios is due to profit shifting. With this assumption in mind, IMF (2014) estimate a rough measure of the revenue loss (if negative) or gain (if positive) from profit shifting as the difference between the actual ($R_i = \tau_i G_i E_i$)

and the simulated CIT revenue ($R_i^* = \tau_i G_i \bar{E}$), i.e. $\tau_i G_i$ multiplied by $\bar{E}$, a GOS-weighted average of countries' CIT-efficiencies, for each country as:

$$\Delta_i = R_i - R_i^* = \tau_i G_i (E_i - \bar{E})$$

Through multiplication by this weighted average, $\bar{E}$, they argue that they allow for base erosion or expansion other than profit shifting, but it can also be considered an arbitrary setting of the cut-off point (possibly as an alternative to setting the simulated CIT revenue as equal to $\tau_i G_i$ only, which would imply the value of $\bar{E}$ as unity and make the revenue estimates substantially higher, assuming mean efficiency below 100 per cent as is the case in this sample with the value of $\bar{E}$ being 43 per cent). It follows that they de facto use the weighted average as the benchmark for zero profit shifting and any negative or positive profit shifting follows from differences of countries' efficiency with the sample's weighted average. The estimated revenue impact, Δ_i, can thus only be negative if the country's share of the world's implicit CIT base exceeds its share of the world's GOS, i.e. its CIT-efficiency is lower than the weighted average.

IMF (2014) is aware of a number of important shortcomings of their approach. For example, it can capture only profit shifting between countries in the sample, which does not include many countries, including those considered tax havens (and therefore the revenue impact might be underestimated if the group of countries in the sample together lose profits to third countries such as tax havens). IMF (2014) discusses the crucial assumption in some detail. They argue that to the extent that such variation reflects differences in the prevalence of incentives that are themselves a strategic response to the tax policies of others, it can be seen as capturing base erosion from international tax competition. But they realise that variations in CIT-efficiency may also reflect such unrelated features as differences in compliance and enforcement and they show that revenue impact underestimates the loss from profit shifting if a country has more exemptions or compliance problems relative to its GOS compared to the sample average (so the estimate could in theory be improved by adjusting it for differences in compliance or enforcement across countries). Bach (2013) made a similar comparison of the tax base reported in tax statistics with the corporate income derived from national accounts for Germany (the difference amounted to 90 billion euros or 3.7 per cent GDP in 2008) to observe considerable tax base erosion; neither he nor IMF (2014) have further accounting data of sufficient extent to give precise reasons for the erosion.

EPRS (2015)

EPRS (2015) in chapter 1 follows a similar methodological approach as IMF (2014), but focuses on the EU member states. We include them despite their regional focus on the EU, especially due to their relevance in following IMF (2014) and improving on their approach in some respects, such as when presenting more details including the country-level estimates. Separately, EPRS (2015) in chapter 3 further conclude that if a complete solution to the problem of base erosion and profit shifting were available and implementable across the EU, it would have an estimated positive impact of 0.2 per cent of the total tax revenues of the member states, assuming that the total tax revenues collected over the EU as a whole were 5.74 trillion euro in 2011, a comprehensive solution would add another 11.5 billion euro in revenues. They believe that this estimate underplays the amount of revenue that is recoverable through a cost-effective regulatory response.

In their main estimates and similarly to IMF (2014), the calculation is based on differences in countries' corporate income tax efficiency (here defined as a country's actual CIT revenue relative to a potential CIT revenue estimated by the multiplication of CIT rate and a theoretical tax base derived from operating surplus) compared to the average ratio in the sample countries. EPRS (2015) defines the CIT-efficiency as (to simplify the comparison we are using the notation from IMF (2014), rather than the one used by EPRS (2015)):

$$E_i = \frac{R_i}{\tau_i G_i}$$

where, again, E_i is the CIT-efficency, R_i is the actual CIT revenue, τ_i is the CIT rate, G_i is the reference, here called theoretical, tax base. Together with IMF (2014), EPRS (2015) shares a number of drawbacks and realises that lower CIT-efficiency might be due to not only profit shifting, but also due to, for example, special tax initiatives.

Similarly to IMF (2014), EPRS (2015) estimates the revenue loss or gain from profit shifting as the difference between the actual ($R_i = \tau_i G_i E_i$) and the simulated (i.e. supposedly without profit shifting) CIT revenue ($R_i^* = \tau_i G_i \bar{E}$), i.e. $\tau_i G_i$ lowered by multiplying by $\bar{E}$, in their case a non-weighted average of countries' CIT-efficiencies to allow for base erosion or expansion other than profit shifting), for each country as:

$$\Delta_i = R_i - R_i^* = \tau_i G_i (E_i - \bar{\bar{E}})$$

The methodological differences with IMF (2014) are nuanced, but important. EPRS (2015) use a different sample (only EU members; Spain, Hungary and Finland are excluded due to data unavailability) and data source (Eurostat and the European Commission's publications on taxation trends in the EU). EPRS (2015) uses a non-weighted average of sample countries' CIT-efficiencies (the weighted average used by IMF (2014) seems more reasonable to enable larger countries to have a bigger impact on others and it is not clear why EPRS (2015) uses a non-weighted average). Importantly, EPRS (2015) use the net operating surplus (NOS) as a theoretical base rather than the gross one (GOS) used by IMF (2014). EPRS (2015) argues that the NOS is closer to the theoretical base and thus more suitable for the task at hand (with which IMF (2014) agree, but lack the data); they subtract depreciation from the GOS to create it. Furthermore, they prefer and use NOS adjusted for imputed compensation for self-employed workers (who are treated for tax purposes as being external contractors and not subject to payroll taxes or pensions).

4.8.4. Results

Both IMF (2014) and EPRS (2015) focus on estimations of tax revenue losses rather than the underlying scale of profits and our presentation of their results follow this approach (however, it is possible to derive the scale of profit shifting from their tables and graphs with some imprecision, which would be especially high for IMF (2014) because of their results being communicated mostly via graphs). In the results of IMF (2014), mean CIT efficiency is 43 per cent, while they provide country-level mean values of CIT efficiency for the period between 2001 and 2012 only in a graph (rather than a table) as Figure 2 in the Appendix of IMF (2014). For example, average CIT efficiency exceeds 100 per cent for Cyprus, is also high in Ireland and Luxembourg, and is lowest in some of the African countries.

In terms of estimated revenue losses, IMF (2014) reports an unweighted average revenue loss across all countries in the sample of 5 per cent of current CIT revenue, but almost 13 per cent in the non-OECD countries. They do not include detailed country-level estimates and so the approximate relative results can be derived from country-level mean values of CIT-efficiency in Figure 1. We derive from the graph that Egypt and other countries to the left with lower values of CIT-efficiency than 43 per cent are, according to these estimates, losers of corporate income tax profit shifting. There are also some of the world's big economies—from Germany and Japan to India and China—some developing countries as well as some countries, such as the Netherlands, which are being viewed in other existing research as those benefiting from profit shifting (Janský & Kokeš, 2016; Weyzig, 2014). In contrast, Brazil and other countries to the right with higher values of CIT-efficiency than 43 per cent are beneficiaries of corporate income tax profit shifting.

There are also three EU member states which are often considered tax havens and have the highest values of CIT-efficiency in the sample: Cyprus, Ireland, Luxembourg. Behind these three tax havens are countries that are usually not considered as such: the Czech Republic, Tunisia, Bulgaria and Ukraine. This diverse group of countries further includes other tax havens such as Malta and Switzerland, as well as some of the biggest developed economies: United Kingdom and United States; the inclusion of the latter being surprising in the light of evidence suggesting otherwise (Cobham & Janský, 2017d).

EPRS (2015) estimates the mean CIT efficiency at around 75 per cent over the period 2009–2013. Their estimate based on NOS is comparable to 86 per cent estimated by IMF (2014) using GOS over the period 2001–2012 (and reported for a sample of 20 European countries in footnote 134 on page 62). EPRS (2015) estimate revenue losses for the EU as a result of profit shifting to be around 50–70 billion euro, which they think is a lower-end estimate and interpret it as the amount lost due to profit shifting. Moreover, if they assume that profit shifting is the only source of lower CIT-efficiency than 100 per cent, they estimate that revenue losses for the EU could amount to around 160–190 billion euro (which EPRS (2016) interpret as the amount lost due to aggressive tax planning) and they interpret this as including other tax regime issues, such as special tax arrangements, inefficiencies in tax collection and other practices. Although they compare it to an estimate of similar scale by Murphy (2012), who provides annual estimates of 150 and 850 billion euros for total EU tax avoidance and evasion, respectively (the latter being based mostly on shadow economy estimates of Schneider, Buehn, & Montenegro (2010)), they are aware that this is likely an over-estimate because there are cross-country differences in compliance and enforcement as well as strategic responses to the tax policies of other countries (what some would call international tax competition) that are not directly related to profit shifting.

The detailed results by EPRS (2015) show not only country-level estimates, but also that a weighted (weighted by NOS-derived theoretical revenue) average is substantially lower at 60 per cent (and this estimate might be more suitable for comparison with the average of 86 per cent estimated by IMF (2014) for the EU). This is partially because three countries with highest CIT-efficiency, all above 100 per cent (Cyprus, Slovenia, Croatia), have together a weight of only 1.1 per cent, whereas five countries with highest weights (Germany, United Kingdom, France, Italy, Netherlands), altogether above two fifths of total, have all values below the unweighted average.

4.8.5. Conclusions

Corporate income tax efficiency estimates are some of the most readily available profit-shifting-related estimates for a wide range of countries with the coverage likely to increase in the future. However, it is important to keep in mind that both IMF (2014) and EPRS (2015) are based on differences in countries' estimated corporate income tax efficiency and this provides a wide scope for other interpretations than international corporate tax avoidance, so these results should be interpreted cautiously and might be of little more than indicative value for discussions of revenue implications.

4.9. Tørsløv, Wier, & Zucman (2018)

4.9.1. Overview

In a recent contribution, Tørsløv, Wier, & Zucman (2018) present novel research on tax havens, including new estimates of the tax revenue losses related to profit shifting.

4.9.2. Data

Tørsløv, Wier, & Zucman (2018) use balance of payments (including newly available bilateral data on service payments such as royalties and FDI interest payments), foreign affiliate statistics (FATS) and national accounts data. They use data on 81 countries covering 90 per cent of world GDP. To support the use of this data, they convincingly show that most of some MNEs' profits are not included in the often used Orbis data (in fact they show that only a weighted average of 17 per cent of global profits is included in Orbis and for more than a quarter of MNEs there are no profits at all included in Orbis).

4.9.3. Methodology

In their main empirical analysis, Tørsløv, Wier, & Zucman (2018) use two indicators to make two observations. First and most importantly, they argue (following the standard Cobb-Douglas production function) that the ratio of corporate profits to the compensation of employees in the corporate sector should be constant. A similar argument has been used by Hines & Rice (1994) and the ensuing vast body of profit shifting literature as well as by the EuropeanCommission (201a) in their proposal for the Common Consolidated Corporate Tax Base and the related analysis of misalignment between profits and economic activity by Cobham & Janský (2019). Tørsløv, Wier, & Zucman (2018) then, as a novelty, use national account data (main source is OECD, Table 14a, and webpages of national statistical offices) to calculate country-level corporate profit measures (corporate gross operating surplus, less net interest paid, less depreciation).

They find that tax havens are abnormally profitable compared to the compensation of employees (up to a factor of 10). They then show, using foreign affiliate statistics, that all of the abnormal profitability in tax havens can be explained by foreign subsidiaries operating in tax havens. That is, whereas local firms have comparable profitability to the global average profitability, foreign firms operating in tax havens are substantially more profitable. For example, in Ireland, local firms earn roughly 70 cents per wage paid while foreign firms earn more than 8 dollars per wage paid. Their benchmark estimate of profit shifting is simply to set the foreign sector profitability in tax havens equal to the local sector profitability. They argue that their estimate accounts for all shifting of parent firms and subsidiaries to subsidiaries in tax havens. In contrast, their estimate does not capture profit shifting from subsidiaries to parent firms in tax havens, which, however, the authors argue, is a second order issue.

Second, the authors observe that tax havens have high trade surpluses relative to gross national income, a vast majority of which seems to be paid back to foreign parents (GNI is the often used denominator in this case, more suitable than GDP, since it is not affected so much by profit shifting, but both GNI and GDP include both corporate and non-corporate economic activity). Importantly, they assume that all 'abnormal' profitability of foreign affiliates in tax havens (that is, profitability above that of local firms) reflects inward profit-shifting. A similar, crucial assumption is made by the IMF (2014) staff paper's Appendix IV and both UNCTAD (2015) and Janský & Palanský (forthcoming). In line with the previous research, they acknowledge that high profitability could be due to other factors, but argue that the assumption can be supported with a correlation between the abnormal profitability and dividends payments and retained earnings of ultimate owners (i.e. profits are shifted to tax havens and then paid out to owners in high-tax countries). Finally, they arrive at comparable estimates of worldwide profit shifting scale through two alternative approaches: first, they assume that all net foreign income in tax havens is profit shifting and, second, they assume that excessive high risk exports (such as royalty payments) and FDI interest paid reflect profit shifting.

Tørsløv, Wier, & Zucman (2018) allocate the above-average (i.e. artificially shifted) profits based on which countries import from (and pay interest to) tax havens. They exploit the detailed Eurostat data of service trade for six EU's tax havens (Netherlands, Ireland, Luxembourg, Malta, Cyprus and Belgium). For non-EU tax havens they rely on Eurostat and BEA data for the US and the EU and bilateral FDI data for the remaining countries. They argue that profit shifting of information and communications technology companies often goes directly from companies to consumers (such as customers paying Uber Netherlands directly or Skype customers paying Skype Luxembourg directly), which was supported by the LuxLeaks revelations. The issue with companies to consumer exports are that they are rarely reported in the importing countries (in line with the Balance of Payments 6 manual). Strikingly, they document clear discrepancies in service export and import data in the EU only for the most important tax havens (e.g. Luxembourg). They thus argue that exporting countries' export data are more reliable than the lower imports reported by the other countries. They also show that some profits by US MNEs are missing in EU havens' national accounts.

We set out one part of their methodology in simple algebra, in line with their labelling. π is profit relative to a compensation of employees defined as:

$$\pi = \frac{Taxable\ corporate\ profits}{Compensation\ of\ employees}$$

Within each country, π_f is this ratio for foreign companies (affiliates) and π_l for local companies. They estimate average π among non-haven at 36 per cent in 2015.

They assume that for a preselected group of tax havens, any π_f above π_l have been artificially shifted into these tax havens:

$$Profits\ shifted\ into\ tax\ haveni = (\pi_f - \pi_l)^* \\ Taxable\ corporate\ profits\ of\ foreign\ companies$$

4.9.4. Results

Tørsløv, Wier, & Zucman (2018) find that 15 per cent of global profits are made by multinationals abroad (and as little as 5 per cent in the 1980s). They define MNEs' profits as the sum of FDI equity income receipts across all countries (with corrections for taxes paid and depreciation). They subtract income received by tax havens to avoid double counting. They find that MNEs' profits are around 1.74 trillion USD in 2015, while global corporate profits are around 11.5 trillion USD.

They conclude that 40 per cent of multinationals' profits are artificially shifted to tax havens, i.e. more than 600 billion USD in 2015. They also estimate global corporate tax revenue loss around 200 billion USD per year (around 10 per cent of global corporate tax revenue). This scale is broadly comparable to global estimates of other recent research contributions: IMF's Crivelli et al. (2016) and a follow-up study by Cobham & Janský (2018), UNCTAD (2015) and a follow-up study by Janský & Palanský (forthcoming), OECD (2015b), Clausing (2016), Cobham & Janský (2019) and IMF (2014).

Under their preferred apportionment rule, the European Union is the main loser (with around 20 per cent of its revenue at risk). They argue that as the ratio of taxable corporate profits to a compensation of employees is increasing for some tax havens (e.g. Ireland), a growing amount of profits is artificially shifted to them and that low tax rates in combination with this huge tax base leads to a lot of revenue for these tax havens. The countries benefiting most are Ireland, Netherlands and Luxembourg (which impose low rates on huge tax bases), which is in line with earlier results presented by Zucman (2014) and Cobham & Janský (2019).

4.9.5. Conclusions

The results of Tørsløv, Wier, & Zucman (2018) offer a more deliberate and comprehensive assessment of the global, multinational tax base than others. Their findings suggest a pattern of profit shifting that are partly, they innovatively argue, due to the fact that European tax enforcement focuses on other high-tax countries rather than tax havens—allowing the latter to flourish. The argument is supported with information about the counterparts in OECD's mutual agreement procedures within the EU. While the revenue loss estimates are lower than some, they sit within the range of other work.

4.10. Conclusions on International Corporate Tax Avoidance

To conclude this chapter on international corporate tax avoidance, we draw the main lessons from the extensive and still expanding academic and policy literature reviewed in detail above.

First, profit shifting of MNEs to tax havens and associated international corporate tax avoidance falls under illicit financial flows, as we argue at the beginning of the chapter as well as in the book's introduction. These should be seen in total as illicit flows, since they rest on a combination of criminal, unlawful and socially forbidden practices. We leave the question of strict legality mostly to others, to deal with on a case by case basis. Low- and middle-income countries seem to be more intensively affected by profit shifting, with predictable results for public spending and access to health, education and so forth; and this makes even stronger the case for its inclusion in the Sustainable Development Goals' target to curtail illicit financial flows.

In addition, the international policy consensus, expressed in the G20/OECD BEPS project, is that multinationals' profit misalignment should be curtailed: 'The G20 finance ministers called on the OECD to develop an action plan to address BEPS issues in a co-ordinated and comprehensive manner. Specifically, this Action Plan should provide countries with domestic and international instruments that will *better align rights to tax with economic activity*' (OECD, 2013a, p.11, emphasis added).

This international consensus that profit shifting should be addressed *in general* is compounded by consensus in the SDG process, and most visibly in the High Level Panel on Illicit Financial Flows from Africa, and the High Level Panel of Eminent Persons on the Post-2015 Framework, that profit shifting should be addressed specifically within the SDGs. It is, moreover, clear that the intention of the global agreement on the SDGs was that this be done within SDG 16.4 on illicit financial flows, rather than SDG 17.1 on tax. We can see arguments to address profit shifting under either; but it is clear that 16.4 is what was agreed, and we see no reason to unpick this now. Profit shifting is an integral element of the wider problem of illicit financial flows, and like others should be curtailed.

Second, profit shifting is a real phenomenon. Second, profit shifting is a real phenomenon, and there is now a large body of evidence consistent with MNEs shifting profits illicitly from where economic activity occurs to tax havens. A clear conclusion emerges that the international tax system provides MNEs with opportunities to decrease their taxes through intra-company transfer prices, strategic management of the location of intangible assets or distortion of the corporate debt structure. The research confirms that many MNEs do often make use of these opportunities and do shift income to tax havens (Clausing, 2003; Hines & Rice, 1994; Huizinga & Laeven, 2008). However, until recently, the literature had been less conclusive in respect of scale and revenue implications. The quality and coverage of estimates has improved substantially in recent years, and for coverage of countries in particular—with direct relevance to estimates of the scale and harms of illicit financial flows. havens. A clear conclusion emerges from the existing research that the international tax system provides MNEs with opportunities to decrease their taxes through intra-company transfer prices, strategic management of the location of intangible assets or distortion of the corporate debt structure. The research confirms that many MNEs do often make use of these opportunities and do shift income to tax havens (Clausing, 2003; Hines & Rice, 1994; Huizinga & Laeven, 2008). However, until recently at least, the literature has been less conclusive in respect of scale of profit shifting flows and revenue implications.

Third, profit shifting is an important phenomenon of substantial scale—economically, statistically, as well as in terms of revenues lost. The various studies estimate that governments worldwide lose more than 100 billion USD annually. The existing research indicates that the scale of shifted profits and revenue losses are widely distributed across jurisdictions, with the highest values in high-income countries but the most intense losses in relation to GDP and especially to tax revenues, in lower-income countries. In contrast, only a small number of jurisdictions are consistently the recipients of disproportionate volumes of profit related to economic activity elsewhere. Furthermore, Guvenen, Mataloni Jr, Rassier, & Ruhl (2017) and Tørsløv, Wier, & Zucman (2018) provide estimates of profit shifting impacts on macroeconomic aggregates such as gross domestic product that are statistically important.

Fourth and perhaps more obviously, profit shifting can be curbed. Although it has over the past couple of decades grown into an important economic phenomenon, it has not always been so big. Some studies, such as Cobham & Janský (2019) and Tørsløv, Wier, & Zucman (2018), show that in the 1990s profit shifting was a much smaller concern. This historical account can thus help us understand that profit shifting is not an inherent feature of the global economy and that it can work well (or, indeed, better) without it. How to measure progress in reducing profit shifting is an important matter that has been increasingly addressed since 2013 both by academics and policy experts, so far without clear recommendations—although as we write in 2019, the 'BEPS 2.0' process at the OECD has committed to going beyond the arm's length principle, and is actively considering unitary tax approaches which have the potential to deliver both meaningful change in the international rules and also clearer measures of progress.

Fifth, in terms of methodology, three recent studies stand out as particularly useful when thinking about an indicator for the SDG. Although each of Tørsløv, Wier, & Zucman (2018), Cobham & Janský (2019) and IMF (2014) uses different methodology and reaches different results, all three of them have much in common that is desired for an indicator of the SDG target. They all rely on official statistical sources, largely national accounts data and official statistics of foreign affiliates of MNEs. Their methodological approaches are relatively straightforward, which makes them feasible and transparent. All of them rely on basic ratios of various economic variables. None of them uses regression analysis, which might be hard to implement as a part of the SDG target indicator, whereas all the other four studies rely on regressions in reaching their conclusions. Another methodological similarity is that they all make use of the comparison between what the profits or tax revenues are, and a counterfactual of what they would be in the absence of profit shifting. Also, all of them take quite literally the BEPS objective of better aligning rights to tax with economic activity, useful aligning the approaches with the policy consensus (this also helps guide our proposal in chapter 6). In sum, IMF (2014), Cobham & Janský (2019) and Tørsløv, Wier, & Zucman (2018) apply straightforward methodologies to publicly available, official, government-sponsored data. We are confident that these observations can help us design a new indicator that overcomes some remaining drawbacks these estimates have, such as data quality and selection of specific economic variables.

Sixth, there is no perfect indicator operationalised in the literature that could be used as it is and applied for the SDG target. Some of the research reviewed is promising, and we believe that a workable indicator is within reach. Perhaps the biggest challenge is the necessary consensus of national statistical offices on which specific version of a profit shifting indicator should be used for the target. We return to this question in chapter 6.

PART 3

PROPOSALS FOR IFF MONITORING

5

Beyond Scale

Risk- and Policy-based Indicators

In Part 3, we turn from scale estimates to the alternatives. While chapter 6 presents two direct measures of scale, our proposals for SDG 16.4 indicators, chapter 5 lays out the non-scale alternatives. First, in section 5.1 we consider a set of policy-based indicators that were originally proposed before the SDG process settled on a scale measure. These offer the scope to track global progress on transparency measures that are key to curtailing illicit financial flows, and also offer the jurisdiction-level disaggregation to support accountability for policies that maintain opacity.

We then explore two related sets of IFF risk measure, which extend the logic of evaluating IFF-facilitating secrecy jurisdictions, to evaluate the exposure of each country to the IFF risks of secrecy elsewhere. Both approaches build on the global ranking constructed by the Tax Justice Network, the Financial Secrecy Index (section 5.2). The first is a Bilateral Financial Secrecy Index, replicating the global approach at the national level (5.3). The second, operating in a similar way and pioneered by the High Level Panel on Illicit Financial Flows from Africa, emphasises granular analysis of each countries' vulnerabilities to IFF, to support policy prioritisation (5.4).

Overall, these measures present a range of approaches to the multi-faceted problem of illicit financial flows which have the potential to support national, regional and international policymakers in prioritising their responses and ensuring appropriate accountability.

5.1. Policy Measures

Following the formal establishment of the Tax Justice Network in 2003, internationally engaged experts from law, accounting, economics and other fields contributed to the development of a policy platform to challenge the problems of tax havens and associated evasion and avoidance—not least by addressing the power and inequality associated with the uncounted at the top (Cobham, 2019).

Estimating illicit financial flows: A critical guide to the data, methodologies and findings. Alex Cobham and Petr Janský, Oxford University Press (2020). © Alex Cobham and Petr Janský.
DOI: 10.1093/oso/9780198854418.001.0001

The core of this policy platform is the 'ABC of tax transparency':

- Automatic, multilateral exchange of tax information
- Beneficial ownership (public registers for companies, trusts and foundations); and
- Country-by-country reporting by multinational companies, in public.

The A and B relate primarily to the financial secrecy sphere. Automatic exchange of tax information was intended as a direct challenge to the then OECD standard of information exchange 'upon request'. This required requesting authorities to lay out substantial detail of the individual they were examining, and whose bank account information they sought. This in turn allowed secrecy jurisdictions multiple opportunities to stall and to reject requests on spurious grounds. In contrast, automatic exchange provides for regular multi-lateral exchange of data about all relevant accountholders—literally, the end of banking secrecy if fully delivered.

Public registers of beneficial ownership are intended to eliminate secret ownership of assets. This can occur through the anonymously held vehicles including companies, trusts and foundations, or other legal structures that can play the equivalent role of separating a warm-blooded individual from that which they control and/or from which they benefit financially. As the World Bank's *Puppet Masters* research powerfully demonstrated (van der Does de Willebois, Halter, Harrison, Park, & Sharman, 2011), and as successive leaks including the Panama Papers and Paradise Papers have confirmed to a global public, this secrecy lies at the heart not only of much offshore tax evasion but a range of other criminal and corrupt practices. Public registers are a critical step to end the associated impunity.

The C of tax transparency refers to public, country-by-country reporting by multinational companies. This requires data, for each jurisdiction of operation, on the absolute levels of economic activity including sales and employment; on declared profits and tax paid; and the names of each entity operating there which forms part of the multinational group in question. Making this public would put multinationals on a similar transparency footing to single-country businesses, and demonstrate the extent and nature of engineered divergence between where activity takes place, and where the resulting profits are declared—a powerful tool for accountability of both multinationals themselves and of the jurisdictions that set out to procure profit shifting at the expense of their global neighbours.

While international organisations such as the OECD initially wrote off the proposals as utopian and unrealistic, they quickly gained traction and by 2013 had become the basis for a global policy agenda with broad support and indeed leadership from the G20, G8 and G77 groups of countries.

The shift to automatic information exchange was confirmed with the creation of the OECD Common Reporting Standard, a fully multilateral instrument with more than 100 signatories exchanging information by September 2018 at the latest, including all the major financial centres except the United States. There is work to do in countering efforts at circumvention, and ensuring full inclusion of low-and middle-income countries, but it is major progress that the structure and expectations of transparency are now in place.

On beneficial ownership, public registers are now emerging as the international standard—despite the concerted resistance of a range of small jurisdictions and individual US states that profit from selling secrecy structures. Gradually, including through the UK establishment of a public register for companies in 2016; subsequent revisions to the EU anti-money laundering directive which now requires public registers for trusts as well as companies; related measures such as new requirements in the Extractive Industry Transparency Initiative, and successive albeit small steps in the approach of the OECD Global Forum; public registers are becoming the norm.

Finally, substantial progress has also been made in respect of country-by-country reporting. The G20 mandated the OECD in 2013 to deliver a standard, which follows in outline the original Tax Justice Network proposals except in one crucial aspect: the data need only be delivered to the headquarters country tax authority, not made public. As detailed in section 6.1 below, however, there is considerable momentum to take the next step to require publication. In the meantime, there a range of opportunities for tax authorities to use the data, and the OECD has committed to publish partially aggregated statistics that will reveal the jurisdiction-level pattern of profit shifting.

The ABC arguably provides the key policy measures to counter illicit financial flows, and to assess jurisdictions' commitment to the agenda. But this recent progress—including policymaker familiarity with the technical measures—largely post-dates the critical discussions around the SDG target, and so was not reflected there. The UN Secretary-General's High Level Panel of Eminent Persons on the Post-2015 Development Agenda (2013) proposed the following, attractively simple target:

'12e. Reduce illicit flows and tax evasion and increase stolen-asset recovery by $x'

In doing so, this group set the basis for the eventual SDG 16.4. Even at the time, however, the proposal faced questions in relation to technical accuracy, measurability and accountability. Cobham (2014, 2018) proposed three policy targets, to be considered either as a direct alternative or as additional detail to sit underneath this high-level aim. The three targets draw directly on the ABC:

i. Reduce to zero the legal persons and arrangements for which beneficial ownership information is not publicly available;
ii. Reduce to zero the cross-border trade and investment relationships between jurisdictions for which there is no bilateral automatic exchange of tax information; and
iii. Reduce to zero the number of multinational businesses that do not report publicly on a country-by-country basis.

Zero targets are proposed on the grounds that partial responses to financial secrecy are somewhat like squeezing a sausage: the total volume (of IFF) does not change, only the distribution as agents seek alternative secrecy jurisdictions if one becomes transparent.

The targets aim to provide global numbers, but by their construction would support disaggregation to allow jurisdiction-level accountability. Data collated would highlight the extent to which each jurisdiction had met their responsibilities, so accountability for financial secrecy affecting others (the related risk of IFF elsewhere) would be clear. The proposed target (ii) is framed differently, in that it aims to highlight not the existence of jurisdictions with no information exchange but also no economic or financial relationship, but rather the jurisdictions that have major bilateral relationships yet provide no information—since the latter rather than the former are the source of IFF risk. In addition, at the national level, such reporting would identify the major partner jurisdictions with which information exchange should be prioritised.

Cost-benefit analysis for all three targets indicates that the returns are likely to be high in all three cases, notwithstanding the inevitably high uncertainty over dollar estimates of IFF impact. Even consistent reporting on the indicators, at global and jurisdiction level, seems likely to provide a valuable step forward in accountability. Indeed, this is part of the motivation for the Tax Justice Network's Financial Secrecy Index and all the related work.

5.2. Financial Secrecy Literature

The Financial Secrecy Index was first published in 2009, and was created as a response to the consistent failure of attempts to create 'tax haven' blacklists by international organisations. These failures reflected two key issues. First, the absence of objectively verifiable criteria led inevitably to the politicisation of lists, and the inability of international organisations to list their own more politically powerful members—while smaller, less well-connected jurisdictions found themselves targeted. Second, the desire to separate 'tax havens' (bad actors) from all others (good actors, by implication), led to an unhelpful simplification of a complex issue.

Underpinning both issues is the long-recognised difficulty of reaching consensus on a measurable definition for 'tax haven', because of the vagueness and range of uses of the term—and the fact that tax is not always central to the role played. The Tax Justice Network argued instead that the main role played is the provision not of tax breaks but of financial secrecy: the ability to hide from publics and regulators elsewhere, including but not limited to tax authorities.

Cobham, Janský, & Meinzer (2015) extend this argument, providing a definition of the term 'secrecy jurisdiction' and showing how the Financial Secrecy Index makes this operational—and how, assessed on this basis, a secrecy spectrum emerges rather than a binary division of havens versus others.

The most recent biennial edition of the index (Tax Justice Network, 2018) ranks jurisdictions according to their scores on 20 Key Financial Secrecy Indicators (KFSIs, see table 5.1), and combines this with a Global Scale Weight constructed to reflect the size of role of each jurisdiction in the worldwide provision of financial services to non-residents. Central to the approach is the transparency of construction, so that all scores and ranking are objectively verifiable, and any researcher or policy analyst can choose their preferred secrecy indicators and the international sources, to construct their own alternative measures.

Overall, the FSI provides both a ranking of the most important financial secrecy jurisdictions—that is, those that pose the greatest threat of IFF to others—and a consistent reporting of policy progress, aggregate from the jurisdiction to global level.

As such, the FSI has the potential to support a range of approaches to the monitoring of progress against SDG 16.4. In addition, as sections 5.3 and 5.4

Table 5.1. Overview of Key Financial Secrecy Indicators

Ownership Registration	Legal Entity Transparency	Integrity of tax and financial regulation	International Standards and Cooperation
1 Banking secrecy	6 Public company ownership	11 Tax administration capacity	17 Anti-money laundering
2 Trusts and foundations register	7 Public company accounts	12 Consistent personal income tax	18 Automatic information exchange
3 Recorded company ownership	8 Country-by-country reporting	13 Avoids promoting tax evasion	19 Bilateral treaties
4 Other wealth ownership	9 Corporate tax disclosure	14 Tax court secrecy	20 International legal cooperation
5 Limited partnership transparency	10 Legal entity identifier	15 Harmful structures	
		16 Public statistics	

Source: Tax Justice Network (2018)

Table 5.2. Financial Secrecy Index 2018, top ten

Rank	Jurisdiction	FSI Value	FSI Share	Secrecy Score	Global Scale Weight
1	Switzerland	1,589.57	5.01%	76	4.50%
2	USA	1,298.47	4.09%	60	22.30%
3	Cayman Islands	1,267.68	3.99%	72	3.78%
4	Hong Kong	1,243.67	3.92%	71	4.16%
5	Singapore	1,081.98	3.41%	67	4.57%
6	Luxembourg	975.91	3.07%	58	12.13%
7	Germany	768.95	2.42%	59	5.16%
8	Taiwan	743.37	2.34%	76	0.50%
9	UAE (Dubai)	661.14	2.08%	84	0.14%
10	Guernsey	658.91	2.07%	72	0.52%

Source: Tax Justice Network (2018)

explore, the FSI can also support granular policy analysis at the national level, for policymakers seeking to curtail the IFF risks that their own countries face.

5.3. Bilateral Financial Secrecy Index

To evaluate which secrecy jurisdictions are most harmful for which countries, one needs both a measure of the intensity of financial secrecy of a jurisdiction and an indicator showing the strength of the economic relationship between each pair of jurisdictions.[1] In the construction of the BFSI, Janský, Meinzer, & Palanský (2018) follow the FSI's methodology as closely as possible to maintain consistency. The BFSI uses the same information for secrecy scores as published in the 2018 version of the FSI (adjusted for intra-EU relationships), but it applies a bilateral scale weight (BSW) specific for each country instead of the GSW. Because the data on exports of financial services used for the original GSW is not available in bilateral country-level breakdown, the IMF's 2015 CPIS data on total portfolio assets are used as an approximation for the strength of the economic link between country i and jurisdiction j. As an indicator of the scale of the relationship between two jurisdictions, the authors use data on total portfolio investments, since this data fulfils the condition of being relevant for the provision of financial services that can be abused under conditions of secrecy, while at the same time being available for many relevant countries worldwide and on a bilateral basis. The BSW thus estimates the share of each country's total portfolio investment in a jurisdiction as a ratio to the total global cross-border portfolio investment. More formally, they define the BSW as:

$$BSW_{ij} = \frac{Cross-border\ portfolio\ assets_{ij}}{Sum\ of\ all\ global\ cross-border\ portfolio\ assets}.$$

for each country i and each partner jurisdiction j. They then define the BFSI, using secrecy scores from the 2018 FSI and the same transformation as in the FSI, as:

$$Bilateral\ Financial\ Secrecy\ Index_{ij}$$
$$= Secrecy\ Score_j^{\ 3} * \sqrt[3]{Bilateral\ Scale\ Weight_{ij}}$$

and thereby they obtain one value of the BFSI for each country i and partner jurisdiction j.

Janský, Meinzer, & Palanský (2018) estimate the BFSI for 86 countries with available data by quantifying the financial secrecy supplied to their residents by 112 secrecy jurisdictions. Their results are in line with the finding of the FSI that some major global economies are responsible for the bulk of global harmful financial secrecy. For most countries, the United States, Switzerland, and Cayman Islands are among the most important secrecy jurisdictions.

---

[1] This subsection draws on a working paper (Janský, Meinzer, & Palanský, 2018).

From the detailed results of the BFSI, it emerges that certain countries are affected relatively more by specific secrecy jurisdictions, such as European economies by Luxembourg and the Netherlands, or the United States and Japan by the Cayman Islands. Generally, their results point to many countries supplying harmful secrecy and they argue that only extensive cooperation of countries at the global scale is capable of taming the bulk of harmful financial secrecy.

The authors then evaluate two major recent policy efforts by comparing them with the results of the BFSI. First, they focus on the blacklisting process of the European Commission and find that most of the important secrecy jurisdictions for EU member states have been identified by the lists. Second, they link the results to data on active bilateral automatic information exchange (AIE) treaties to assess how well-aimed are the policymakers' limited resources. They argue that while low-secrecy jurisdictions' gains are maximized if a large share of received secrecy is covered by AIE, tax havens aim not to activate these relationships with countries to which they supply secrecy. Their results show that so far, some major secrecy jurisdictions successfully keep their most prominent relationships uncovered by AIE, and activating these relationships may thus be an effective tool to curb secrecy.

As an example, Figure 5.1 from Janský, Meinzer, & Palanský (2018) shows the share of BFSI accounted for by countries which are covered by an existing activated AIE treaty versus the number of AIE relationships set up with these jurisdictions. They observe that while some countries, such as Greece, Slovakia or Czechia, have already covered around 85 per cent of the financial secrecy received (and, if we treated FATCA for the United States equally to AIE, the United States would likely come out with even higher shares of its financial secrecy covered), other countries, despite having activated more than 60 AIE relationships, have only covered less than 60 per cent of the received secrecy. Except for the notorious outlier tax havens of Hong Kong, Cyprus, Singapore and Isle of Man, all jurisdictions cover more than 50 per cent of the received secrecy.

Drawing on these results Janský, Knobel, Meinzer, & Palanský (2018) discuss the EU as an example of a regional policy prioritisation mechanism. They highlight that EU member states have on average covered 82 per cent of the financial secrecy targeting their jurisdictions by having automatic exchange of information treaties in place with the countries supplying financial secrecy structures targeting them. Other regions, especially lower-income ones, will have much lower levels of protection of this form.

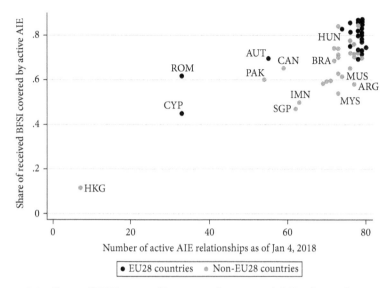

Figure 5.1. Share of BFSI covered by currently activated AIE relationships vs. the number of activated AIE relationships.

Notes: In this figure they only show the 81 countries for which they have BFSI scores for at least 10 counterpart countries.

Source: Janský, Meinzer, & Palanský (2018).

5.4. IFF vulnerability measures

Risk-based approaches have the potential to offer both a more granular analysis, and also to go beyond overall monitoring and accountability, to support policy prioritization at the national level. The central idea behind this approach, pioneered in the work of United Nations Economic Commission for Africa & African Union (2015), the High Level Panel on Illicit Flows from Africa aka 'Mbeki report', is this: that precisely because illicit financial flows are, by definition, hidden, the likelihood of an illicit component will be increasing in the degree of financial opacity in any given transaction.

The assumption is that all else being equal, the easier it is is to hide something, the more likely that something will be hidden: trading with Switzerland, or accepting investment from the British Virgin Islands, exposes a country to a greater risk of IFF than trading with Denmark or accepting investment from France. This does not of course imply that all trade with Switzerland is illicit, nor that all multinationals with BVI subsidiaries are committing tax evasion. However, the greater is the transparency of the partner jurisdiction in a given bilateral transaction, then the lower, all other things being equal, will be the

Box: Calculating 'Exposure' to IFF risk

Partner Opacity	Scale	Exposure
$V_i = \dfrac{\sum F_{i,j}.SS_j}{F_i}$	$I_i = \dfrac{F_i}{Y_i}$	$E_i = \dfrac{\sum F_{i,j} \bullet SS_j}{Y_i}$

Where:

	$i:\{1,...,I\}$	Country of interest
	$j:\{1,...,j\}$	Partner country
	$F_{i,j}$	Flow between reporter i and partner j
	Y_i	GDP of country of interest
	SS_j	Secrecy Score of partner country. Ordinal, 0–100.

risk of something being hidden. Not all transactions of a less transparent nature will be illicit; but the likelihood of illicit transactions within a less transparent flow will be higher. The greater the degree of opacity, in other words, the higher the risk of IFF.

To the extent that financial opacity of partner jurisdictions can be measured, this provides the basis to assess the risk of IFF facing a given country or region, according to the pattern of partners in economic and financial cross-border activity. The first step is therefore to create a measure of average Partner Opacity in each stock or flow for which data are available on a bilateral basis. This measure reflects the extent to which countries face a risk of 'hiddenness' in each stock or flow.

Multiplying Partner Opacity with 'Scale' (the importance of a given bilateral stock or flow in relation to the GDP of the country of concern) yields values of 'Exposure' (see Box). If all possible partner jurisdictions were either completely transparent, or completely secretive, the Exposure values would simply be the share of GDP involved in transactions with pure secrecy jurisdictions. Exposure scores can therefore be interpreted as measures of the overall risk to an economy from financial secrecy, or equivalently as measures of IFF risk.

Exposure scores have been calculated for African countries, subject to data availability, in respect of flows of trade in goods and services (figure 5.2); stocks of direct investment (figure 5.3) and stocks of portfolio investment (figure 5.4). Underlying data are for 2011 and sourced from UN Comtrade, IMF CDIS and IMF CPIS respectively. One immediate suggestion of figure 3 is that trade exposure tends to be higher in imports, with the exception of major commodity exporters. Indeed, as would be expected, countries with

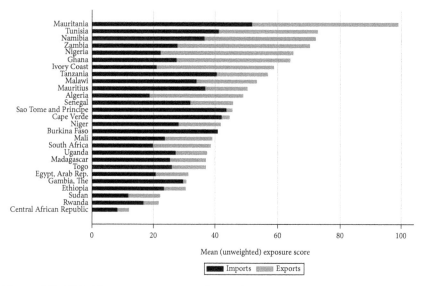

Figure 5.2. IFF risk exposure, commodity trade.
Source: Cobham (2014).

great natural resource wealth are among the most exposed in all categories. Inward direct and portfolio investment exposure dominates outward, although this in part reflects weaknesses in international reporting of outward positions. In addition, many countries are simply missing altogether. Enhanced regional data collation and reporting would offer clear advantages in terms of policymakers' ability to track and manage IFF exposure in different areas. Comprehensive IFF vulnerability analysis, using the most recent data, will be made available by Tax Justice Network in 2020. Updated results for African countries have already been published (Abugre et al., 2019).

Note that exposure on investment stocks should not be compared directly with that in trade flows; and in addition, note from the typology that illicit flows in trade are likely to be a relatively small proportion of the total value (i.e. the mispriced element), while illicit flows in investment may be 100 per cent of the total where ownership is hidden for illicit purposes. Policymakers are likely to have more detailed data with which to carry out this assessment, and should consider carefully the specific circumstances in their country in making decisions to prioritise particular areas.

Such vulnerability measures provide the potential to track the exposure of countries to IFF risk on a consistent basis over time, using existing data. While not a full alternative to estimates of the scale of IFF, the consistency and granularity for policy prioritisation may offer useful complementarity. An alternative to using the full Financial Secrecy Index would be to focus on

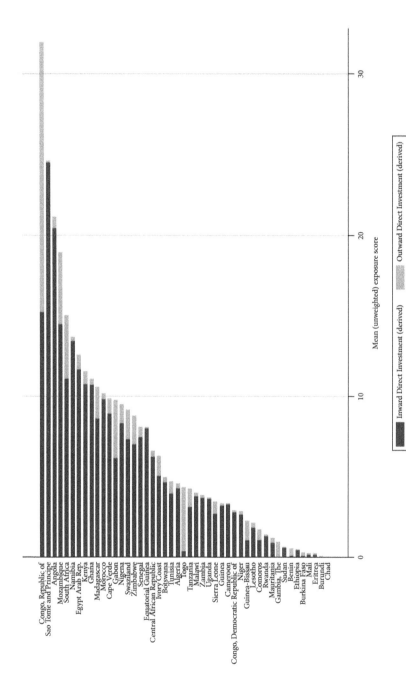

Figure 5.3. IFF risk exposure, direct investment.
Source: Cobham (2014).

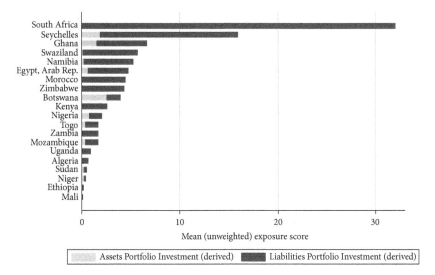

Figure 5.4. IFF risk exposure, portfolio investment.
Source: Cobham (2014).

the ABC of tax transparency, identifying more narrowly the concerns there, in line with the targets discussed in section 5.1.

The Tax Justice Network has recently released its new Corporate Tax Haven Index, which provides a complementary approach to the Financial Secrecy Index, focused on the efforts of jurisdictions to attract profit shifting by multinational companies. In a similar way to the FSI, the Corporate Tax Haven Index combines 20 indicators of haven aggressiveness, with a measure of global scale (in this case based on jurisdictions' shared of foreign direct investment flows). Similarly again, it will be possible to construct risk-based measures of vulnerability to tax avoidance, including a bilateral corporate tax haven index.

5.5. Conclusions

There is now a range of options available to national authorities, to evaluate the IFF risks faced and to prioritise policy responses at a more granular level. On the principle that the more is hidden, the higher risk of illicit flows, policymakers can target access to information as well as investigation of particular irregularities. While these non-scale measures do not offer flow estimates in currency terms, they do allow significantly more precise measures of proxies for illicit flow risk.

6

New Proposals for IFF Indicators in the Sustainable Development Goals

As discussed in chapter 1, the illicit flows target in the Sustainable Development Goals (16.4) leaves much to be desired. Politically, it made sense to maintain the overall framing that the Mbeki panel had set. But technically, the combination of the quite different issues under the IFF umbrella creates a challenge. That challenge is exacerbated by the proposed, single IFF indicator:

16.4.1 Total value of inward and outward illicit financial flows (in current USD)

The various types and channels of IFF have different implications in terms of tax revenue loss, damage to governance and political representation, and effective market functioning. They also create different patterns of inflow and outflow from a given jurisdiction. Summing across every type, and treating inflows and outflows as equivalent, will provide at best a blunt measure of the scale of the underlying phenomena.

The target is, however, politically significant. It reflects political leadership from the global South, and the African region in particular. It would be unfortunate if the UN system were to fail to deliver meaningful progress— beginning with agreed indicators.

Looking ahead, the target is of substantive importance. While there is uncertainty associated with many individual estimates, there are literally no results for the scale of any type or channel of illicit financial flow which support the view that the phenomena should not be considered a sizeable obstacle to development. The international nature of IFF requires, by definition, international coordination as well as national action; the SDG target represents the best opportunity to drive progress.

If IFF were readily separable by type and/or by channel, it would be possible to create sub-indicators that summed to the proposed indicator 16.4.1. For example, given separability by IFF type and robust estimates of each, 16.4.1 could be the sum of 16.4.1.1: market-abusive IFF; 16.4.1.2: tax-abusive IFF; 16.4.1.3: abuse of power IFF; and 16.4.1.4: IFF due to laundering of the

Estimating illicit financial flows: A critical guide to the data, methodologies and findings. Alex Cobham and Petr Janský, Oxford University Press (2020). © Alex Cobham and Petr Janský.
DOI: 10.1093/oso/9780198854418.001.0001

proceeds of crime. An equivalent but more complex structure could be envisaged on the basis of the IFF channels in table 1.1.

In theory, either of these would offer not only a comprehensive indicator for monitoring and accountability purposes, but also a disaggregable basis for policy prioritisation at any and all of the global, regional and national levels. In practice, however, as we have seen in the foregoing chapters, current estimates provide neither the robustness nor the separability necessary to support such an approach. The one broad IFF approach that could be relatively straightforwardly generated on a global basis is that of Global Financial Integrity. But neither the capital account component, nor the trade component of this approach, appear robust; and nor, then, are any conclusions about the relative importance of trade-based IFF.

The risk approaches outlined in chapter 5 do provide a more granular basis for policy prioritisation, and sidestep the problems of estimates by relying instead on proxy measures that can be directly calculated. They do not, however, offer indicators of scale of the type required by SDG 16.4.1.

To meet the constraints of the SDG process, we have therefore proposed two measures—*measures*, rather than estimates—that capture the scale of two key outcomes of IFF. These reflect, first, the volume of profit shifting; and second, the extent of undeclared offshore assets (Cobham & Janský, 2017d, 2018b). These form part of basis for national pilots in the process led by UNCTAD and the UN Economic Commission for Africa to develop and test SDG indicators of tax-related illicit flows (UNODC and the UN Economic Commission for Latin America and the Caribbean are leading work on illegal market IFFs).

Rather than inevitably imprecise estimates of the scale of illicit flows, our two preferred indicators (or indicator components) address instead the measurable consequences. In this chapter we lay out the two measures, evaluate their strengths and weaknesses including in respect of data availability and potential work-arounds at national level, and consider the scope to combine the measures, if necessary, into a single indicator 16.4.1.

6.1. Profit Shifting: SDG 16.4.1a

6.1.1. Overview

'Another governance dimension of IFFs relates to the unequal burden of citizenship imposed on other sectors of society, both in terms of tax fairness and 'free-riding'. When large companies, particularly multinational corporations, engage in base erosion and profit-shifting activities, the bulk of the tax burden as a result falls on small and medium-scale enterprises and individual taxpayers. This runs counter to the idea of progressive taxation, in which those who earn more income contribute a larger percentage of tax revenues. Just as pernicious to governance is the 'free-riding' that results when entities evade or avoid taxes where they undertake substantial economic activities and yet benefit from the physical and social infrastructure, most of which is still provided by the public sector in Africa.'

- African Union/Economic Commission for Africa, 2015, *Report of the High Level Panel on Illicit Financial Flows from Africa*, (p.52).

'We will make sure that all companies, including multinationals, pay taxes to the Governments of countries where economic activity occurs and value is created, in accordance with national and international laws and policies.'

- United Nations, 2015, *Addis Ababa Action Agenda of the Third International Conference on Financing for Development* (p.12).

'The G20 finance ministers called on the OECD to develop an action plan to address specific BEPS issues in a coordinated and comprehensive manner. Specifically, this Action Plan should provide countries with domestic and international instruments that will better align rights to tax with economic activity.'

- OECD, 2013a, *Action Plan on Base Erosion and Profit Shifting* (p.11).

'Developed countries…have special responsibilities in ensuring that there can be no safe haven for illicit capital and the proceeds of corruption, and that multinational companies pay taxes fairly in the countries in which they operate.'

- United Nations, 2013, *Report of the High Level Panel of Eminent Persons on the Post-2015 Development Agenda* (p.11).

As seen in chapter 4, estimates of multinational companies' profit shifting may be the robust of all the IFF areas. The revenue losses associated with these tax abuses may very well be the largest. But for a consistent basis of annual monitoring and accountability, with near-global coverage, these estimates too remain lacking.

For the SDG indicator, we therefore propose an approach which differs from most of the literature. Rather than a necessarily imperfect estimate of the profit shifting flow, we construct a more precise measure of a somewhat broader phenomenon: the ultimately achieved misalignment of profits with the underlying real economic activity.

As the quotations illustrate, reduction of this misalignment is the now well established and unique aim of international attempts to combat these abuses. As discussed in chapter 1, the exact nature of profit misalignment means that this measure will necessarily include a degree of licit activity. Recall that profit *shifting* is made up of lawful and unlawful avoidance, along with criminal evasion. Profit *misalignment*—the phenomenon that can be measured, rather than estimated—is a broader term, including these three elements but also misalignment that may arise simply from the fact that national and international tax rules do not explicitly seek alignment.

The result is that, since some divergence from full alignment might therefore be expected even in the absence of tax-motivated shifting, the value of the indicator consistent with IFF elimination need not be zero. There is, however, no reason to expect any systematic change over time in the overall, global degree of non-tax-motivated misalignment. There is also no reason to expect that individual jurisdictions would experience particular swings in non-tax-motivated misalignment over time. On this basis, we favour tracking a relatively precise measure which includes some noise, in preference to more uncertain and imprecise estimates of a more closely defined phenomenon.

6.1.2. Data

To construct a global measure of profit misalignment requires data on profits declared and real economic activity at the country level, plus ideally data on tax paid to understand the likely motivation.

Now for a company operating in a single jurisdiction, as was the case for all companies at the time when corporate law and accounting norms began to emerge, most of this information will be contained in the annual accounts. Those annual accounts in many jurisdictions, have long been required to be placed in the public domain. This reflects a crucial decision in the development of entrepreneurship, by which governments allowed the liability of those running companies to be capped—so that commercial activity was not held back, for example, by the risk that business failure would also mean the loss of one's family home. While having sporadic use across millennia, it was only from the early 19th century that limited liability companies were the subject of formal legislation followed by widespread use.

The effective quid pro quo for this protection was the publication of company accounts, signed off by an approved auditor. Where limited liability socialises (some of) the private risks of business failure, the publication of audited accounts provides transparency to allow external stakeholders and investors to manage their own exposure to those risks.

In the 20th century, the growing emergence of business groups operating transnationally necessitated major changes to national regulatory frameworks that had hitherto been purely domestically focused. Most obviously, this process saw the League of Nations take leading role in establishing the basis for international tax rules that first governed the imperial interactions in the multinational tax sphere, and were later taken up by the OECD.

Perhaps unsurprisingly, compared to tax, there was less pressure to ensure transparency regulations were adapted for the globalising world. With most multinationals headquartered in and owned from current or former imperial powers, these OECD country governments were largely able to ensure domestic regulatory compliance and to access any data they required to ensure appropriate tax was paid—in their own jurisdictions.

And so it fell, eventually to the G77 group of countries to force the question of greater corporate disclosure (Ruffing & Hamdani, 2015; Meinzer & Trautvetter, 2018). Following growing anger at the apparent impunity of multinationals operating in lower-income countries, and after lengthy negotiations at the United Nations, the Center for Transnational Corporations (UNCTC) was established in 1975. The Center in turn convened a Group of Experts on International Standards of Accounting and Reporting (GEISAR), to increase the financial transparency of multinationals and their global networks, including proposals for publication of the accounts of each entity in each country of operation.

While the work of GEISAR was eventually blocked through the mobilisation of business lobbyists, major accounting firms and OECD member states, and the UNCTC shut down in 1992, the issues remained unaddressed. The International Accounting Standards Board in London, and in the US the Federal Accounting Standards Board, allowed during some periods for geographic segment reporting—but typically this did not break out more than a handful of individual countries of operation, if that, and left the rest aggregated by broad region.

Then in the early 2000s, the lack of jurisdiction-level reporting by multinationals become the subject of discussions among a small expert group in what would soon become the Tax Justice Network. And so it was that some months before the network was formally established, the first ever draft accounting standard for country-by-country reporting was published (Murphy, 2003). This set out the basis for public data to ensure that multinationals, too, would provide effective disclosure about their activities and risks at the jurisdiction level. Although swiftly taken up by civil society transparency advocates, initially focusing on the extractive sector and subsequently looking at tax avoidance more broadly, the proposals were consistently resisted at the International Accounting Standards Board and at the OECD.

In just ten years, however, the powerful G20 group of countries had required the OECD to put aside any misgivings and deliver a standard for country-by-country reporting, to apply to all multinationals in the world over a certain size threshold. The eventual standard in most technical respects hewed closely to the proposals developed by the Tax Justice Network, but with one, crucial difference: the OECD data was not to be made public, but provided privately only to home country tax authorities.

This limitation, despite the complex information sharing arrangements constructed since, largely defeats the purpose of the proposal. Above all, it prevents any public scrutiny by stakeholders including investors, labour, and people in the communities where companies' activities take place. But on top of that, the OECD approach manages to take a measure designed to level the playing field between the tax authorities of lower- and higher-income jurisdictions, and instead to exacerbate the inequalities faced. By construction, the information sharing arrangements result in systematically worse access to information in those (low- and middle-income) countries that suffer the most intense revenue losses (Knobel & Cobham, 2016).

Aside from the question of access, the data itself is not perfect. Table 6.1 compares the OECD standard with civil society proposals, and a range of other existing requirements: CRD IV (limited country-by-country reporting for EU financial institutions, under the fourth Capital Requirements Directive); the now-repealed Dodd-Frank requirement for US-listed extractive sector firms; the Canadian and EU equivalents; and the standard of the Extractive Industries Transparency Initiative (EITI). Indeed, EITI and the extractive industries sector has been discussed recently in comparison with other reporting requirements for extractive industries (Porsch et al., 2018) and within a broader discourse on illicit financial flows in extractive industries (Lemaître, 2018). While most of the key variables are included in the OECD

Table 6.1. Comparison of data fields in CBCR standards

	Civil Society Proposal	OECD CBCR	CRD IV	Dodd Frank	Canada	EITI	EU
Identity	Group name	Group name	Group name	Group name	Payee name	Payee name	Group name
	Countries	Countries	Countries	Countries	Countries	Legal and institutional framework	Countries
	Nature of activities	Nature of activities	Nature of activities	Projects (as in: by contract)	Same data required per project as well as per country	Allocation of contracts and licenses	Projects (as in: by contract)
	Names of constituent companies	Names of constituent companies		Receiving body in government	Subsidiaries if qualifying reporting entities	Exploration and production	
						Social and economic spending	
Activity	Third party sales	Third party sales	Turnover				
	Turnover	By the process of addition	Number of employees				
	Number of employees FTE	Number of employees FTE					
	Total employee pay						
	Tangible assets						
Intra-group transactions	Intra-group sales	Intra-group sales					
	Intra-group purchases						
	Intra-group royalties rec'd						

Key financials	Intra-group royalties paid			Profits taxes
	Intra-group interest recd			taxes levied on the income, production or profits of companies
	Intra-group interest paid			
	Profit or loss before tax	Profit or loss before tax	Profit or loss before tax	
Payments to/from governments	Tax accrued	Tax accrued	Income taxes paid	Tax paid
	Tax paid	Tax paid	Tax paid	
	Any public subsidies received	Any public subsidies received	Any public subsidies received	

Source: Cobham, Gray, & Murphy (2017)

standard, there are important absences: notably, of economic activity indicators (employee remuneration and tangible assets), and of intra-group transactions including interest and royalties.

In addition, the OECD standard has faced criticism over the failure to require that the data be reconciled with the published, global consolidated accounts of multinationals; and that it currently applies only to the largest 10–15 per cent of multinationals, those with a turnover above three quarters of a billion euro. The Global Reporting Initiative (GRI) has now launched on a technical standard for voluntary public reporting which addresses this question and a number of others, and sets the basis for future improvements to the OECD standard also. Vodafone, a participant in the GRI working group, have also become the first major multinational to commit to publish their OECD standard reporting, from 2019.

Notwithstanding its weaknesses, the OECD standard marks a turning point in the debate. Previous arguments that such data was not held by companies, or would be prohibitively expensive to collate, have been eliminated. This in turn means that the opportunity is there for the data to be made available.

The OECD BEPS Action 11 team, tasked with generating consistent measures to track progress in reducing base erosion and profit shifting by multinationals, soon recognized that existing estimates cannot provide such measures—and, moreover, that this can only be done with country-by-country reporting data. But BEPS Action 13, which includes the responsibility to introduce country-by-country reporting, had already been the subject of energetic lobbying. Major multinational lobby groups, the big four professional services firms and certain OECD member states (Meinzer & Trautvetter, 2018) were successful in having country-by-country reporting data designated as confidential, with removal of access for states that violate this.

For this reason, it took until the OECD Secretary-General's report to G20 finance ministers of July 2018—some five years after the start of the BEPS project and three years after its formal end—for the BEPS 11 team to obtain agreement that it would collate and publish the partially aggregated country-by-country reporting received by each relevant home jurisdiction tax authority. Even then, the commitment is only to publish data by end-2019. But this is potentially a great step forward delivering not transparency of individual multinationals, but the ultimately more important accountability of individual jurisdictions for their role in promoting and/or tackling profit shifting.

The difficulty, of course is that BEPS Action 11 can only publish the data that states provide—and this will include at least some regional aggregation to accommodate confidentiality concerns. It remains to be seen to what extent any further aggregation is imposed, and to what extent it limits the value of the data for the proposal made here.

Consider a country with few multinationals above the reporting size threshold (annual turnover of $750 million), such as the Czech Republic. Here, tax authorities may find that data aggregated to the country level (e.g. the total employment of all reporting Czech multinationals in France) could threaten confidentiality.

For a major headquarters jurisdiction like the US, with a large number of reporting multinationals, there may be no obstacle. But with a range of (e.g. lower-income) countries in which only a smaller number of US-headquartered, reporting multinationals operate, the problem may still arise. In fact, the current Bureau of Economic Analysis survey of *all* US multinationals has many data suppressions for this reason (Cobham & Janský, 2019).

Before that data is scheduled to be available in early 2020, three other channels are under exploration. One is the voluntary route. There are potential champions here—Vodafone, for example, has committed to publish its OECD standard reporting from 2019, and its fellow members of the 'B Team' alliance have indicated some interest. The Global Reporting Initiative's new standard is likely to see broad take-up from 2020. But voluntary approaches are difficult, since the data will inevitably focus attention on the absolute levels of a given multinational's profit misalignment—rather than any relative superiority to less transparent rivals.

A second channel is that of unilateral requirement for publication. The UK parliament has already legislated to allow publication, but the government has not yet chosen to impose the requirement. The French parliament had passed a measure mandating publication, before the previous government reversed this with an archaic, technical manoeuvre. In the absence of multilateral agreement at the OECD, pressure will continue for others such as the EU to take a lead—albeit that Germany has now emerged as the key blocker.

The third channel is for the issue of corporate disclosure to return to the UN system (on which see Cobham, Janský, & Meinzer, 2018). One possibility here would be for ISAR, the successor to GEISAR, to develop a mandatory public standard. Another would be for the requirement to be embedded within the draft treaty on multinationals and human rights. Perhaps the most obvious channel, however, given the organisation's central role in analysing data on the investment (and more recently, profit shifting) behaviour of multinationals, would be for UNCTAD to become the repository for country-by-country reporting data, and the guardian of a strong standard delivering the data to underpin an indicator of profit misalignment for the SDGs.

Only this latter channel, of course, has the potential to generate consistent data of sufficient coverage to support the proposed SDG indicator, should the OECD release prove insufficient. An additional channel, for countries involved in the initial pilot studies at least, is to construct nationally-relevant equivalent measures by requiring local filing of OECD standard data, and/or by creating work-around approaches using nationally filed tax returns and additional data (public and privately filed) on the global operations of each multinational. Figure 6.1 compares the current OECD arrangements to access the data, with an alternative proposal put forward by the Tax Justice Network.

For the moment, we may optimistically assume that states providing data to the OECD as now agreed will not spuriously use confidentiality arguments to downgrade the quality of data supplied. Were this the case, however, it is possible that a delegated UN body such as UNCTAD could—in tandem with the OECD or quite separately—obtain additional data direct from member states' tax authorities, with the guarantee of protecting confidentiality of individual reporting multinationals.

Even in a more pessimistic view, however, the overall transparency provided is likely to far exceed any current public information about the activities and profit declaration of multinationals. Unnecessary aggregation aside, the quality of the data required is high. Although not currently required to be audited and consolidated to global accounts, the basis in reporting by individual multinationals to their home tax authorities sets the likely standard well above any current alternative—from the limited, publicly available company balance sheet data, to elements of national accounts data or bilateral aggregates. Misreporting faces potentially criminal consequences.

In terms of coverage, the capturing of multinationals above the threshold is expected to be complete—and therefore global in terms of their operations.

Finally, in the discussion of data, we note that reliance on country-by-country reporting would reflect a central policy position of the High Level Panel on Illicit Financial Flows from Africa (AU/UNECA, 2015), whose work underpins the global agreement on SDG 16.4.

"We were encouraged by the emergence of discussions on country-by-country reporting of employees, profits, sales and taxes as a means of ensuring transparency in cross-border transactions. Country-by-country reporting, publicly available, will help to show where substantial activity is taking place and the

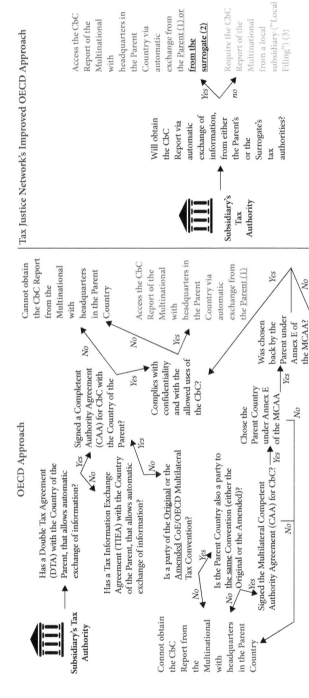

Figure 6.1. Approaches to sharing country-by-country (CbC) data.
Source: Knobel & Cobham (2016).

relative profits generated and taxes paid. In the absence of a universal tax administration, country-by-country reporting will enable tax and law enforcement agencies to gain a full picture of a company's activities and encourage companies to be transparent in their dealings with African countries." (p.45)

"African States should require multinational corporations operating in their countries to provide the transfer pricing units with a comprehensive report showing their disaggregated financial reporting on a country-by-country or subsidiary-by-subsidiary basis. African governments could also consider developing a format for this reporting that would be acceptable to multiple African revenue authorities." (p.81)

"The Panel calls for partner countries to require publicly available disaggregated, country-by-country reporting of financial information for multinational companies incorporated, organized or regulated in their jurisdictions." (p.85)

These policy positions provide further confirmation, of course, that those responsible for this globally leading work saw multinational profit shifting as a major component under the IFF umbrella. At the same time, the approach proposed for SDG indicators allows full separation of the profit shifting component, to support the distinct policy approaches needed.

6.1.3. Methodology

The misaligned profit indicator is defined as the value of profits reported by multinationals in countries, for which there is no proportionate economic activity of MNEs. It is defined for each jurisdiction and it can be summed across some or all countries. For each jurisdiction we define the misaligned profit as:

$$\chi_i = \pi_i - \omega_i \Pi \tag{1}$$

where:

π_i is the value of all multinationals' gross profits declared in jurisdiction i;

ω_i is the share of all multinationals' economic activity in jurisdiction i; and

Π is the global, gross profits of all multinationals, such that $\Pi = \sum_{i=1}^{n} \pi_i$.

We propose to capture economic activity as the simple average of single indicators of production (the share of full-time equivalent employees in a jurisdiction, ι_i) and consumption (share of final sales within each jurisdiction, γ_i). We define, for all i:

$$\omega_i = \frac{1}{2}(\iota_i + \gamma_i)$$

It follows that the global sum of misaligned profits, X, is equal to zero:

$$X = \sum_{i=1}^{n} \chi_i = 0$$

We propose that the profit misalignment indicator for use in SDG target 16.4 is the global sum of *positively misaligned* profits—that is, the total excess profits declared in jurisdictions with a greater share of profits than would be aligned with their share of economic activity. Equivalently, this can be calculated as half the sum of the absolute values of misaligned profit:

$$SDG_{16.4.1a} = \frac{1}{2}\sum_{i=1}^{n} |\chi_i| \tag{2}$$

Note that the SDG indicator as defined in the current framework is expressed as the sum of inward and outward IFF, so the sum of absolute profit misalignment could be used; this seems inelegant at best. Note also that the underlying country-level misalignment measures provide monitoring and accountability for individual states seeking to reduce the (negative) misalignment suffered—for example, to demonstrate to citizens and domestic businesses that multinationals are being fairly taxed; and for states that benefit from profit-shifting at the expense of others, an accountability mechanism to demonstrate their own commitment to global progress.

Although not proposed as an element of the SDG framework, such a profit misalignment indicator can also be constructed at the firm level. Equation (2), calculated with the data from a single multinational group, will provide a measure of the value of profit that is misaligned. The χ_i for individual jurisdictions will show the group-specific pattern of misalignment, including which jurisdictions are suffering and benefiting.

In addition, a further indicator can be constructed to allow easier comparison across multinationals and of a given multinational over time. This is simply the level of the group's global profit misalignment, per Equation (2), expressed not in currency terms but as a proportion of total group profits: in other words, a comparable measure of the intensity of profit misalignment at multinational group j:

$$\mu_j = \frac{\sum_{i=1}^{n} |\chi_i|}{2\Pi_j} \tag{3}$$

Note that, perhaps counter-intuitively, this intensity ratio can easily exceed 100 per cent. This is because the sum of positive profits declared at jurisdiction level (and so potentially able to be misaligned) will exceed the global profit total if there are also losses declared in some jurisdictions.

We can explore the methodology at the firm level by applying it to one of multinationals currently leading the way in publishing some form of country-by-country reporting. Vodafone, who for many years were subject to campaigning by tax justice activists in the UK over a questionable deal with the tax authority, have become the first multinational to commit to publish their OECD standard country-by-country reporting, from 2019. In the meantime, they publish data on a roughly equivalent basis (Vodafone, 2018) which we use here for illustrative purposes.

In Vodafone's case, for 2016–17 data, the sum of positive, declared profits at the jurisdiction level is €4.128bn. This is 221 per cent of the overall, (net) global profit of €1.867bn. Applying the approach in equations (1) and (2) reveals misaligned profit of €3.574bn, or an intensity of profit misalignment, per equation (3), of 191 per cent of global profit.

Figure 6.2 shows the extent of misaligned profit and the effective tax rate paid, for the ten jurisdictions in which more than 1 per cent of the global profit is declared and where there is positive profit misalignment. Of the nearly €1.5bn declared in Luxembourg, more than 99.5 per cent is not aligned with the real economic activity taking place there (as captured by employment and sales). The effective tax rate on these profits, according to Vodafone's data, is around 0.3 per cent.

On the other hand, South Africa appears to benefit from a 33 per cent effective tax rate on declared profit of around €1.08bn, of which nearly 90 per cent is misaligned. Egypt, Kenya and at a lower effective rate, Italy, appear to follow a similar pattern; while Malta sees misalignment on an effective rate around 6 per cent. Not shown are the range of EU states and the US and Australia, where losses are declared in significant, long-established markets with major activity.

In a series of basic simulations, using constrained, randomly generated values for activity and profit in the jurisdictions of hypothetical multinational groups, we confirm that while misalignment intensities in excess of 100 per cent are not necessarily common, they are certainly plausible—especially, as noted, when a group records losses in a number of jurisdictions.

The same simulations confirm, as would be expected, that aggregation of the country-by-country reporting of multiple multinationals will tend to result in substantially lower, overall profit misalignment. For example, aggregating

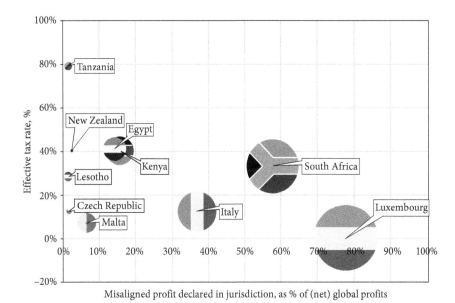

Figure 6.2. Major jurisdictions in Vodafone's profit misalignment.

Notes: Figure shows ten jurisdictions for which declared profit exceeds 1 per cent of Vodafone's ultimate, global profit. The size of the bubbles is in proportion to the absolute value of misaligned profit (the largest, Luxembourg, is equivalent to €1.44bn). An eleventh jurisdiction with 1 per cent of Vodafone's global profit, Romania, is excluded, since it sees negative profit misalignment (i.e. lower profit than its share of economic activity indicates).

Source: authors' calculations, using Vodafone data for 2016–17. We are grateful to Tommaso Faccio for providing the data.

across 10 simulated multinationals operating in the same 26 jurisdictions, with misalignment intensity varying between 55 per cent (44 per cent) and 135 per cent (129 per cent), we obtained an overall misalignment of 22 per cent (17 per cent) of global profits.

The limitations of these basic simulations aside, we would expect actual misalignment to be higher, however, if the patterns of positive misalignment are not in fact random—if, for example, multinationals in general are likely to use a particular set of jurisdictions for tax-motivated profit shifting. The methodology here is broadly comparable to the approach of Cobham & Janský (2019) surveyed in section 4.6, in which we use data on US multinationals and find a level of aggregate misalignment that rises from 5–10 per cent of global profits in the 1990s, to 25–30 per cent by the early 2010s. Tørsløv, Wier, & Zucman (2018) use a different but not unrelated methodology, evaluated in section 4.9, to reach a finding that 40 per cent of the profits declared by foreign affiliates are misaligned (note: this is substantially lower than 40 per cent of multinationals' global profits, since it excludes home jurisdiction entities).

The data available for banks under CRD IV (limited country-by-country reporting for EU financial institutions, under the fourth Capital Requirements Directive) provide an opportunity for a case study. Banks in the European Union recently started publicly reporting data on profit, number of employees, turnover and tax on a country-by-country basis. Janský (2018) introduces the largest, hand-collected, public data set of its kind, which covers almost 50 banks for up to 5 years between 2013 and 2017. he identifies the main locations of European bank's profits, which include the largest European economies as well as tax havens. He focuses on answering the question of how geographically aligned these profits are with economic activity. He finds that some of the tax havens have maintained high shares of profits in contrast with their much lower shares of employees. Figure 6.3 below illustrates this point for Ireland and Luxembourg, for which there are ample data and both of which are important locations of profit. Janský (2018) concludes that his results indicate that banks are likely shifting their profits to tax havens, but for the profit shifting to be directly observed, regulators will need to ask banks to publish even better data.

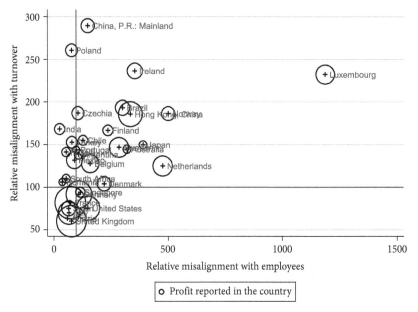

Figure 6.3. Relative misalignment between profits and employees and turnover, respectively (% of gross profits), 2013–2017 mean for countries with at least 1000 million euro in profits reported in at least one of the years.

Source: Janský (2018).

6.1.4. Conclusions

The proposed SDG indicator is a measure, rather than an estimate, of the global total of country-level profit misalignment of multinationals with annual turnover in excess of $750 million. There are three potential criticisms, and one area of significant uncertainty.

The first criticism would take the form of a claim that some estimate, specifically of profit *shifting*, could more closely capture the scale of the problem. As discussed in chapter 4, we do not believe that there is *currently* an estimate which combines a robust methodology with sufficiently high quality data of near-global coverage, that could justify being put forward as part of the SDG framework.

A second criticism relates to just what is being measured. Given that profit misalignment is broader than profit shifting, is a direct measure of the former really preferable to an estimate of the latter—which is the IFF concern? While a direct measure of the specific phenomenon would of course be preferable, it is also unlikely—if the IFF were directly observable, it would not represent such a threat and would likely tend toward zero. The choice is therefore between a measure of a related phenomenon, and a less precise estimate of the specific phenomenon.

As figure 1.2 shows, profit shifting IFF are made up of the cross-border components of corporate tax evasion; unlawful tax avoidance; and lawful tax avoidance. Profit misalignment comprises these three elements, plus that of misalignment which is not tax-related—which, in other words, reflects simply that the current international tax rules do not have alignment as their goal or inevitable outcome, absent any tax-motivated behaviour.

Cobham & Janský (2019) find that by the 2010s, around 25–30 per cent of the global profit of US multinationals was misaligned. Tørsløv, Wier, & Zucman (2018) estimate that around 40 per cent of the profits of multinationals' foreign affiliates is misaligned. In both cases, tax motivations drive the misalignment, and would support the assumption that overall, the non-tax-related component is likely to be small *and* should not be expected to demonstrate any systematic trend over time, or even across countries.

The extent of misalignment captured by the indicator in error (that is, not related to profit shifting) is therefore likely to be both small and random. As such, the indicator should provide a broadly consistent indicator of the scale of the IFF in question, allowing meaningful comparison across countries and of progress over time.

The third criticism is related and something of a truism: namely, that the measure is not a fair evaluation of the current international tax rules, but instead a measure of how far they deviate from a unitary tax approach. The current tax rules rely on the arm's length principle: namely, that entities within a multinational group should transact with each other at genuine market prices (assuming these exist for the goods or services in question), and the resulting distribution of taxable profits will be the 'right' one. The OECD's separate accounting approach therefore takes each entity within the group as individually profit maximising.

A unitary approach, in contrast, identifies the unit of profit maximisation as the group itself—recognising that it may be in the group's interest for some entities to make no profit, or even a loss, on paper. The total global profit is then allocated as potential tax base between jurisdictions where the group's activity takes place, according to some formula. That formula could reflect, for example, the shares of a group's tangible assets, sales, employee numbers and remuneration in each country (as the EU's proposed Common Consolidated Corporate Tax Base does); or, say, sales and employee numbers (as the formula for apportionment between Canadian provinces does).

In this way, a unitary approach allows precisely the alignment of economic activity and profit that is sought, according to the global consensus reflected in the quotations in section 6.1.1. However, the indicator here simply reflects that consensus on the need to reduce misalignment—it does not set unitary tax as a global goal. Policymakers looking to move beyond the failed arm's length principle might, of course, reflect on the alignment potential of unitary approaches.

Finally, this approach faces remaining uncertainty around the availability of data. It is unclear, first, whether the partially aggregated country-by-country reporting data provided to the OECD by national governments, for publication in early 2020 and annually thereafter, will be sufficiently consistent and of high quality and coverage to support the approach proposed here. Second, it is unclear whether a UN agency such as UNCTAD could or would step in to ensure better data if the OECD is unable to deliver. A further possibility would be to establish the range of necessary variables as part of the system of national accounts, and so to ensure their publication for the longer term. Third, it is uncertain to what extent tax authorities can generate their own national analyses—especially in lower-income countries which have least access to company reporting, and may be more likely to see their data suppressed in host countries' reporting to the OECD. Immediate opportunities will depend on the quality of submitted tax returns and publicly available, global consolidated accounts; and a willingness to follow non-OECD countries such as China, India and Uruguay (Knobel, 2018b) in requiring direct filing of country-by-country data.

6.2. Undeclared Offshore Assets: SDG 16.4.1b

6.2.1. Overview

With multinational profit shifting addressed by the proposed indicator SDG 16.4.1a, Table 6.2 shows the range of illicit flows outstanding. It is immediately clear that the range is wide indeed. Recall, too, that the underlying channels as set out in table 1.1 show greater detail and variety.

While each of the behaviours are unlawful, the main split is between the illicit use of legally generated funds, on the one hand, and the flow of criminal funds on the other. In the first category, the most iconic IFF behaviour is that of outright, cross-border tax evasion: the use of secrecy jurisdictions to hide, and to hold, undeclared assets and income streams resulting from legitimate business activity. We also find here illicit transfers of licit income, for example to circumvent capital controls; and licit transfers for illicit purposes, for example the financing of terrorist activity.

The third channel of illicit flows of legitimate income, however, is perhaps the largest and only in recent years has begun to receive greater public and policymaker attention. This is the use of anonymous ownership vehicles

Table 6.2. A simple outline of illicit financial flows, excluding multinational profit shifting

Legal category	Origin of assets	Behaviour type
Unlawful Criminal	Legally generated profits, capital gains and income	Market/regulatory abuse Illicitly transferred, and/or transferred for illicit purposes Tax evasion
	Proceeds of corruption	*Bribery; Grand corruption; Illicit enrichment; Embezzlement*
	Proceeds of theft/related crime	*Theft; Extortion; Kidnapping; Fraud; Bankruptcy*
	Proceeds of illegal markets	*Drug trafficking; Counterfeiting; Firearms trafficking; Trafficking in persons; Smuggling of migrants; Wildlife trafficking*

Source: Extract from table 1.2.

to circumvent market regulations—for example, anti-monopoly limits on ownership concentration, or to hide potential conflicts of interest—for example, policymakers' financial interests in regulated entities or in companies benefiting from political discussions such as the granting of mining rights, or telecoms licenses, or tax incentives. Most famously, in 2016 Iceland's Prime Minister Sigmundur Davíð Gunnlaugsson stepped down after the Panama Papers revealed an anonymous company owned with his wife. The pivotal revelation was that the company held bonds in three major Icelandic banks—the value of which, after the financial crisis, was largely dependent on decisions taken by Gunnlaugsson's government.

The second category includes three types of flows of illegally earned funds: the proceeds of corruption, the proceeds of theft, kidnapping and related crimes; and the proceeds of criminal markets including trafficking in narcotics, humans and firearms, illegal wildlife, waste, and illegal logging and fishing. As explained in chapter 1, this book has not sought to survey the literature on criminal market IFFs, surveyed recently in the crime-focused World Atlas of Illicit Flows (Nellemann, Stock, & Shaw, 2018). While work continues at organisations like UNODC to refine the approaches to estimation for specific, individual markets in individual countries, the gap is great indeed to build from these to credible, robust measures with broad coverage both of countries and of markets.

Overall, the sheer range of IFF types here raise problems for measurement or estimation. In addition, none of the approaches surveyed has suggested a comprehensive approach. The GFI and Ndikumana & Boyce approaches do aim to cover both capital account- and trade-based IFF, but even if perfect would not necessarily capture e.g. payments made offshore for trafficked goods or people; or hidden ownership through anonymous 'foreign' investment.

These IFF channels do, however, have a common element: the creation of undeclared offshore assets and/or income streams of domestic taxpayers. This varies in its centrality to each IFF type. For tax evasion, the creation of undeclared offshore assets is the essence of the IFF. For regulation-circumventing anonymous ownership, undeclared offshore assets are almost a byproduct of the process, which aims to hold domestic assets. For IFF relating to the proceeds of illegal markets, undeclared offshore wealth is a result that it is often unwanted, with further laundering used in an attempt to overcome it.

The proposed indicator takes the sum of undeclared assets as a potentially measurable proxy for the scale of IFF other than multinational profit shifting. In this way it collates the range of quite different IFF into a single indicator of scale, of the type envisaged by the SDG drafters.

6.2.2. Data

As with the proposed profit-shifting indicator, so too in the area of undeclared offshore wealth there is a new possibility due to the recent adoption at global level of a key tax justice proposal. In this case, it relates to the 'A' of the Tax Justice Network's ABC of tax transparency: the *a*utomatic exchange of tax information. This measure requires jurisdictions that are signatories to the OECD Common Reporting Standard to provide bilaterally to other jurisdictions, detailed reporting on financial assets of the other's citizens—for example, for Switzerland to report to Germany the Swiss bank holdings of German citizens.

This policy measure is intended above all to address offshore tax evasion by individuals. The category of undeclared assets, however—and hence the proposed indicator—should include the results of the great majority of illicit flows as set out in Table 6.2. With only certain exceptions, maintaining the success of the illicit flow will require continuing not to declare ownership of the results offshore assets to the home authorities.

More than 100 of the leading financial centres are committed to exchange financial information under the CRS, starting either in September 2017 or September 2018, and annually thereafter. Unfortunately, the OECD has allowed jurisdictions to breach the originally understood commitment to exchange automatically with all other CRS signatories, leading Switzerland and others to restrict their detailed reporting to only economically and politically powerful states. But as with 16.4.1a, the proposal here does not require full access to the detailed data.

Since financial institutions are required for CRS effectiveness to confirm the citizenship of accountholders, reporting of aggregate data is straightforward—that is, not the data on individual German citizens with Swiss bank accounts, but on the totality of their holdings. At the same time, to participate in the CRS requires tax authorities to organise their own data on citizens' self-declaration in an equivalent manner. This therefore makes it reasonable to publish aggregate data on the totality of holdings in each other jurisdiction—e.g. of German citizens in Switzerland, in France, in Austria, and so on.

The major financial secrecy jurisdiction that has not committed to the CRS is the United States, which ranks second in the Tax Justice Network's Financial Secrecy Index 2018. The major financial secrecy jurisdiction that has committed to the CRS, but used the bilateral 'dating' approach to ensure that it only provides data to a small number of fellow signatories, is Switzerland, ranked first in the Financial Secrecy Index. But both Switzerland and the US publish aggregate data which is broadly equivalent to what would be required in the form of aggregate CRS reporting: the liabilities to foreigners, by jurisdiction, of financial firms in the reporting country (Knobel, 2018c).

The Tax Justice Network (Knobel, 2018a, Meinzer & Knobel, 2017) has published proposals for aggregate CRS reporting, to provide consistent data in support of global monitoring and accountability—just as the SDG indicator should ideally do. The complexity of the CRS approach, hinted at in figure 6.4, means that full accountability requires consistent data on the assets and income of the whole range of both reported and non-reported accounts, by jurisdiction of account-holder.

A particular concern relates to the ongoing activity to create non-reportable asset classes such as insurance 'wrappers' that may allow circumvention of the CRS. In this sense, automatic information exchange can be thought of as a form of capital control, and in common with all such measures will require ongoing strengthening as financial institutions and others 'innovate' to avoid (in this case) transparency. The standard should be expected to evolve over time for this reason, potentially raising issues for comparability in the longer term. In addition, the somewhat narrow range of financial assets currently covered makes leakage inevitable; but there is no serious alternative in terms of data quality with wider range.

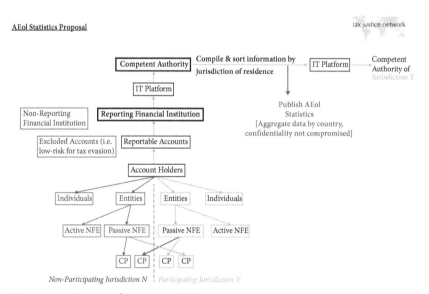

Figure 6.4. Proposed aggregate CRS statistics.
Source: Meinzer & Knobel (2017).

The benefits of having all major financial centres bar the US collate data for exchange on a consistent basis should not be understated. The quality of the data required is expected to be generally high.

In terms of coverage, comprehensive data would require some improvement in implementation. Some implementing jurisdictions have sought to limit the data gathered by requiring their reporting financial institutions only to collect data for the jurisdictions with which they will initially be exchanging information—ensuring that no data is available, even in the aggregate, on the assets of citizens of other jurisdictions. In addition, the current systematic exclusion of lower-income jurisdictions must be addressed—either through pressure on the OECD to implement the fully multilateral instrument that the G20 first sought, or through an alternative UN measure to require it.

The most consistent data currently available is that from the Bank of International Settlements (BIS). For many years, the BIS published bilateral data only on a consolidated basis. This consolidation of bank branches around the world up to the jurisdiction of their parent produced largely unhelpful data. For example, the sums held by an Ethiopian account-holder at Credit Suisse in Addis Ababa would be shown in the consolidated statistics as a Swiss-Ethiopian stock.

Following civil society pressure, the BIS now also publishes data on a locational basis—so that the Swiss-Ethiopian stock shows only the funds of Ethiopian account-holders at Credit Suisse branches in Switzerland—or indeed those of HSBC, etc.

In order to complement international reporting on bilateral funds held by financial institutions, domestic data are required on the extent of declared assets and income streams. For various reasons, some of which underpin non-reportable categories in the CRS and some of which reflect decisions not to seek the relevant information for tax purposes at home, not all accounts held offshore need always be declared to the home tax authority. But good practice suggests that, at a minimum, any decision not to collect all such data should be made clear.

The High Level Panel on Illicit Financial Flows from Africa (pp.65–66) is again clear in its findings on the importance of automatic exchange, and of engagement by lower-income countries:

Transparency is key to achieving success in the fight against IFFs. The admonition of the late Justice Louis D. Brandeis of the United States mentioned earlier that 'sunlight is the best disinfectant' is especially pertinent in this regard. The importance of transparency is evident in ongoing approaches to tackle IFFs, whether through the automatic exchange of information, country-by-country reporting...

Policy implication: *The policy implication of increased transparency is that it should ensure access to such information and the right to obtain it. While various countries and regions are developing mechanisms for information sharing, there is a need to move to a common global mechanism. African countries in turn need to show commitment to the various voluntary and mandatory initiatives by joining them and mainstreaming their requirements nationally and region-ally, including through legislation and adoption of common standards. They also need to develop the capacity to request, process and use the information that they obtain.*

In keeping with this, the construction of an IFF indicator that requires the collation of tax authorities' own data on declarations, and may over time require a wider range of declarations, will have benefits above and beyond the indicator itself.

6.2.3. Methodology

The undeclared offshore assets indicator is defined as the excess of the value of citizens' assets declared by participating jurisdictions under the CRS, over the value declared by citizens themselves for tax purposes. For each jurisdiction we define the undeclared assets as:

$$\phi_i = \textstyle\sum_{j=1}^{n} \beta_{j,i} - \alpha_i \qquad (4)$$

where:

α_i is the sum of assets declared by citizens of jurisdiction i as being held in jurisdictions $j = 1, \ldots, n$ where $j \neq i$; and

$\beta_{j,i}$ is the sum of assets of citizens of jurisdiction i reported as being held in jurisdiction j.

We propose that the undeclared offshore assets indicator for use in SDG target 16.4 is the global sum of jurisdiction-level undeclared assets:

$$SDG_{16.4.1b} = \textstyle\sum_{i=1}^{n} \phi_i \qquad (5)$$

Again, the underlying jurisdiction-level measures will allow monitoring and accountability in a number of ways. Individual states seeking to reduce the under-declaration suffered, for example, will be able to demonstrate to taxpayers that the economic elites who make disproportionate use of 'tax havens' are being fairly taxed. For example, the underlying data would allow France's tax authority to show progress in closing the undeclared assets gap, thereby bolstering revenues and also confidence in the system, with wider benefits for tax morale and compliance.

For states that benefit from providing financial secrecy at the expense of others, the measures offer an accountability mechanism to demonstrate their own commitment to global progress. This would allow Switzerland, for example, to be held to account over the number of countries and the volume of assets for which it still refuses to provide automatic information exchange.

6.2.4. Results

Without systematic publication by tax authorities of the jurisdiction-level aggregate data from declarations of taxpayers' offshore holdings, it is not yet possible for independent researchers to construct the proposed indicator. It is, however, possible to see how it would work.

Knobel (2018c) considers the example of Argentina:

[T]he Argentine media outlets reported that Argentina, an early adopter of the CRS, in 2017 received information about 35,000 foreign accounts, mainly in Belgium, Bermuda, Cayman, France, Isle of Man, Luxembourg, the Netherlands, Spain, and the UK. Interestingly, the US and Switzerland aren't mentioned— because Argentina has no agreement to automatically exchange banking information with the US, and exchanges with Switzerland will only start in 2019.

But because of the data those two countries publish, Argentine authorities still have cards to play. On the one hand, they can check if the total amount of money Argentines declared in US banks matches what the US Treasury reports as belonging to Argentines. If Argentines declared less, then authorities can start investigating who has failed to declare their holdings, or make specific requests for information. The same goes for Switzerland.

. . . If all or most countries (or at least all major financial centres) published these details, a world of new patterns and knowledge would emerge, upon which citizens and responsible governments could act. Now imagine if all CRS adopting countries published this data not just at the legal owner level—as the US and Switzerland currently do (still allowing individuals to hide behind e.g. a company that is holding the bank account), but if countries also published this data at the

beneficial owner level (identifying also the individuals who may be hiding behind a shell company that holds the bank account). The CRS framework already requires beneficial ownership information to be collected and exchanged, so countries are already in a position to publish this aggregated banking data (both at the legal and beneficial ownership level) at no extra cost. A lot more data would emerge, no confidentiality would be breached, and a host of benefits could flow.

An engaged tax authority could construct a range of measures, comparing the gaps between taxpayer declarations of offshore holdings with public BIS data on the bilateral position of financial institutions elsewhere, and with received CRS data. Public, aggregate CRS data would complete the picture.

6.2.5. Conclusions

Like SDG 16.4.1a, this second proposed SDG indicator is a measure, rather than an estimate. In this case the indicator is a measure of the global total of undeclared offshore financial assets, which we take as one result of, and therefore a broad proxy for, the scale of illicit financial flows excluding multinationals' profit shifting.

This second indicator is more ambitious, in two ways. First, it relies on financial centres being willing (or being required) to publish aggregate CRS data. The alternative, of potentially less consistent data from unilateral reporting (as e.g. the US and Switzerland currently do), or from reporting to the Bank for International Settlements, may provide an acceptable alternative in the meantime. Second, the indicator relies on tax authorities being able and willing to collate data on offshore assets declared by taxpayers, in order to demonstrate the gap vis-à-vis CRS reported totals.

6.3. Combining the Two Components

Overall, we believe that the two proposed indicators have the potential to provide global measures, respectively, of the scale of multinationals' profit shifting and of undeclared offshore assets (a key result of all other illicit financial flows). In addition, both indicators are fully decomposable to support jurisdiction-level accountability for those that procure the underlying illicit flows, and those that suffer them—in some cases at least, without sufficient challenge. As such, the adoption of these indicators into the UN SDG framework, after the county pilots, could go a long way to ensuring policy focus and eventually progress against illicit flows.

A final issue to consider is that the proposed measure for undeclared assets is not of a form consistent with the profit shifting indicator. To align the two—so that, for example, they could be added to form a single number as the currently framed UN target envisages—would require a conversion of undeclared asset (stock) into undeclared income (flow).

There are two possible approaches. One would be to assume some rate of return on the measured stock, to estimate the associated annual income flow—much as Henry (2012) and Zucman (2013) do. The fact that those two studies reach similar values for global revenues lost to tax evasion, despite a threefold difference in the asset base, speaks to the sensitivity of such approaches to the assumed rates of return.

The other approach would be to track the growth in total undeclared assets, year to year, as effectively a net flow of undeclared assets. This approach could also be adapted, à la Henry (2012), to allow for given rates of consumption of assets.

A weakness here is that if CRS circumvention through asset class innovation is effective, the data are likely to show falling flows even as the stock of undeclared assets (in non-CRS classes) grows more strongly. This is, of course, also ultimately a weakness of the approach in equation (4)—and so continuing tightening of the asset class definitions will be needed to maintain effectiveness. Using the potentially less sensitive BIS data to provide backup measures of overall scale may be valuable.

Since either conversion of the undeclared assets measure to a flow approach would introduce complications, we would propose to report separately on 16.4.1a and 16.4.1b, rather than seeking to combine the two—but as indicated, conversion and combination are possible if deemed strictly necessary.

In combination, the two measures respond to the main components of illicit flows as presented, most simply, in Table 1.2. Proposed indicator 16.4.1a captures the level of achieved profit shifting by multinationals. Proposed indicator 16.4.1b captures the level of achieved creation of illicit (undeclared) assets offshore, an important result of the remaining IFF types.

7

Conclusion

Estimating illicit financial flows

We began this book by asking: Which flows fall under the umbrella term, 'illicit financial flows'? How will progress in reducing them be measured? How will that progress be achieved? And who is ultimately accountable?

In this closing chapter, we aim to summarise the findings of the volume on these questions. We have reviewed the quality of existing estimates, their methodology and data and the likely scope for progress; and assessed the potential for scale and non-scale indicators of illicit financial flows for global targets, including the Sustainable Development Goals, and for national policy prioritisation.

7.1. Definition of Illicit Financial Flows

To begin with the definitional question, we have argued that IFF are composed of four main elements. Two types typically involve legally-generated capital in illicit transactions. These are 'market abuse' IFF, such as the circumvention of laws constraining monopoly power or political conflicts of interest; and tax abuse IFF. The other two IFF types depend on funds that are illegally obtained at the outset: 'abuse of power' IFF, including the theft of state funds and assets; and the laundering of the proceeds of crime.

The one major controversy around the umbrella term relates to the inclusion of multinational corporate tax avoidance. In UN settings, some OECD member states and lobbyists for some business interests have sought retrospectively to exclude avoidance from the IFF agenda. The argument has been that 'illicit' should be interpreted to mean strictly 'illegal', thereby excluding the lawful component of avoidance behaviour; and that there was no agreed political basis to include avoidance.

The facts speak otherwise. The original promoter of the term, Raymond Baker, did so to promote analysis supporting his important book, *Capitalism's*

Estimating illicit financial flows: A critical guide to the data, methodologies and findings. Alex Cobham and Petr Janský, Oxford University Press (2020). © Alex Cobham and Petr Janský.
DOI: 10.1093/oso/9780198854418.001.0001

Achilles Heel. The thesis of the book is that commercial tax abuses in lower-income countries, above all by companies based in OECD countries, are the largest part of the problem. And 'illicit' is a specifically chosen term with a broader definition than 'illegal'. Per the dictionary, 'illicit' flows include those that are socially forbidden as well as those that are legally forbidden. In this case, that means at least part of the *lawful* avoidance practices, as well as the unlawful. Given the existence of both, there can be no argument for the exclusion of multinationals' tax behaviour in total from the scope of the work.

Nor is there any doubt that this was the intention of the politics underpinning the emergence of the umbrella term, including the creation of target 16.4 in the globally agreed UN Sustainable Development Goals. The driving force, African Union and UN Economic Commission for Africa's High Level Panel on Illicit Financial Flows from Africa, takes multinational tax avoidance (lawful or otherwise) as a central concern. The UN Secretary-General's High Level Panel of Eminent Persons on the Post-2015 Development Agenda shared this emphasis.

Nonetheless, there are genuine and important differences in the nature of multinational tax avoidance and a range of other IFF. To this end, while the umbrella term has carried the issues forward together to international policy prominence, we generally support more closely defined policy approaches to the individual types.

The common feature that unites all IFF is the use of financial secrecy to obscure the true nature of the transactions, or their underlying ownership, precisely because of their socially or legally forbidden nature. That same feature, of course, makes measurement problematic. If IFF were easily quantified, they would equally be easily seen—and so, by definition, less likely. While this points towards greater financial transparency as a major element of the necessary policy response, it also underlines the difficulties of the work surveyed in Part 2: estimation of the deliberately hidden is challenging.

The common impacts of vulnerability to IFF are, broadly, two-fold. First, in extracting and hiding capital, IFF erode the resource available for development—whether through exploitation of state assets or contracts, or through direct tax revenue losses. Second, IFF tend to be associated, both through the tax channel and otherwise, with weakening governance. The combination of lower resources for public spending, and a less effective, less representative state governing their expenditure, creates a doubly damaging impact on the prospects for human development and efforts to curtail inequality.

7.2. Estimates of IFF

7.2.1. Trade estimates

From the analysis of trade-based IFF estimates in chapter 2, we draw three main conclusions. First, international trade is an active channel for illicit financial flows and the research leading to trade estimates has been useful in a number of respects. From numerous case studies as well as indicatively from a number of aggregate studies reviewed here we learn about the use of trade mispricing to transfer funds illicitly across borders. The trade estimates have been helpful in shedding light on international trade data discrepancies. Also, many of the relevant studies have proven useful for customs officers in highlighting cases suitable for more detailed audit and for policy makers in underlying areas of potential concern. We consider most of the recent transaction-level studies credible for estimation of the scale of trade-based illicit flows. In contrast, the estimates based on the trade mirror statistics approach and country-level data might have been helpful in the past for raising awareness about these issues, but we do not consider them credible enough to inform us about the scale of illicit financial flows over time. We consider some of the abnormal pricing estimates useful as indicators for audit and other purposes, but we would not rely on them for the estimates on overall scale.

Second, we observe improvements in the methodology applied by Global Financial Integrity and other researchers in their quest to provide more reliable trade data-based estimates of illicit financial flows. Nevertheless, the employment of the trade estimates for the SDG target is not straightforward. We recognise that much of research has been carried out recently on trade mis-invoicing and on trade as a channel of illicit financial flows for many countries, and that there is an argument for its inclusion in the indicator of the target as discussed by, among others, the United Nations Economic Commission for Africa (ECA) (2015), Economic Commission for Latin America and the Caribbean (2016) and, most recently, by Kravchenko (2018) of the United Nations Economic and Social Commission for Asia and the Pacific (ESCAP). However, we find that their estimates are still not of sufficient reliability, and allow for a wider interpretation than illicit financial flows. There is also a new research frontier generating stronger trade estimates based on relatively high-quality data and methods. We judge the quality of these research estimates as sufficient, but their country coverage is poor and it does not seem feasible to extend them to many more countries in a foreseeable future. Indeed, there seems to be a trade-off for the trade estimates—either they are available for many countries but not credible or they are of relatively high quality but available only for a few countries (and, furthermore, it is difficult to compare the estimates across the few countries). Clearly, more research in this area is required. For the time being, no indicator from the group of trade estimates seems to be workable as the indicator of the SDG target.

Third, identify a number of few promising areas of further research, but none of them seem promising enough in the medium term to enable their inclusion as the SDG target indicator. One option is to improve the current methods, either at the country level—as exemplified by the GFI recent changes or Kellenberg & Levinson (2016)—or at more detailed, commodity-level such as ECA (2015). Another promising area of future policy-relevant research is extending the current transaction-level methods to more countries, while making sure that they are comparable, ideally, across both countries and years. Even more reliable than the current one-country one-data-source studies would be estimates based on customs data from both countries of the trading pair involved in any given transaction examined for illicitness. Before transactions-level data are available in most countries, to reach near-global coverage it might be worth trying to adapt these methodologies for trade data sets (e.g. UN Comtrade) with less detailed data but better country coverage. Indeed, something similar is what Kellenberg & Levinson (2016) did with trade mirror statistics method and UN Comtrade data. But so far, given the data limitations, a better country coverage can be attained to some extent only at the expense of credible methodology.

7.2.2.   Capital and offshore wealth

From the analysis of capital estimates in chapter 3, we conclude that while they allow a good coverage of countries and years and are feasible (perhaps explaining their use in the most prominent estimates so far), they lack the required quality and should not be seen as reliable indicators of illicit financial flows. Capital estimates can be useful in specific cases, as exemplified by Novokmet, Piketty, & Zucman (2018), but at the moment this does not seem promising as a basis for an indicator of the SDG target.

In relation to estimates of offshore wealth, we identify five main findings. First, offshore wealth estimates are and should be an integral part of the mission to estimate the scale of illicit financial flows. Wealth held in tax havens is a direct consequence of some of the illicit financial flows heading from onshore to offshore. The Panama Papers and other offshore leaks have highlighted the importance of financial secrecy and offshore wealth. A country should be clearly better off when a lower share of its wealth is held offshore. Illicit financial flows that result in offshore wealth in be reduced and this should contribute to sustainable development.

Second, offshore wealth is clearly important and the scale seems to be substantial. The recent estimates of Alstadsaeter, Johannesen, & Zucman (2018) put the scale of financial offshore wealth at 10 per cent of world GDP, with some countries much more vulnerable. This is supported by other estimates, including the capital estimates, that usually arrive at even higher projections of offshore wealth. Some current estimates are not based on official data or require crucial assumptions to arrive at specific-country estimates. Some other current estimates—namely capital estimates on the basis of balance of payments data—are not so reliable. From the point of view of the SDG target indicator, it would be useful if these strengths were combined in one reliable indicator—based on official statistical data, and without the need for important assumptions.

Third, undeclared offshore wealth can be reduced and this makes it policy-relevant as a basis for the SDG target indicator. Offshore wealth estimates vary widely across countries and tax havens. On the one hand, there is a lot of heterogeneity among countries having wealth in tax havens. On the other hand, the role of Switzerland seems to be declining which might be due to changes in international regulations influencing offshore wealth, such as exchange of information, to which Switzerland, in the end, agreed. Furthermore, recent research has shown that a focus by tax authorities on wealth held by individuals offshore might bring the wealth onshore. For example, Johannesen, Langetieg, Reck, Risch, & Slemrod (2018) find that the US Internal Revenue Service's enforcement efforts initiated in 2008 caused approximately 60 thousand people to disclose offshore accounts with a combined value of around $120 billion. Overall, a reduction in undeclared, offshore wealth seems a suitable policy target.

Fourth, the SDG target is set in terms of illicit financial flows, while offshore wealth is usually estimated as a stock. This creates a technical challenge in harmonising the expectations of the target and the actual estimates. One potential solution is to estimate the income streams (perhaps comparable to the notion of illicit financial flows) that may accrue on offshore assets. For example, Johannesen & Pirttilä (2016) provide a comparison of these: both

Henry (2012) and Zucman (2013) estimate an offshore income stream of around $190 billion annually (Henry assumes a much more cautious rate of his return, on his much higher estimated stock). However, the additional extrapolations (from outflows to stocks, and then to potential income streams) inevitably add a higher degree of uncertainty.

Fifth and overall, the offshore wealth estimates are promising with respect to the indicator of the SDG target with some of the leading estimates—Alstadsaeter, Johannesen, & Zucman (2018)—being of very high quality. Although the offshore wealth estimates are not so strong in the coverage of countries and years, it might be feasible to extend them given the expected improvement in the availability of the relevant data and we discuss these opportunities in our proposal for new indicators.

7.2.3.   International corporate tax avoidance

From chapter 4, we draw six key points of conclusion. First, profit shifting by multinationals to tax havens and associated international corporate tax avoidance falls under illicit financial flows, as we argue at the beginning of the chapter as well as in the book's introduction. These are illicit rather than illegal flows and thus inclusion of profit shifting is appropriate because we consider the practice of profit shifting illicit and leave the question of legality mostly to others. Our concern is a zemiological one, focused on the harm done. Low- and middle-income countries seem to be more intensively affected by profit shifting and this makes even stronger the case for its inclusion in the Sustainable Development Goals' target to curtail illicit financial flows. Also, the international policy consensus, expressed in the G20/OECD BEPS project, is that multinationals' profit misalignment should be curtailed: 'The G20 finance ministers called on the OECD to develop an action plan to address BEPS issues in a co-ordinated and comprehensive manner. Specifically, this Action Plan should provide countries with domestic and international instruments that will *better align rights to tax with economic activity*' (OECD, 2013a, p.11, emphasis added). We thus see profit shifting as an integral part of the scale of illicit financial flows that should be reduced.

Second, profit shifting is a real phenomenon, and there is now a large body of evidence consistent with MNEs shifting profits illicitly from where economic activity occurs to tax havens. A clear conclusion emerges that the international tax system provides MNEs with opportunities to decrease their taxes through intra-company transfer prices, strategic management of the location of intangible assets or distortion of the corporate debt structure. The research confirms that many MNEs do often make use of these opportunities and do shift income to tax havens (Clausing, 2003; Hines & Rice, 1994; Huizinga & Laeven, 2008). However, until recently, the literature had been less conclusive in respect of scale and revenue implications. The quality and coverage of estimates has improved substantially in recent years, and for coverage of countries in particular - with direct relevance to estimates of the scale and harms of illicit financial flows.

Third, profit shifting is an important phenomenon of substantial scale— economically, statistically, as well as in terms of revenues lost. The various studies estimate that governments worldwide lose more than 100 billion USD annually. The existing research indicates that the scale of shifted profits and revenue losses are widely distributed across jurisdictions, with the highest values in high-income countries but the most intense losses in relation to GDP and especially to tax revenues, in lower-income countries. In contrast, only a small number of jurisdictions are consistently the recipients of disproportionate volumes of profit related to economic activity elsewhere. Furthermore, Guvenen, Mataloni Jr, Rassier, & Ruhl (2017) and Tørsløv, Wier, & Zucman (2018) provide estimates of profit shifting impacts on macroeconomic aggregates such as gross domestic product that are statistically important.

Fourth and perhaps more obviously, profit shifting can be curbed. Although it has over the past couple of decades grown into an important economic phenomenon, it has not always been so big. Some studies, such as Cobham & Janský (2019) and Tørsløv, Wier, & Zucman (2018), show that in the 1980s profit shifting was a much smaller concern. This historical account can thus help us understand that profit shifting is not an inherent feature of global economy and that it can work well (or, indeed, better) without it. How to measure progress in reducing profit shifting is an important matter that has been increasingly addressed since 2013 both by academics and policy experts, so far without clear recommendations.

Fifth, in terms of methodology, three recent studies stand out as particularly useful when thinking about an indicator for the SDG. Although each of Tørsløv, Wier, & Zucman (2018), Cobham & Janský (2019) and IMF (2014) uses different methodology and reaches different results, all three of them have much in common that is desired for an indicator of the SDG target. They all rely on official statistical sources, mostly either national accounts data or official statistics of foreign affiliates of MNEs. Their methodological approaches are relatively straightforward, which makes them feasible and transparent. All of them rely on basic ratios of various economic variables. None of them uses regression analysis, which might be hard to implement as a part of the SDG target indicator, whereas all the other four studies rely on regressions in reaching their conclusions. Another methodological similarity is that they all make use of the comparison between what the profits or tax revenues are and what they should be in the absence of profit shifting. Also, all of them take quite literally the BEPS objective of better aligning rights to tax with economic activity that will help guide our proposal when we make it in chapter 6. In sum, IMF (2014), Cobham & Janský (2019) and Tørsløv, Wier, & Zucman (2018) apply straightforward methodologies to publicly available, official, government-sponsored. We are confident that these observations help us design a new indicator that would overcome some remaining draw-backs these estimates have, such as data quality and selection of specific economic variables.

Sixth, there is no perfect indicator operationalised in the literature that could be used as it is and applied for the SDG target. Some of the research reviewed is promising, and we believe that a workable indicator is within reach. Perhaps the biggest challenge is the necessary consensus of national statistical offices on which specific version of a profit shifting indicator should be used for the target. This, again, fuels the thinking for proposals for new indicators.

7.3. IFF Indicators

7.3.1. Non-scale IFF indicators

In chapter 5, we survey the range of policy indicators and risk-based IFF indicators that have been proposed. The last fifteen years have seen important progress towards a global agenda for greater financial transparency in key areas, including the Tax Justice Network's ABC of tax transparency:

- Automatic, multilateral exchange of tax information
- Beneficial ownership (public registers for companies, trusts and foundations); and
- Country-by-country reporting by multinational companies, in public.

Alongside has come a growth in data on jurisdictions' adherence to these and broader measures of transparency and international cooperation in the sphere of financial regulation and tax. The Financial Secrecy Index includes 20 secrecy indicators, each based on a range of sub-indicators from international organisations and direct research, and so provides a broad snapshot of progress at jurisdiction and global level.

The set of policy targets for the SDGs proposed by Cobham (2014), as an alternative or complement to the scale-based target then under consideration, provides one set of possible indicators of jurisdictions' performance against the ABC. One attraction of this approach is that it identifies clearly the accountabilities of jurisdictions that resist transparency, and thereby heighten IFF risks for others. The disadvantages are that the approach neither generates scale measures as SDG 16.4 requires, nor provides an immediate basis for policy decisions in jurisdictions that suffer from IFF.

The risk-based measures aim to address the latter point. The approach of the Bilateral Financial Secrecy Index allows policymakers to identify clearly the secrecy jurisdictions that pose the greatest IFF threat, not globally but to their specific jurisdiction or region. The IFF vulnerability measures pioneered in the report of the High Level Panel on Illicit Financial Flows from Africa provide granular policy analysis, identifying both the relative risk in various trade, investment and banking channels, and also the bilateral partners responsible for those risks in each. Overall, these approaches can empower policymakers to undertake the most effective responses to the specific IFF risks faced—and at the same time allow progress to be demonstrated, and also for the spotlight of accountability to be shone on those jurisdictions that impose risks on others.

7.3.2. SDG proposals

In chapter 6, we present the two proposed indicators that now form part of the country pilot process for SDG 16.4. These draw on the analysis presented throughout this volume, in a range of ways. First, despite the common elements of exploiting financial secrecy to circumvent laws and social oversight, there is an important distinction in IFF related to multinational tax avoidance and other types. This leads us to propose two indicators, separating these out.

Second, the proposals reflect the broad conclusion that *at present* there is no approach that can generate sufficiently robust and broadly global IFF scale estimates. For that reason, both draw on potentially newly available data to construct direct measures, rather than estimates.

Third, the assessment of policy- and risk-based measures leads us to the conclusion that the SDG indicators will best support accountability if they are fully disaggregable to the jurisdiction level, and allow tracking of progress both by those who exacerbate illicit flows from elsewhere, and those who suffer IFF.

The first indicator relates to the profit shifting of multinationals. While estimates of shifting continue to develop apace, none as yet provide the consistency that would be required for SDG indicators. But the most promising approaches point the way, by seeking to measure profit *misalignment* (i.e. profits declared in other jurisdictions than those of the underlying economic activity)—which thanks to new country-by-country reporting requirements can now be measured.

The second proposed indicator captures a core outcome of other illicit flows—namely, the creation of undeclared assets held offshore, following the insights of Henry (2012). Once again, using newly available data that is now feasible due to the multilateral instrument for automatic exchange of information on financial accounts, we propose a direct measure of the gap between what is reported to tax authorities, and what is notified elsewhere by financial institutions.

In each case we identify potential sources of data for national-level work-around solutions, where international arrangements may not yet give rise to full access in each country. Overall, of course, there is a powerful case for a consistent, global effort to raise the standard of data available—perhaps, ultimately, through changes to the system of national accounts to ensure comparable data worldwide.

7.4. Conclusions

This book has laid out the 'state of the art' in the literature that aims to assess the scale of key channels of illicit financial flows. Our intention, in part, has been to create a reference text that is otherwise absent, to help to guide researchers, activists and policymakers through the maze of the many numbers out there—to find the right ones that can best support appropriate responses.

We have also identified the most promising approaches for further development, including where methodological improvements or enhanced data can give rise to new insights. We have surveyed the leading non-scale indicators, based on policy measures and IFF risks associated with exposure to other jurisdictions' financial secrecy, that may ultimately provide the strongest basis for national and international counter-measures and accountability.

Finally, we have presented our proposed indicators for target 16.4 of the UN Sustainable Development Goals, which represents the single best chance for global progress against these damaging phenomena which undermine both the resources available for states to support development, and the capacity of states to pursue inclusive, politically representative development strategies.

As we write in 2019, the degree of lobbying of UN agencies by multinational companies poses a serious threat to the prospect for meaningful indicators being agreed under SDG 16.4. In addition, the United States and some EU members have increasingly sought in UN negotiations to exclude multinational companies from the scope of any measures relating to illicit financial flows. At the same time, however, the OECD has embarked upon a new reform of the international tax rules which seeks explicitly to address the distribution of taxing rights between countries.

Recognising that progress on indicators for SDG 16.4 is not certain, and that wider measures will be needed in any case to achieve the target, two policy instruments are proposed in addition (see Cobham, 2019, for a longer exposition). One is a convention on tax and transparency. This could include commitments around the tax rules for multinationals, but would at a minimum set international standards for the full inclusion of countries at all income levels in the application and benefits of the ABC of transparency.

The other proposal is for a UN centre to monitor taxing rights. This would be charged with curating and publishing data with global coverage on the cross-border patterns of profit misalignment and of financial asset ownership—that is, the detailed data underlying the proposed indicators for SDG 16.4, and based on the extension of the ABC of transparency to all jurisdictions regardless of income level. An annual report would reveal the extent to which each country is able to exert taxing rights over profits associated with economic activity in their jurisdiction, and over the offshore financial assets of their tax residents.

The assessment here of methodologies to estimate illicit financial flows is not, and cannot be the last word. Such is the research attention in this field now that new papers appear increasingly frequently, often with quite new approaches and data sources. At the same time, international progress against financial secrecy continues to open new possibilities for better data and ultimately to curtail illicit flows themselves. Our hope is for strong indicators in the SDGs, to underpin accountability for the jurisdictions and actors driving illicit flows—and strong progress to follow.

References

Abugre, C., Cobham, A., Etter-Phoya, R., Lépissier, A., Meinzer, M., Monkam, N., & Mosioma, A. (2019). *Vulnerability and Exposure to Illicit Financial Flows risk in Africa.* Retrieved from https://www.taxjustice.net/wp-content/uploads/2019/08/Vulnerability-and-Exposure-to-Illicit-Financial-Flows-risk-in-Africa_August-2019_Tax-Justice-Network.pdf

Alstadsaeter, A., Johannesen, N., & Zucman, G. (2017). *Tax Evasion and Inequality.* Retrieved from Working Paper website: http://www.nielsjohannesen.net/wp-content/uploads/AJZ2017.pdf

Alstadsaeter, A., Johannesen, N., & Zucman, G. (2018). Who Owns the Wealth in Tax Havens? Macro Evidence and Implications for Global Inequality. *Journal of Public Economics, 162*(2018), 89–100.

Alvarez-Martinez, M., Barrios, S., d'Andria, D., Gesualdo, M., Nicodème, G., & Pycroft, J. (2018). *How Large is the Corporate Tax Base Erosion and Profit Shifting? A General Equilibrium Approach* (CEPR Discussion Paper No. 12637). Retrieved from C.E.P.R. Discussion Papers website: https://econpapers.repec.org/paper/cprceprdp/12637.htm

Andersen, J. J., Johannesen, N., Lassen, D. D., & Paltseva, E. (2017). Petro rents, political institutions, and hidden wealth: Evidence from offshore bank accounts. *Journal of the European Economic Association, 15*(4), 818–60.

Bach, S. (2013). *Has German Business Income Taxation Raised Too Little Revenue Over the Last Decades?* Retrieved from http://www.diw-berlin.de/documents/publikationen/73/diw_01.c.421801.de/dp1303.pdf

Baker, R. W. (2005). *Capitalism's Achilles heel: Dirty money and how to renew the free-market system.* Retrieved from http://books.google.com/books?hl=en&lr=&id=Wkd0—M6p_oC&oi=fnd&pg=PA1&dq=baker+Capitalism%27s+Achilles+Heel&ots=lhWaH-yU4T&sig=x4bDn0uTB86PJCY99Zvbr29_8ps

Bartelsman, E. J., & Beetsma, R. M. (2003). Why pay more? Corporate tax avoidance through transfer pricing in OECD countries. *Journal of Public Economics, 87*(9–10), 2225–52.

Beer, S., Mooij, R. de, & Liu, L. (2019). International Corporate Tax Avoidance: A Review of the Channels, Magnitudes, and Blind Spots. *Journal of Economic Surveys.* https://doi.org/10.1111/joes.12305

Beja, E. (2005). Capital flight: Meanings and measures. *Capital Flight and Capital Controls in Developing Countries* in Epstein, G. A. (Ed.). (2005). *Capital flight and capital controls in developing countries* (pp. 58–82). Edward Elgar Publishing.

Beja, E. L. (2008). Estimating Trade Mis-invoicing from China: 2000–2005. *China & World Economy, 16*(2), 82–92. https://doi.org/10.1111/j.1749-124X.2008.00108.x

Berger, H., & Nitsch, V. (2012). Gotcha! A profile of smuggling in international trade. In C. C. Storti & P. De Grauwe (Eds.), *Illicit Trade and the Global Economy.* Retrieved from https://papers.ssrn.com/sol3/papers.cfm?abstract_id=1310068

Bernard, A. B., Jensen, J. B., & Schott, P. K. (2006). *Transfer Pricing by U.S.-Based Multinational Firms* (Working Paper No. 12493). https://doi.org/10.3386/w12493

Bhagwati, J. (1964). On the underinvoicing of imports. *Oxford Bulletin of Economics and Statistics, 27*(4), 389–97.

Bhagwati, J. N. (1974). On the underinvoicing of imports. In *Illegal Transactions in International Trade* (pp. 138–47). Elsevier.

Bilicka, K. A. (2019). Comparing UK Tax Returns of Foreign Multinationals to Matched Domestic Firms. *American Economic Review, 109*(8), 2921–53.

Blankenburg, S., & Khan, M. (2012). Governance and illicit flows. Draining development, 21–68. In Reuter, P. *Draining development?: Controlling flows of illicit funds from developing countries.* https://elibrary.worldbank.org/doi/abs/10.1596/978-0-8213-8869-3#page=39

Bloomquist, K. M., Hamilton, S., & Pope, J. (2014). Estimating Corporation Income Tax Under-Reporting Using Extreme Values from Operational Audit Data. *Fiscal Studies, 35*(4), 401–19. https://doi.org/10.1111/j.1475-5890.2014.12036.x

Boston Consulting Group (2017). *Global Wealth 2017: Transforming the Client Experience.* Boston.

Boyce, J., & Ndikumana, L. (2000). Is Africa a net creditor? New estimates of capital flight from severely indebted African countries, 1970–1996. *Working Paper 2000–01,* Department of Economics, University of Massachusetts at Amherst, MA.

Brautigam, D., Fjeldstad, O.-H., & Moore, M. (2008). *Taxation and state-building in developing countries: Capacity and consent.* Cambridge University Press.

Broms, R. (2011). Taxation and government quality. *QoG Working Paper Series, 2011*(16), 16.

Brülhart, M., Kukenova, M., & Dihel, N. (2015). More than copper: toward the diversification and stabilization of Zambian exports. *World Bank Policy Research Working Paper,* (7151).

Buettner, T., & Wamser, G. (2013). Internal debt and multinational profit shifting: Empirical evidence from firm-level panel data. *National Tax Journal, 66*(1), 63.

Carbonnier, G., & Mehrotra, R. (2019). Abnormal Pricing in International Commodity Trade: Empirical Evidence from Switzerland. *Discussion Paper.*

Carbonnier, G., & Zweynert de Cadena, A. (2015). Commodity Trading and Illicit Financial Flows. *International Development Policy|Revue internationale de politique de développement.* Retrieved from http://journals.openedition.org/poldev/2054

Carter, P., & Cobham, A. (2016). *Are taxes good for your health?* WIDER Working Paper.

Carton, C., & Slim, S. (2018). Trade misinvoicing in OECD countries: what can we learn from bilateral trade intensity indices?

Cathey, J., Hong, K. P., & Pak, S. J. (2018). Estimates of undervalued import of EU Countries and the U.S. from the Democratic Republic of Congo during 2000–2010. *The International Trade Journal, 32*(1), 116–28. https://doi.org/10.1080/08853908.2017.1377650

Celasun, M., & Rodrik, D. (1989a). IV: Debt, Adjustment, and Growth: Turkey. In *Developing Country Debt and Economic Performance, Volume 3: Country Studies-Indonesia, Korea, Philippines, Turkey* (pp. 615–16). Retrieved from http://www.nber.org/chapters/c9056.pdf

Celasun, M., & Rodrik, D. (1989b). Turkish experience with debt: macroeconomic policy and performance. In *Developing country debt and the world economy* (pp. 193–211). Retrieved from http://www.nber.org/chapters/c7526.pdf

Chalendard, C., Raballand, G., & Rakotoarisoa, A. (2019). The use of detailed statistical data in customs reforms: The case of Madagascar. *Development Policy Review, 37*(4), 546–563.

Christensen, J., Kapoor, S., Murphy, R., Pak, S., & Spencer, D. (2007). Closing the floodgates–collecting tax to pay for development (Commissioned by the Norwegian Ministry of Foreign Affairs and Tax Justice Network). London: Tax Justice Network.

Christian Aid. (2008). *Death and Taxes: The True Toll of Tax Dodging.* Retrieved from Christian Aid website: http://www.christianaid.org.uk/images/deathandtaxes.pdf

Christian Aid. (2009). *False Profits: robbing the poor to keep the rich tax-free.* Retrieved from Christian Aid website: www.christianaid.org.uk/Images/false-profits.pdf

Claessens, S., & Naude, D. (1993). *Recent estimates of capital flight.* World Bank Washington, DC.

Clausing, K. A. (2003). Tax-motivated transfer pricing and US intrafirm trade prices. *Journal of Public Economics, 87*(9–10), 2207–23. https://doi.org/10.1016/S0047-2727(02)00015-4

Clausing, K. A. (2007). Corporate tax revenues in OECD countries. *International Tax and Public Finance, 14*(2), 115–33.

Clausing, K. A. (2009). Multinational Firm Tax Avoidance and Tax Policy. *National Tax Journal, 62*(4), 703–25.

Clausing, K. A. (2011). The revenue effects of multinational firm income shifting. *Tax Notes, March, 28.* Retrieved from http://papers.ssrn.com/sol3/papers.cfm?abstract_id=2488860

Clausing, K. A. (2016). The Effect of Profit Shifting on the Corporate Tax Base in the United States and Beyond. *National Tax Journal, 69*(4), 905–34. https://doi.org/10.17310/ntj.2016.4.09

Cloke, J., & Brown, E. (2019). Speaking in riddles: The Panama Papers and the global financial services sector. *Area, 51*(1), 190–2. https://doi.org/10.1111/area.12431

Cobham, A. (2005). Tax evasion, tax avoidance and development finance. *Queen Elizabeth House, Série Documents de Travail,* (129). Retrieved from http://www.gazdasagkifeheritese. uni-corvinus.hu/images/0/0c/Gazdasagi_fejlodes_es_adozas.pdf

Cobham, Alex. (2005). *Tax evasion, tax avoidance and development finance* (No. 129; pp. 1–20). Retrieved from University of Oxford, Queen Elizabeth House website: http:// www3.qeh.ox.ac.uk/pdf/qehwp/qehwps129.pdf

Cobham, Alex. (2007). *The tax consensus has failed! Recommendation to policymakers and donors, researchers and civil society.* Retrieved from Oxford Council on Good Governance website: http://www.oxfordgovernance.org/fileadmin/Publications/ER008.pdf

Cobham, Alex. (2014). *Benefits and Costs of the IFF Targets for the Post-2015 Development Agenda.* Retrieved from https://www.copenhagenconsensus.com/sites/default/files/ iff_assessment_-_cobham_0.pdf

Cobham, Alex. (2018). Benefits and Costs of the IFF Targets for the Post-2015 Development Agenda. In B. Lomborg (Ed.), *Prioritizing Development: A Cost Benefit Analysis of the United Nations' Sustainable Development Goals* (pp. 171–91). https://doi. org/10.1017/9781108233767.010

Cobham, Alex (2019). *The Uncounted.* Cambridge: Polity Press.

Cobham, Alex, Davis, W., Ibrahim, G., & Sumner, A. (2016). Hidden Inequality: How Much Difference Would Adjustment for Illicit Financial Flows Make to National Income Distributions? *Journal of Globalization and Development, 7*(2). https://doi.org/10.1515/ jgd-2016-0022

Cobham, Alex, & Gibson, L. (2016). *Ending the Era of Tax Havens. Why the UK government must lead the way.* Retrieved from http://oxfamilibrary.openrepository.com/ oxfam/bitstream/10546/601121/4/bp-ending-era-tax-havens-uk-140316-en.pdf

Cobham, Alex, Gray, J., & Murphy, Richard. (2017). *What Do They Pay? Towards a Public Database to Account for the Economic Activities and Tax Contributions of Multinational Corporations.* City Political Economy Research Centre, Working Paper Series, 1. Retrieved from www.city.ac.uk/__data/assets/pdf_file/0004/345469/CITYPERC-WPS-201701.pdf

Cobham, Alex, & Janský, P. (2017a). *Global distribution of revenue loss from tax avoidance: Re-estimation and country results* (UNU-WIDER Working Paper No. 55; pp. 1–28). Helsinki: UNU-WIDER.

Cobham, Alex, & Janský, P. (2017b). *Illicit financial flows: An overview* (pp. 1–50) [Background paper for the Intergovernmental Group of Experts on Financing for Development, first session, 8–10 November 2017]. Retrieved from UNCTAD website: http://unctad.org/en/Pages/MeetingDetails.aspx?meetingid=1442

Cobham, Alex, & Janský, P. (2017c). *Measurement of Illicit Financial Flows* [Background paper Prepared for UNCTAD. UNODC-UNCTAD Expert consultation on the SDG Indicator on Illicit financial flows 12–14 December 2017.].

Cobham, Alex, & Janský, P. (2017d). Measurement of Illicit Financial Flows [Background paper Prepared for UNCTAD. UNODC-UNCTAD Expert consultation on the SDG Indicator on Illicit financial flows 12–14 December 2017.].

Cobham, Alex, & Janský, P. (2018a). Global distribution of revenue loss from corporate tax avoidance: re-estimation and country results. *Journal of International Development, 30*(2), 206–32. https://doi.org/10.1002/jid.3348

Cobham, Alex, & Janský, P. (2018b). *Measurement of Illicit Financial Flows: Towards SDG indicators* [Background paper Prepared for UNECA.].

Cobham, Alex, & Janský, P. (2019). Measuring misalignment: The location of US multinationals' economic activity versus the location of their profits. *Development Policy Review, 37*(1), 91–110. https://doi.org/10.1111/dpr.12315

Cobham, Alex, Janský, P., & Meinzer, M. (2015). The financial secrecy index: Shedding new light on the geography of secrecy. *Economic Geography, 91*(3), 281–303.

Cobham, Alex, Janský, P., & Meinzer, M. (2018). A half-century of resistance to corporate disclosure. *Transnational Corporations, 25*(3), 1–26.

Cobham, Alex, & Loretz. (2014). International distribution of the corporate tax base: Implications of different apportionment factors under unitary taxation. *International Centre for Tax and Development Working Paper, 2014*(27).

Collier, P., Hoeffler, A., & Pattillo, C. (2001). Flight capital as a portfolio choice. *The World Bank Economic Review, 15*(1), 55–80.

Collins, J., Kemsley, D., & Lang, M. (1998). Cross-jurisdictional income shifting and earnings valuation. *Journal of Accounting Research, 36*(2), 209–29.

Comtrade. (2018). United Nations Statistics Division—Commodity Trade Statistics Database (COMTRADE). Retrieved March 9, 2018, from https://comtrade.un.org/db/help/ureadMeFirst.aspx

Cristea, A. D., & Nguyen, D. X. (2016). Transfer Pricing by Multinational Firms: New Evidence from Foreign Firm Ownerships. *American Economic Journal: Economic Policy, 8*(3), 170–202.

Crivelli, E., de Mooij, R., & Keen, M. (2016). Base Erosion, Profit Shifting and Developing Countries. *FinanzArchiv: Public Finance Analysis, 72*(3), 268–301. https://doi.org/10.162 8/001522116X14646834385460

Cuddington, J. T. (1987). Capital flight. *European Economic Review, 31*(1–2), 382–8.

Davies, R. B., Martin, J., Parenti, M., & Toubal, F. (2017). Knocking on Tax Haven's Door: Multinational Firms and Transfer Pricing. *The Review of Economics and Statistics.* https://doi.org/10.1162/REST_a_00673

De Boyrie, M. E., Pak, S. J., & Zdanowicz, J. S. (2005). Estimating the magnitude of capital flight due to abnormal pricing in international trade: The Russia–USA case. *Accounting Forum, 29*(3), 249–70.

de Boyrie, M. E., Pak, S., & Zdanowicz, J. S. (2005). The Impact of Switzerland's Money Laundering Law on Capital Flows Through Abnormal Pricing in International Trade. *Applied Financial Economics*, 15(4), 217–30.

Devereux, M. (2007). *Developments in the Taxation of Corporate Profit in the OECD since 1965: Rates, Bases and Revenues*. Retrieved from http://eureka.sbs.ox.ac.uk/3393/

Dharmapala, D. (2014). What Do We Know about Base Erosion and Profit Shifting? A Review of the Empirical Literature. *Fiscal Studies*, 35(4), 421–48. https://doi.org/10.1111/j.1475-5890.2014.12037.x

Dharmapala, D., & Riedel, N. (2013). Earnings shocks and tax-motivated income-shifting: Evidence from European multinationals. *Journal of Public Economics*, 97, 95–107.

Dischinger, M., & Riedel, N. (2011). Corporate taxes and the location of intangible assets within multinational firms. *Journal of Public Economics*, 95(7), 691–707.

Dooley, M. P. (1988). Capital Flight: A Response to Differences in Financial Risks. *Staff Papers*, 35(3), 422–36. https://doi.org/10.2307/3867180

Dorling, D., Gordon, D., Hillyard, P., Pantazis, C., Pemberton, S., & Tombs, S. (2008). *Criminal obsessions: Why harm matters more than crime*. Centre for Crime and Justice Studies.

Dowd, T., Landefeld, P., & Moore, A. (2017). Profit shifting of U.S. multinationals. *Journal of Public Economics*, 148, 1–13. https://doi.org/10.1016/j.jpubeco.2017.02.005

Dyreng, S., & Markle, K. (2013). *The effects of taxes and financial constraints on income shifting by US multinationals*. Retrieved from http://areas.kenan-flagler.unc.edu/conferences/2013cfea/Documents/Markle-Dyreng.pdf

Economic Commission for Africa. (2018a). A study on the global governance architecture for combating illicit financial flow. Addis Ababa: Ethopia. https://www.uneca.org/sites/default/files/PublicationFiles/global-governance_eng_rev.pdf

Economic Commission for Africa. (2018b). Base Erosion And Profit Shifting In Africa: Reforms to Facilitate Improved Taxation of Multinational Enterprises.

Economic Commission for Latin America and the Caribbean. (2016). *Economic Survey of Latin America and the Caribbean 2016: The 2030 Agenda for Sustainable Development and the challenges of financing for development* [Text]. Retrieved from https://www.cepal.org/en/publications/40327-economic-survey-latin-america-and-caribbean-2016-2030-agenda-sustainable

EPRS. (2015). *Bringing transparency, coordination and convergence to corporate tax policies in the European Union: Assessment of the magnitude of aggressive corporate tax planning*. Retrieved from http://www.europarl.europa.eu/thinktank/en/document.html?reference=EPRS_STU(2015)558773

EPRS. (2016). *Bringing transparency, coordination and convergence to corporate tax policies in the European Union: II—Evaluation of the European Added Value of the recommendations in the ECON legislative own-initiative draft report*. Retrieved from http://www.europarl.europa.eu/RegData/etudes/STUD/2016/558776/EPRS_STU(2016)558776_EN.pdf

Erbe, S. (1985). The flight of capital from developing countries. *Intereconomics*, 20(6), 268–75.

Erskine, A. (2018). *3-part series on Illicit Financial Flows: Making Sense of Confusion*. Retrieved from https://erskinomics.com/2018/10/12/3-part-series-on-illicit-financial-flows-making-sense-of-confusion/

European Commission. (2013). *Proposal for a Council Directive on a Common Consolidated Corporate Tax Base (CCCTB)*. Retrieved from https://ec.europa.eu/taxation_customs/business/company-tax/common-consolidated-corporate-tax-base-ccctb_en

European Commission. (2016a). *Proposal for a Council Directive on a Common Consolidated Corporate Tax Base (CCCTB)*. Retrieved from https://ec.europa.eu/taxation_customs/business/company-tax/common-consolidated-corporate-tax-base-ccctb_en

European Commission. (2016b). *The concept of tax gaps—report on VAT gap estimations*. Retrieved from http://ec.europa.eu/taxation_customs/resources/documents/common/publications/studies/tgpg_report_en.pdf

Evers, L., Miller, H., & Spengel, C. (2015). Intellectual property box regimes: effective tax rates and tax policy considerations. *International Tax and Public Finance*, 22(3), 502–30.

Finke, K. (2014). Tax Avoidance of German Multinationals and Implications for Tax Revenue. *Mimeo*. Retrieved from http://www.sbs.ox.ac.uk/sites/default/files/Business_Taxation/Events/conferences/doctoral_meeting/2013/finke.pdf

FISCALIS Tax Gap Project Group. (2018). *The concept of tax gaps. Corporate Income Tax Gap Estimation Methodologies* (Working Paper No. 73; pp. 1–104). Luxembourg: European Commission.

Fisman, R., & Wei, S.-J. (2009). The Smuggling of Art, and the Art of Smuggling: Uncovering the Illicit Trade in Cultural Property and Antiques. *American Economic Journal: Applied Economics*, 1(3), 82–96.

Flaaen, A. (2017). The Role of Transfer Prices in Profit-Shifting by US Multinational Firms: Evidence from the 2004 Homeland Investment Act. *FEDS Working Paper*, 2017(55).

Fontana, A. (2010). *"What does not get measured, does not get done". The methods and limitations of measuring illicit financial flows*. Retrieved from http://www.u4.no/publications/what-does-not-get-measured-does-not-get-done-the-methods-and-limitations-of-measuring-illicit-financial-flows-2/

Forstater, M. (2015). Can Stopping "Tax Dodging" by Multinational Enterprises Close the Gap in Development Finance? *CGD Policy Paper*, (069). Retrieved from http://www.cgdev.org/publication/can-stopping-tax-dodging-multinational-enterprises-close-gap-development-finance

Forstater, M. (2016a). Illicit Flows and Trade Misinvoicing: Are we looking under the wrong lamppost? *CMI Insight*.

Forstater, M. (2016b, August 1). The Great Gold Heist That Never Was. Retrieved March 9, 2018, from Hiya Maya website: https://hiyamaya.wordpress.com/2016/08/01/the-great-gold-heist-that-never-was/

Forstater, M. (2018). Tax and Development: New Frontiers of Research and Action.

Fuest, C., Hebous, S., & Riedel, N. (2011). International debt shifting and multinational firms in developing economies. *Economics Letters*, 113(2), 135–8.

Fuest, C., & Riedel, N. (2012). Tax Evasion and Tax Avoidance: The Role of International Profit Shifting. In P. Reuter (Ed.), *Draining Development? Controlling Flows of Illicit Funds from Developing Countries* (pp. 109–42). Retrieved from https://openknowledge.worldbank.org/handle/10986/2242

Fuest, C., Spengel, C., Finke, K., Heckemeyer, J., & Nusser, H. (2013). Profit shifting and'aggressive'tax planning by multinational firms: Issues and options for reform. *ZEW-Centre for European Economic Research Discussion Paper*, (13–044). Retrieved from http://papers.ssrn.com/sol3/papers.cfm?abstract_id=2303676

Gara, M., Giammatteo, M., & Tosti, E. (2018). *Magic mirror in my hand.... how trade mirror statistics can help us detect illegal financial flows* (Questioni Di Economia e Finanza (Occasional Papers) No. 445). Retrieved from Bank of Italy, Economic Research and International Relations Area website: https://econpapers.repec.org/paper/bdiopques/qef_5f445_5f18.htm

Garcia-Bernardo, J., Fichtner, J., Heemskerk, E. M., & Takes, F. W. (2017). Uncovering Offshore Financial Centers: Conduits and Sinks in the Global Corporate Ownership Network. *ArXiv Preprint ArXiv:1703.03016*. Retrieved from https://arxiv.org/abs/1703.03016

Garcia-Bernardo, J., Fichtner, J., Takes, F. W., & Heemskerk, E. M. (2017). Uncovering Offshore Financial Centers: Conduits and Sinks in the Global Corporate Ownership Network. *Scientific Reports, 7*(1), 6246. https://doi.org/10.1038/s41598-017-06322-9

Global Financial Integrity. (2019). *Illicit Financial Flows to and from 148 Developing Countries: 2006–2015*. Retrieved from https://www.gfintegrity.org/report/2019-iff-update/

Graham, J. R., Raedy, J. S., & Shackelford, D. A. (2012). Research in accounting for income taxes. *Journal of Accounting and Economics, 53*(1), 412–34.

Gravelle, J. G. (2013). *Tax Havens: International Tax Avoidance and Evasion*. Retrieved from http://fas.org/sgp/crs/misc/R40623.pdf

Gumpert, A., Hines, J. R., & Schnitzer, M. (2016). Multinational Firms and Tax Havens. *The Review of Economics and Statistics, 98*(4), 713–27. https://doi.org/10.1162/REST_a_00591

Guvenen, F., Mataloni Jr, R. J., Rassier, D. G., & Ruhl, K. J. (2017). *Offshore profit shifting and domestic productivity measurement*. National Bureau of Economic Research.

Hebous, S., & Johannesen, N. (2015). *At Your Service! The Role of Tax Havens in International Trade with Services* (SSRN Scholarly Paper No. ID 2627083). Retrieved from Social Science Research Network website: https://papers.ssrn.com/abstract=2627083

Heckemeyer, J. H., & Overesch, M. (2017). Multinationals' profit response to tax differentials: Effect size and shifting channels. *Canadian Journal of Economics/Revue Canadienne d'économique, 50*(4), 965–94. https://doi.org/10.1111/caje.12283

Henry, J. S. (2012). *The Price of Offshore Revisited. New Estimates for Missing Global Private Wealth, Income, Inequality and Lost Taxes*. Retrieved from www.taxjustice.net/cms/upload/pdf/Price_of_Offshore_Revisited_26072012.pdf

Henry, J. S. (2016). More than $12 trillion stuffed offshore, from developing countries alone.

Herrigan, M., Kochen, A., & Williams, T. (2005). Analysis of asymmetries in intra-community trade statistics with particular regard to the impact of the Rotterdam and Antwerp effects. *Edicom Report. Statistics & Analysis of Trade Unit (SATU) HM Revenue & Customs*.

Hillyard, P. (Ed.) (2004). Beyond criminology. In *Beyond criminology: Taking harm seriously*. London: Pluto Press.

Hines, J. (2014). How Serious Is the Problem of Base Erosion and Profit Shifting? *Canadian Tax Journal, 62*(2), 443–53.

Hines, J. R. (2010). Treasure Islands. *Journal of Economic Perspectives, 24*(4), 103.

Hines, J. R., & Rice, E. M. (1994). Fiscal paradise: Foreign tax havens and American business. *The Quarterly Journal of Economics, 109*(1), 149–82.

Hogg, A., Baird, R., Mathiason, N., & Cobham, A. (2010). *Blowing the Whistle: Time's Up for Financial Secrecy*. Retrieved from http://www.christianaid.org.uk/images/blowing-the-whistle-caweek-report.pdf

Hogg, A., McNair, D., & Pak, S. (2009). *False profits: robbing the poor to keep the rich tax-free* (Christian Aid Report). Retrieved from http://www.christianaid.org.uk/Images/false-profits.pdf

Hollingshead, A. (2010). *The Implied Tax Revenue Loss from Trade Mispricing*. Retrieved from http://www.gfintegrity.org/content/view/292/156/

Hong, K., H. Pak, C., & J. Pak, S. (2014). Measuring abnormal pricing–an alternative approach: The case of US banana trade with Latin American and Caribbean Countries. *Journal of Money Laundering Control, 17*(2), 203–18.

Hong, K. P., & Pak, S. J. (2017). Estimating Trade Misinvoicing from Bilateral Trade Statistics: The Devil is in the Details. *The International Trade Journal*, *31*(1), 3–28.

Huesecken, B., & Overesch, M. (2015). *Tax Avoidance through Advance Tax Rulings— Evidence from the LuxLeaks Firms* (SSRN Scholarly Paper No. ID 2664631). Retrieved from Social Science Research Network website: http://papers.ssrn.com/abstract= 2664631

Huizinga, H., & Laeven, L. (2008). International profit shifting within multinationals: A multi-country perspective. *Journal of Public Economics*, *92*(5), 1164–82.

IBFD. (2015). *IBFD Spillover Analysis. Possible Effects of the Irish Tax System on Developing Economies*. Retrieved from http://www.budget.gov.ie/Budgets/2016/Documents/IBFD_ Irish_Spillover_Analysis_Report_pub.pdf

Inter-agency Expert Group on SDG Indicators. (2015). *IAEG-SDG's Open Consultation for Members and Observers* (p. 388).

International Monetary Fund. (2014). *Spillovers in international corporate taxation*. Retrieved from http://www.imf.org/external/np/pp/eng/2014/050914.pdf

Janský, P. (2018). European Banks and Tax Havens: Evidence from Country-by-Country Reporting. *IES Working Papers*, (38), 1–30.

Janský, P., Knobel, A., Meinzer, M., & Palanský, M. (2018). Financial Secrecy affecting the European Union: Patterns across member states, and what to do about it. *COFFERS Policy Paper*, 1–64.

Janský, P., & Kokeš, O. (2016). Profit-shifting from Czech multinational companies to European tax havens. *Applied Economics Letters*, *23*(16), 1130–3. https://doi.org/10.1080 /13504851.2015.1137543

Janský, P., Meinzer, M., & Palanský, M. (2018). Is Panama really your tax haven? Secrecy jurisdictions and the countries they harm. *IES Working Paper Series*, *2018*(23), 1–29.

Janský, P., & Palanský, M. (forthcoming). Estimating the scale of profit shifting and tax revenue losses related to foreign direct investment. *International Tax and Public Finance*. https://doi.org/10.1007/s10797-019-09547-8

Janský, P., & Palanský, M. (2017). Estimating the Scale of Profit Shifting and Tax Revenue Losses Related to Foreign Direct Investment. *IES Working Paper Series*, *2017*(25), 1–43.

Javorcik, B. S., & Narciso, G. (2008). Differentiated products and evasion of import tariffs. *Journal of International Economics*, *76*(2), 208–22.

Johannesen, N., Langetieg, P., Reck, D., Risch, M., & Slemrod, J. (2018). *Taxing Hidden Wealth: The Consequences of U.S. Enforcement Initiatives on Evasive Foreign Accounts* (Working Paper No. 24366). National Bureau of Economic Research. https://www.nber. org/papers/w24366

Johannesen, N., & Pirttilä, J. (2016). Capital flight and development: An overview of concepts, methods, and data sources. *UNU-WIDER Working Paper Series*, *2016*(19), 1–18.

Johannesen, N., Tørsløv, T., & Wier, L. (forthcoming). Are less developed countries more exposed to multinational tax avoidance? Method and evidence from micro-data. *World Bank Economic Review*.

Johannesen, N., & Zucman, G. (2014). The End of Bank Secrecy? An Evaluation of the G20 Tax Haven Crackdown. *American Economic Journal: Economic Policy*, *6*(1), 65–91.

Johansson, A., Skeie, O. B., Sorbe, S., & Menon, C. (2017). Tax planning by multinational firms: Firm-level evidence from a cross-country database. *OECD Economics Department Working Papers*, *2017*(1355), 64. http://dx.doi.org/10.1787/9ea89b4d-en

Kar, D. (2011). *Illicit financial flows from the least developed countries: 1990–2008* (pp. 1–68). New York: UDNP.

Kar, D., & Cartwright-Smith, D. (2008). *Illicit Financial Flows from Developing Countries: 2002–2006*. Retrieved from Global Financial Integrity website: http://www.gfintegrity. org/storage/gfip/economist%20-%20final%20version%201-2-09.pdf

Kar, D., & Cartwright-Smith, D. (2009). Illicit Financial Flows from Developing Countries: 2002–2006. *SSRN ELibrary*. Retrieved from http://papers.ssrn.com/sol3/papers.cfm? abstract_id=1341946

Kar, D., & Cartwright-Smith, D. (2010). Illicit financial flows from Africa. Hidden resources for development. *Global Financial Integrity*. Washington DC. https://gfintegrity.org/ report/briefing-paper-illicit-flows-from-africa/

Kar, D., Cartwright-Smith, D., & Hollingshead, A. (2010). *The Absorption of Illicit Financial Flows from Developing Countries: 2002–2006* (SSRN Scholarly Paper No. ID 2335028). Retrieved from Social Science Research Network website: http://papers.ssrn.com/ abstract=2335028

Kar, D., & Freitas, S. (2012). *Illicit Financial Flows from Developing Countries: 2001–2010. A December 2012 Report from Global Financial Integrity*. Retrieved from http://iff. gfintegrity.org/iff2012/2012report.html

Kawano, L., & Slemrod, J. (2015). How do corporate tax bases change when corporate tax rates change? With implications for the tax rate elasticity of corporate tax revenues. *International Tax and Public Finance*, *23*(3), 401–33. https://doi.org/10.1007/s10797-015-9375-y

Kee, H. L., & Nicita, A. (2016). Trade Frauds, Trade Elasticities and Non-Tariff Measures. *5th IMF-World Bank-WTO Trade Research Workshop, Washington, DC, November, 30.*

Keightley, M. P., & Stupak, J. M. (2015). Corporate Tax Base Erosion and Profit Shifting (BEPS): An Examination of the Data. *Congressional Research Service*. Retrieved from https://www.fas.org/sgp/crs/misc/R44013.pdf

Kellenberg, D., & Levinson, A. (2016). *Misreporting Trade: Tariff Evasion, Corruption, and Auditing Standards*. Retrieved from National Bureau of Economic Research website: http://www.nber.org/papers/w22593

Kessler, M., & Borst, N. (2013). Did China really lose $3.75 trillion in illicit financial flows? *China Economic Watch, 10.*

Khan, M., Roy, P., & Andreoni, A. (2019). Illicit Financial Flows: theory and measurement challenges. *Anti-Corruption Evidence (ACE) Working Paper*, *2019*(10), 1–38.

Klassen, K. J., & Laplante, S. K. (2012). Are US multinational corporations becoming more aggressive income shifters? *Journal of Accounting Research*, *50*(5), 1245–85.

Knobel, A. (2018a). Automatic Information Exchange: a trove of useful new data. Here's a template for using it. Retrieved May 27, 2019, from https://www.taxjustice.net/ 2016/01/05/global-automatic-exchange-of-information-a-trove-of-relevant-new-data/, https://www.taxjustice.net/2016/01/05/global-automatic-exchange-of-information-a-trove-of-relevant-new-data/

Knobel, A. (2018b). Country by country reports: why "automatic" is no replacement for "public." Retrieved May 27, 2019, from https://www.taxjustice.net/2018/07/17/country-by-country-reports-why-automatic-is-no-replacement-for-public/, https://www.taxjustice. net/2018/07/17/country-by-country-reports-why-automatic-is-no-replacement-for-public/

Knobel, A. (2018c). It's time for countries to start publishing the data they're collecting under OECD's Common Reporting Standard. Retrieved May 27, 2019, from https:// www.taxjustice.net/2018/07/11/its-time-for-countries-to-start-publishing-the-data-theyre-collecting-under-oecds-common-reporting-standard/, https://www.taxjustice. net/2018/07/11/its-time-for-countries-to-start-publishing-the-data-theyre-collecting-under-oecds-common-reporting-standard/

Knobel, A. and Cobham, A. (2016), Country-by-Country Reporting: How Restricted Access Exacerbates Global Inequalities in Taxing Rights. Retrieved August 5, 2019, from https://ssrn.com/abstract=2943978 or http://dx.doi.org/10.2139/ssrn.2943978 https://papers.ssrn.com/sol3/papers.cfm?abstract_id=2943978

Kravchenko, A. (2018). Where and how to dodge taxes and shift money abroad using trade misinvoicing: A beginner's guide. *Trade, Investment and Innovation Working Paper Series, 2018*(1), 1–30.

Lemaître, S. (2018). Illicit financial flows within the extractive industries sector: a glance at how legal requirements can be manipulated and diverted. *Crime, Law and Social Change.* https://doi.org/10.1007/s10611-018-9791-x

Liu, L., Schmidt-Eisenlohr, T., & Guo, D. (2017). International transfer pricing and tax avoidance: Evidence from linked trade-tax statistics in the UK. *Oxford University Centre for Business Taxation, Working Paper Series, 17*(15). Retrieved from https://www.sbs.ox.ac.uk/sites/default/files/Business_Taxation/Docs/Publications/Working_Papers/Series_17/WP1715.pdf

Mahon, J. E. (2005). Liberal states and fiscal contracts: Aspects of the political economy of public finance. *Prepared for the 2005 Annual Meeting of the American Political Science Association, September,* 1–4.

Meinzer, M., & Knobel, A. (2017). *Delivering a Level Playing Field for Offshore Bank Accounts. What the New OECD/Global Forum Peer Reviews on Automatic Information Exchange Must Not Miss* (SSRN Scholarly Paper No. ID 2934156). Retrieved from Social Science Research Network website: https://papers.ssrn.com/abstract=2934156

Meinzer, M., & Trautvetter, C. (2018). Accounting (f) or Tax: The Global Battle for Corporate Transparency. *Tax Justice Network.*

Miller, H. (2014). Current Issues in Corporate Tax. *Fiscal Studies, 35*(4), 397–400. https://doi.org/10.1111/j.1475–5890.2014.12035.x

Mooij, R. A. de, & Ederveen, S. (2008). Corporate tax elasticities: a reader's guide to empirical findings. *Oxford Review of Economic Policy, 24*(4), 680–97. https://doi.org/10.1093/oxrep/grn033

Morgenstern, O. (1950). *On the accuracy of economic observations.* Princeton University Press.

Morgenstern, O. (1974). Chapter 7: On the accuracy of economic observations: foreign trade statistics. In Jagdish N. Bhagwati (Ed.), *Illegal Transactions in International Trade* (pp. 87–122). North-Holland: Amsterdam. https://doi.org/10.1016/B978-0-444-10581-3.50014-8

MSCI. (2015). *Re-examining the tax gap.* Retrieved from https://www.msci.com/documents/10199/4043da8b-4d49-4449-ac0e-28b09df3b220

Murphy, R. (2003). *A Proposed International Accounting Standard: Reporting Turnover and Tax by Location.* Retrieved from Association for Accountancy and Business Affairs website: http://visar.csustan.edu/aaba/ProposedAccstd.pdf

Murphy, R. (2012). *Closing the European Tax Gap* [A report for the Progressive Alliance of Socialists and Democrats in the European Parliament]. Retrieved from http://www.socialistsanddemocrats.eu/sites/default/files/120229_richard_murphy_eu_tax_gap_en.pdf

Ndikumana, L., & Boyce, J. K. (2008). New estimates of capital flight from Sub-Saharan African countries: linkages with external borrowing and policy options. *PERI Working Papers,* 144.

Ndikumana, Léonce. (2016). Trade misinvoicing in primary commodities in developing countries: The cases of Chile, Côte d'Ivoire, Nigeria, South Africa and Zambia. *New York, United Nations Conference on Trade and Development Special Unit on Commodities, July.*

Ndikumana, Léonce, & Boyce, J. (1998). Congo's odious debt: external borrowing and capital flight in Zaire. *Development and Change, 29*(2), 195–217.

Ndikumana, Léonce, & Boyce, J. K. (2003). Public debts and private assets: explaining capital flight from Sub-Saharan African countries. *World Development, 31*(1), 107–30.

Ndikumana, Léonce, & Boyce, J. K. (2010). Measurement of Capital Flight: Methodology and Results for Sub-Saharan African Countries. *African Development Review, 22*(4), 471–81.

Ndikumana, Léonce, & Boyce, J. K. (2011). Capital flight from sub-Saharan Africa: linkages with external borrowing and policy options. *International Review of Applied Economics, 25*(2), 149–70.

Ndikumana, L. (2016). Trade Misinvoicing in Primary Commodities in Developing Countries: The cases of Chile, Coté d'Ivoire, Nigeria, South Africa and Zambia. Geneva: UNCTAD.

Neiman, B. (2010). Stickiness, synchronization, and passthrough in intrafirm trade prices. *Journal of Monetary Economics, 57*(3), 295–308. https://doi.org/10.1016/j.jmoneco.2010.02.002

Nellemann, C.; Henriksen, R., Pravettoni, R., Stewart, D., Kotsovou, M., Schlingemann, M.A.J, Shaw, M. and Reitano, T. (Eds) (2018). World atlas of illicit flows. *A RHIPTO-INTERPOL-GI Assessment*. RHIPTO -Norwegian Center for Global Analyses, INTERPOL and the Global Initiative Against Transnational Organized crime. International Criminal Police Organization: Vienna. https://globalinitiative.net/wp-content/uploads/2018/09/Atlas-Illicit-Flows-FINAL-WEB-VERSION-copia-compressed.pdf http://iffoadatabase.trustafrica.org/cgi-bin/koha/opac-detail.pl?biblionumber=1093

Nicolay, K., Nusser, H., & Pfeiffer, O. (2016). On the interdependency of profit-shifting channels and the effectiveness of anti-avoidance legislation. *Mimeo*.

Nitsch, V. (2012). Trade mispricing and illicit flows. In *Draining Development? Controlling Flows of Illicit Funds from Developing Countries*. Retrieved from https://openknowledge.worldbank.org/handle/10986/2242

Nitsch, V. (2016). *Trillion dollar estimate: Illicit financial flows from developing countries* (Darmstadt Discussion Papers in Economics No. 227). Retrieved from Darmstadt University of Technology, Department of Law and Economics website: http://econpapers.repec.org/paper/zbwdarddp/227.htm

Nitsch, V. (2017). Trade Misinvoicing in Developing Countries. *CGD Policy Paper, 103*. Retrieved from https://www.cgdev.org/sites/default/files/trade-misinvoicing-developing-countries.pdf

Novokmet, F., Piketty, T., & Zucman, G. (2018). From Soviets to Oligarchs: Inequality and Property in Russia, 1905–2016. *Journal of Economic Inequality, 16*(2), 189–223.

OECD. (2013a). *Action Plan on Base Erosion and Profit Shifting*. OECD Publishing. Retrieved from OECD website: http://www.oecd.org/ctp/BEPSActionPlan.pdf

OECD. (2013b). *Addressing Base Erosion and Profit Shifting*. OECD Publishing. Retrieved from OECD website: www.keepeek.com/Digital-Asset-Management/oecd/taxation/addressing-base-erosion-and-profit-shifting_9789264192744-en

OECD. (2015a). *BEPS 2015 Final Reports*. OECD Publishing. Retrieved from http://www.oecd.org/ctp/oecd-presents-outputs-of-oecd-g20-beps-project-for-discussion-at-g20-finance-ministers-meeting.htm

OECD. (2015b). *Measuring and Monitoring BEPS, Action 11—2015 Final Report*. OECD Publishing. Retrieved from http://www.oecd-ilibrary.org/content/book/9789264241343-en

O'Hare, B., Makuta, I., Bar-Zeev, N., Chiwaula, L., & Cobham, A. (2014). The effect of illicit financial flows on time to reach the fourth Millennium Development Goal in

Sub-Saharan Africa: a quantitative analysis. *Journal of the Royal Society of Medicine*, *107*(4), 148–56. https://doi.org/10.1177/0141076813514575

Ostry, M. J. D., Berg, M. A., & Tsangarides, M. C. G. (2014). *Redistribution, Inequality, and Growth*. International Monetary Fund.

Overesch, M. (2006). Transfer Pricing of Intrafirm Sales as a Profit Shifting Channel–Evidence from German Firm Data. *ZEW Discussion Papers, 6*.

Oxfam. (2000). *Tax Havens: Releasing the hidden billions for poverty eradication*. Retrieved from http://policy-practice.oxfam.org.uk/publications/tax-havens-releasing-the-hidden-billions-for-poverty-eradication-114611

Oxfam. (2009). *Tax haven crackdown could deliver $120bn a year to fight poverty*. Retrieved from http://www.oxfam.org/en/pressroom/pressrelease/2009-03-13/tax-haven-could-deliver-120bn-year-fight-poverty

Oxford University Centre for Business Taxation. (2012). *The Tax Gap for Corporation Tax*. Retrieved from http://www.sbs.ox.ac.uk/sites/default/files/Business_Taxation/Docs/Publications/Reports/TaxGap_3_12_12.pdf

Pak, S. J. (2012). Lost billions. Transfer Pricing in the Extractive Industries. *Oslo: Publish What You Pay Norway*.

Pak, Simon J., Zanakis, S. H., & Zdanowicz, J. S. (2003). Detecting abnormal pricing in international trade: The Greece-USA case. *Interfaces, 33*(2), 54–64.

Pak, Simon J., & Zdanowicz, J. S. (1994). A statistical analysis of the US merchandise trade data base and its uses in transfer pricing compliance and enforcement. *Tax Management Transfer Pricing Report, 3*(1), 50–7.

PastorJr, M. (1990). Capital flight from latin America. *World Development, 18*(1), 1–18.

Picciotto, S. (2018). Why tax avoidance is illicit. Retrieved May 26, 2019, from The International Centre for Tax and Development (ICTD) website: https://www.ictd.ac/blog/why-tax-avoidance-is-illicit/

Piketty, T. (2014). *Capital in the Twenty-First Century*. Cambridge, MA: Harvard University Press.

Ponsford, V., & Mwiinga, I. (2019, January 31). Zambia hones in on fiscal sweet spot for mining. Retrieved May 27, 2019, from Extractive Industries Transparency Initiative website: https://eiti.org/blog/zambia-hones-in-on-fiscal-sweet-spot-for-mining

Porsch, L., Lechardoy, L., Peroz, T., Gavard, C., Vandresse, B., & Haffner, R. (2018). *Review of country-by-country reporting requirements for extractive and logging industries*. European Commission.

Prichard, W. (2015). *Taxation, responsiveness and accountability in Sub-Saharan Africa: the dynamics of tax bargaining*. Cambridge University Press.

Prichard, W., Cobham, A., & Goodall, A. (2014). The ICTD Government Revenue Dataset. *ICTD Working Paper, 2014*(19), 1–64.

Raballand, G., Cantens, T., & Arenas, G. (2012). Mirror Trade Statistics: A Tool t o Help Identify Customs Fraud. In Cantens, T.. Ireland, R., & Raballand, G. (Eds.) (2012) *Reform by Numbers Measurement Applied to Customs and Tax Administrations in Developing Countries,* Chapter 6. Washington, D.C.: The World Bank..

Reeves, A., Gourtsoyannis, Y., Basu, S., McCoy, D., McKee, M., & Stuckler, D. (2015). Financing universal health coverage—effects of alternative tax structures on public health systems: cross-national modelling in 89 low-income and middle-income countries. *The Lancet, 386*(9990), 274–80.

Reuter, P. (Ed.). (2012). *Draining Development? Controlling Flows of Illicit Funds from Developing Countries*. Washington, DC: World Bank.

Reuter, P. (2017). Illicit Financial Flows and Governance: The Importance of Disaggregation. *Background Paper to the World Development Report 2017*.

Reynolds, H., & Wier, L. (2016). Estimating profit shifting in South Africa using firm-level tax returns. *WIDER Working Paper Series, 2016*(128), 1–19.

Riedel, N. (2015). Quantifying International Tax Avoidance: A Review of the Academic Literature. *Policy Paper, 2*. Retrieved from http://www.etpf.org/papers/PP002QuantAvoid.pdf

Riedel, N., Zinn, T., & Hofmann, P. (2015). *Do Transfer Pricing Laws Limit International Income Shifting? Evidence from Europe*. Retrieved from http://www.wiwi.ruhr-uni-bochum.de/fiwipo/mam/content/do_transfer_pricing_laws_limit_international_income_shifting_evidence_from_europe.pdf

Ross, M. L. (2004). Does taxation lead to representation? *British Journal of Political Science, 34*(02), 229–49.

Ruffing, L., & Hamdani, K. (2015). *United Nations Centre on Transnational Corporations*. Retrieved from https://www.book2look.com/book/kRyMcpJ8Hv

Schimanski, C. (2017). 'Earnings shocks and tax-motivated income-shifting: evidence from European multinationals'—revisited. *Applied Economics Letters, 0*(0), 1–9. https://doi.org/10.1080/13504851.2017.1327117

Schneider, F. (2005). *Shadow Economies of 145 Countries all over the World: What do we really know?* (pp. 1–58). Retrieved from Center for Research in Economics, Management and the Arts (CREMA) website: http://www.crema-research.ch/papers/2005-13.pdf

Schneider, F., Buehn, A., & Montenegro, C. E. (2010). Shadow Economies all over the World: New Estimates for 162 Countries from 1999 to 2007. *World Bank Policy Research Working Paper Series, Vol.* Retrieved from http://papers.ssrn.com/sol3/papers.cfm?abstract_id=1645726

Spanjers, J., & Salomon, M. (2017). *Illicit Financial Flows to and from Developing Countries: 2005–2014* (pp. 1–51). Washington DC, USA: Global Financial Integrity.

Swenson, D. L. (2001). Tax reforms and evidence of transfer pricing. *National Tax Journal, 54*(1), 7–25.

Tax Justice Network. (2005). *The Price of Offshore*. Retrieved from http://www.taxjustice.net/cms/upload/pdf/Price_of_Offshore.pdf

Tax Justice Network. (2007). *Closing the floodgates–collecting tax to pay for development* [Commissioned by the Norwegian Ministry of Foreign Affairs and Tax Justice Network]. London: Tax Justice Network.

Tax Justice Network. (2018). *Financial Secrecy Index 2018 Methodology*. Retrieved from https://financialsecrecyindex.com/PDF/FSI-Methodology.pdf

The Economist. (2014, May 3). Uncontained. *The Economist*. Retrieved from https://www.economist.com/news/international/21601537-trade-weakest-link-fight-against-dirty-money-uncontained?frsc=dg%7Ca&fsrc=scn/tw_app_ipad

Tikhomirov, V. (1997). Capital flight from post-Soviet Russia. *Europe-Asia Studies, 49*(4), 591–615.

Tørsløv, T., Wier, L., & Zucman, G. (2018). The Missing Profits of Nations. *National Bureau of Economic Research Working Paper*, (24071). https://doi.org/10.3386/w24701

Transparency International. (2004). *Global Corruption Report 2004*. Retrieved from http://files.transparency.org/content/download/479/1974/file/2004_GCR_PoliticalCorruption_EN.pdf

UNCTAD. (2015). *World Investment Report 2015—Reforming International Investment Governance*. Geneva: United Nations.

United Nations (2013). *A New Global Partnership: Eradicate Poverty and Transform Economies Through Sustainable Development—The Report of the High Level Panel of Eminent Persons on The Post-2015 Development Agenda*. UN: New York City. https://www.un.org/sg/en/management/hlppost2015.shtml

United Nations Economic Commission for Africa, & African Union. (2015). *Report of the High Level Panel on Illicit Financial Flows from Africa ("Mbeki Report")*. Retrieved from www.uneca.org/sites/default/files/PublicationFiles/iff_main_report_26feb_en.pdf

United States Joint Committee on Taxation. (2014). *Technical explanation, estimated revenue effects, distributional analysis, and macroeconomic analysis of the Tax Reform Act of 2014: A discussion draft of the Chairman of the House Committee on Ways and Means to reform the Internal Revenue Code* (Reference No. JCS-1-14.). United States Government Printing Office.

van der Does de Willebois, E., Halter, E. M., Harrison, R. A., Park, J. W., & Sharman, J. C. (2011). *The Puppet Masters. How the Corrupt Use Legal Structures to Hide Stolen Assets and What to Do About It*. Retrieved from http://star.worldbank.org/star/sites/star/files/puppetmastersv1.pdf

Vicard, V. (2015). *Profit Shifting Through Transfer Pricing: Evidence from French Firm Level Trade Data* (SSRN Scholarly Paper No. ID 2614864). Retrieved from Social Science Research Network website: http://papers.ssrn.com/abstract=2614864

Weichenrieder, A. J. (2009). Profit shifting in the EU: evidence from Germany. *International Tax and Public Finance, 16*(3), 281–97. https://doi.org/10.1007/s10797-008-9068-x

Weyzig, F. (2014). The Capital Structure of Large Firms and the Use of Dutch Financing Entities. *Fiscal Studies, 35*(2), 139–64. https://doi.org/10.1111/j.1475–5890.2014.12026.x

Wier, L. (2017). Tax motivated transfer price manipulation in South Africa.

World Bank. (1985). *World Development Report*. New York: World Bank.

World Customs Organisation. (2018). *Illicit Financial Flows via Trade Mis-invoicing Study Report 2018*. Retrieved from http://www.wcoomd.org/-/media/wco/public/global/pdf/media/newsroom/reports/2018/wco-study-report-on-iffs_tm.pdf?la=en

Yang, D. (2008). Can enforcement backfire? Crime displacement in the context of customs reform in the Philippines. *The Review of Economics and Statistics, 90*(1), 1–14.

Zdanowicz, J., Pak, S., & Sullivan, M. (1999). Brazil-United States trade: capital flight through abnormal pricing. *The International Trade Journal, 13*(4), 423–43.

Zdanowicz, J. S. (2009). Trade-based money laundering and terrorist financing. *Review of Law and Economics, 5*(2), 854–78.

Zucman, G. (2013). The Missing Wealth of Nations: Are Europe and the US net Debtors or net Creditors? *The Quarterly Journal of Economics, 128*(3), 1321–64.

Zucman, G. (2014). Taxing across borders: Tracking personal wealth and corporate profits. *Journal of Economic Perspectives, 28*(4), 121–48.

Zucman, G. (2015). *The hidden wealth of nations: The scourge of tax havens*. University of Chicago Press.

Index

Note: Tables, figures, and box are indicated by an italic *t*, *f*, and *b* following the page number.
For the benefit of digital users, indexed terms that span two pages (e.g., 52–53) may, on occasion, appear on only one of those pages.